TO THE NEW 7 WONDERS OF THE WORLD

JAMES A ANDERSON

CONTENTS

FOREWORD

IN NOVEMBER 2007, I came across a web-site on the internet (www.new7wonders.com) which claimed to have identified the new 7 Wonders of the World from a short-list of 21. I discovered that I had already seen all but two of them, including the pyramids at Giza in Cairo which were given a special status outside the "new" list as the only intact survivor of the original 7 Wonders and decided to visit the others the following year. So this is the story of a life-time of travel which took me to these places, rather than a concerted effort to "knock the bastards off" to paraphrase Sir Edmund Hillary about climbing Mount Everest.

If travel is in the blood, I have an excellent pedigree. Born in the Shetland Islands, my DNA traces my ancestors back to the Vikings who arrived in the islands in the late 800s A.D. Those ancestors got to America in open boats 500 years before Columbus, so they knew a bit about travelling the world.

I didn't make an early start to globe-trotting. Until I was 11 years old, I rarely made it off the 5 miles by 2 (8km x 3) island of Whalsay (population then about 800) on which I was born, just after World War II. Communications were limited then; a small steamer, The Earl of Zetland, called in three times a week on her way from the Shetland capital, Lerwick, to the North Isles. Occasionally in summer, the Earl altered her schedule so that a day trip to Lerwick, known as an "excursion", was possible. Although my mother had a sister living in Lerwick, we only got there about half a dozen times in my first 11 years, usually just on excursion days.

Apart from the limited transport links, we couldn't afford to travel. We did have a pot to piss in - just as well, as the draughty, ramshackle, wooden outdoor toilet was over 50m away, past the byre and its steaming midden and propped up against the ponging hen-house and it was a long way to go for a pee on a cold, dark, winter's night. I used to tell gullible people that we used the same pot in the morning to wash our faces and that our mother then used it to boil up the potato and cabbage soup that was all we had to live on. But that was a lie. We were kept meticulously clean and never went hungry. My father was a crofter/fisherman and there was no money in either agriculture or fishing in those days. Our croft (small farm) had only 7 acres (3 ha) of marginally arable land with a share in the open common grazing in the hills where the sheep were kept. We grew potatoes, turnips, carrots and kale and oats and hay to keep two cows alive during the winter. With some hens to supply eggs and the fish my father brought home, we were largely self-sufficient in basic food. Until I was 8 years old, we had to carry water in buckets uphill from a well as there was no piped water supply: I was at university before an undersea cable brought electricity to the island.

At the age of 11, I went to the grammar school in Lerwick. There was a secondary school in Whalsay but if you wanted to go to university, the only option was exile to the Anderson Institute, living in the hostel where the island children and those from the more remote parts of the Shetland Mainland stayed. It was tough being separated from your family at that age – we only got home for the holidays at Christmas, Easter and summer, with a long weekend in October – but it severed the apron strings and was a first step in preparing me psychologically for future travels.

My horizons broadened again at age 17 when I went to Aberdeen University, a 200 miles (320km), 14 hour, often stormy, boat trip away. During my four years there, I still never got beyond Britain. A week-long Geography field trip based in Stoke-on-Trent in the first year and another in Newcastle in the fourth year defined the limits of my known world. But four years studying Geography kindled my interest in the wider world.

When I graduated in 1967, I had no idea what I wanted to do but fancied something to take me overseas. My chance came when I discovered that the Ministry of Overseas Development was recruiting for their Teachers for East Africa (TEA) scheme. This involved taking a post-graduate Diploma in Education at Makerere University in Kampala and then teaching for two years in Uganda, Kenya or Tanzania. My known world extended to London for an interview and before long I was on my way to Uganda. My world travels had begun.

1

THE PYRAMIDS, CAIRO, EGYPT SEPTEMBER 1970

My first Wonder of the World was the only intact survivor of the original 7 Wonders, the Pyramids at Giza, on the outskirts of Cairo. This came at the end of three years in East Africa on my way back to the Shetland Islands.

Arriving at Entebbe Airport in Uganda was the start of a whole new world of experiences. On the bus trip in to the capital, Kampala, we passed women in brightly coloured, intricately patterned "basutis" - voluminous, Victorian style "katenge" cloth dresses with puffed-up, mutton-leg arms – carrying bunches of bananas on their heads. But strangely enough, the most vivid impression was the Coca Cola signs outside the "dukas" (shops) along the road. I hadn't expected that in darkest Africa. And there was the smell of Africa, a mixture of wet earth and wood-smoke which never leaves you.

Makerere University reminded me of pictures of African mission stations I had seen, red tiled roofs and a clock tower on the main hall. Our accommodation was less salubrious: half-round, corrugated iron, American army-surplus Quonset huts, each divided into five rooms and with a cold shower out in the corridor. We ate in New Hall, where some of the local students were housed in more style in a substantial red-brick building. A row of vultures used to sit along the roof-ridge above the kitchens which had open archways. Every now and then, a vulture would swoop down and emerge dragging a lump of meat, pursued by a cursing, "panga" (cutlass-like knife) wielding cook. Not surprisingly, everyone suffered an attack of dysentery in the first few weeks. But it must have acted like a vaccination: I've rarely been afflicted with Delhi Belly since.

The course work for the Diploma in Education was not particularly demanding which left plenty of time for the bars and nightclubs. My favourite nightclub was the Susannah Club on the outskirts of town, with a South African band and hordes of local girls. I bought a Saab 96 from a Swedish doctor who was going back home and at the same time met Marita, the ayah who looked after his children, a beautiful Mutoro girl from Kyenjojo, near Fort Portal in Western Uganda. I arranged to pick her up in the Saab and take her to the Susannah Club and ended up spending more nights in her house near Makerere than in my Quonset hut.

Looking back, I was abysmally ignorant about the political situation in Uganda in my time at Makerere. One incident which gave me a taste of it came on the way back to Makerere from the Susannah Club in the middle of the night. I had gone there with Jasu Patel who was in the room just across from me in the Quonset hut. He had a car as well and we used to take turns providing the transport for our occasional forays out on the town together. Jasu was a Hindu, his ancestors coming from Gujarat in Western India, but his parents now had a shop in Hoima in Western Uganda. He was one of the few Asians on the Diploma course. We had picked up two local girls and were taking them back to the hut when my Saab suddenly spluttered to a halt. "Bloody carburettor," I muttered and pulled the bonnet lever. The girls became very agitated. "We can't stop here" they cried. "It's a restricted area. The Army will come." As Jasu and I got busy under the bonnet, the girls ran off down-hill, the sound of their high heels receding into the distance. Moments later, as they had predicted, the Army came, a jeep-load of them with blazing headlights. They were very belligerent, directing a torrent of Kiswahili at us, interspersed with the English expression "Restricted Area". "Pole sana!" I said. "Gari imeharibika". (Very sorry. The car has broken down.) They calmed down a bit and watched with interest as we dismantled the carburettor, drained it and sucked the jets, spitting petrol out on the road. This had become a bit of a routine, the two-stroke engine of the Saab not coping well with the dust from dirt roads. The engine started and we were away.

Jasu explained what the problem was. We had stopped near the Kabaka's palace, where the Baganda kings had lived, the same dynasty as the despotic Mutesa II whom Burton and Speke had met when Speke discovered the source of the Nile in 1862. In 1966, President Obote, who was a member of the Lango tribe from Northern Uganda, had abolished the traditional kingdoms and taken away the powers they had under the constitution. The Baganda had rebelled and been crushed by the Army under General Amin, the palace being burned down. Since then Bagandan resentment had simmered away and their sacred precincts had been off limits. Their last king, King Freddie, was in exile in London, living in a bed- sit in Bermondsey, where he developed a drink problem and died in the early 1970s. At a military parade, to celebrate Independence Day, somebody pointed out General Amin to me, standing in the back of an armoured car but the horrors of his regime were some years away and if dark deeds were already afoot on the political scene, I was blissfully unaware of them. (As I recall, he was pointed out because he had been the heavy-weight boxing champion of Uganda.)

The same ignorance applied to the crime scene. We had been warned not to walk back to Makerere after dark as there were armed robbers known as "kondos" operating in the city and the local newspapers featured regular lurid accounts of attacks. But at 21 you're fireproof and one night Bob Adams, my next door neighbour in the Quonset hut and I, decided to save a taxi fare and walk back from the cinema in town. (We were both Scottish.) We passed the mosque at "Bat Valley" across from Wandegaya and turned up the hill towards the University gate. There were a lot of tall trees on the left where the bats used to roost and thick undergrowth. Just as we were approaching the gate, a group of dark shapes emerged from the trees. Bob was walking on my right and made a run for the gate where there were two "askaris" (guards) armed with clubs but I was surrounded. I struggled for a bit but they dragged me down and I saw a knife. "Just give us your money, white boy" a voice said in good English. I did. They pulled off my watch as well. Bob was shouting to the askaris to do something but they didn't move. Kondos were known to carry guns so I suppose they felt that discretion was the better part of valour. The robbers melted back into the trees as quickly as they had appeared.

We went back down the road to the Wandegaya police station and reported the robbery. It took one of the duty policemen about an hour to take down my statement in longhand and then a couple of them walked up the road with us to see where the attack had happened. "Of course the thieves will be far away by now" one of them said. The following morning we reported the robbery to the Warden of New Hall so that fresh warnings could be issued. He must have mentioned it to the British High Commission because a couple of days later I had a letter from them – "I was sorry to hear about the attack on yourself and on Adams." Needless to say the thieves were never caught but the fact that the High Commissioner bothered to write to me suggested that such incidents of attacks on Europeans were relatively rare. Certainly I never had any fears about walking around in well lit, busy areas at night and we continued to go to the bars and nightclubs without any problems. Compared to most African cities nowadays the streets were relatively safe.

I had been getting driving lessons from Jasu, who was an excellent teacher and booked myself a driving test. The inspector turned out to be an army officer, carrying a .303 rifle, which he initially stuck out the window but later changed position so that it was pointing at my head. He whistled in a low tuneless way all through the test – I couldn't make out whether he was trying to put me off or just nervous. It all went well until the hill start. He selected what must have been the steepest junction in Kampala, the road leading up on to a busy road past the central market. Just as I was swinging round the corner, an Indian woman in a blue sari stepped off the pavement right in front of me. I slammed on the brakes and managed to avoid mowing her down. She gave me a contemptuous look and continued across the road amidst squealing brakes and irate horn blowing. The inspector made no comment but a little later said: "We needn't bother with an emergency stop." At the end of the test I was in a quandary. Should I offer him a bribe? I'd consulted Jasu about this but he'd just said all I could do was play it by ear. The inspector stopped whistling, his rifle still pointing at my head and said: "Did you see that Muhindi (Indian) woman?" "Yes." I said, "That's why I stopped." He seemed to ruminate for a minute and then said "O.K. I'm putting you through." That night, I took Marita to the Susannah Club and afterwards drove back to her place pissed as a newt. Looking back now on the menace I regularly posed to the population of East Africa by driving under the influence, that inspector, rather than issuing me with a driving licence, would have been perfectly entitled to use his .303 on me instead.

The Saab gave me freedom to explore at the weekends and holidays – the source of the Nile at Jinja, Murchison Falls, where the Nile teemed with hippos and crocodiles and the beautiful Lake Edward. On the trip to Murchison with three other students, we were caught in a tropical monsoon but made it back to our camp near the Game Lodge. We watched the floodwaters rise with some trepidation but the game warden said it wouldn't reach the high ground we were on. In the morning he came to see us and asked if we'd seen the lions. "There were twelve of them just near your tent, sheltering from the floods" he said.

I did my first teaching practice at Nabumale School near Mbale in the foothills of Mount Elgon, a towering extinct volcano on the border with Kenya. The scenery was stunning with rocky escarpments ribbing the mountain side, the cool evenings and mornings scented with wood-smoke and filled with the cries of wood pigeons and cockerels. From Nabumale, I took a trip up to Karamoja, the wild, semi-desert North-East corner of Uganda. The cattle-herding Karamajong tribesmen were still active cattle raiders and went around practically naked. The flat landscape was punctuated with isolated red inselbergs like Ayers Rock (Uluru) and the sparse thorn bush vegetation made it difficult to believe that people could survive there.

Another trip took me to the Ruwenzori Mountains in Western Uganda on the border with Zaire. Sometimes known as the Mountains of the Moon, they were spectacular on the rare occasion when the cloud cover lifted, exposing their white snow-capped summits. I drove around the back of them on the north side through an area of hot springs to visit the pygmy village of Bundibugyo. The diminutive inhabitants didn't look overly friendly with an aggressive sales technique for some wood carvings, monkeys and bananas so I didn't hang about. Further south, in the Queen Elizabeth National Park, I photographed a lion resting half way up a tree.

At Christmas, 1967, a group of us headed off in my Saab, initially making for Mombasa on the Kenyan coast. We spent the night in a farmhouse near Nakuru in the Rift Valley, owned by friends of one of the group, another Scotsman, appropriately enough called Johnny Walker. There were still quite a few European farmers left in Kenya, having survived the Mau Mau rebellion of the 1950s and Uhuru (independence) in 1963, but the numbers were already dwindling. Nairobi was a bustling, modern city with gleaming new high-rise buildings along the wide traffic lanes of Kenyatta Avenue. The New Stanley Hotel with its Thorn Tree Restaurant was a national institution. As in Uganda, the retail trade was dominated by the "Asians" – descendants of Indians brought in to build the railway from Mombasa to Kampala. The shopping streets had the spicy smell of India about them rather than Africa.

You didn't need to go into the game parks in those days to see wild animals. Along the road to Mombasa we saw ostriches and giraffes in the open savannah landscape where the sky seemed immeasurably high and impossibly blue. In the Tsavo National Park we saw elephants, rhinos and some of the famous man-killing lions.

Mombasa at Christmas was hot and sticky. The overwhelming impression was of an Arab city, the men wearing the Arab style dress of "kikois" (brightly coloured lengths of cloth wrapped round the waist like a skirt) or long white robes; and white skull caps. Many of the women wore yasmak face masks and even   black burkas, locally called bui buis. The harbour was full of dhows from Oman and elsewhere in the Arabian Peninsula. The local language, Kiswahili, a mixture of Arabic and the local Bantu languages had spread throughout eastern Africa as a result of Arab trading networks. I was studying it at Makerere as part of my Diploma course and it became the first foreign language in which I was reasonably fluent. The minarets of mosques were prominent on the skyline and the early morning call of the Muezzin calling the faithful to prayer could penetrate the most excruciating hangovers of the infidel. We were staying in the Bristol Hotel, where you had to fight your way through the whores lining the stairs on the way to your room, so the opportunities for sin worthy of stoning to death were endless.

We made our way up the coast to Lamu, another Arab settlement on an island off the coast. No cars were allowed on the island so we had to negotiate a minder's fee at the car park. We took the little ferry across. No beer was allowed either in this strictly Moslem community. Walking on the beach one day we met two women clad in the full black bui buis. The expression in the dark eyes flashing through the slits suggested that perhaps the men had the right idea keeping them under wraps. We came across a wedding dance in the village square, the men rhythmically duelling with wooden sticks to the accompaniment of drums and pipes, like a scene from Sinbad the Sailor. We stayed in a guesthouse built from coral blocks, lime-washed white, with carved ebony doors and balconies overhanging a cool courtyard. With its vehicle free cobbled streets and the sultan's fort dating to 1808, Lamu could have been in a time warp.

A group of us from Makerere had agreed to assemble in Arusha, in Tanzania, to climb Mount Kilimanjaro for Christmas. Someone had even thoughtfully brought a tin of Christmas pudding for consumption on the summit. It was a two day hike up to the upper hut at over 16,000 feet (5000m) starting in rain forest and ending in tundra-like alpine grassland with weird giant lobelia plants distorted by an overdose of ultra-violet light at high altitude. There was very little oxygen in the air at that height and a number of the group were beginning to feel the effects of altitude sickness. It was very difficult to sleep and bitterly cold, almost a relief to get up before dawn for the scramble up the frozen scree slope to the Kibo peak summit at over 19,000 feet (6,000m). I don't think anybody enjoyed the Christmas pudding.

In the last term of the academic year, we were sent out on our long practical teaching practice session. I was posted to Maseno School in Western Kenya, 17 miles from Kisumu and high above Lake Victoria. The equator ran through the school grounds. I stayed in the staff houses in the northern hemisphere and crossed into the southern hemisphere every morning to teach. Unfortunately, I can't remember whether the bath water swirled clockwise or anti-clockwise on the way down the plug hole. I later discovered from Barack Obama's book ' Dreams from my Father' that his father had been expelled from Maseno for smuggling girls into the dormitories and supplementing school dinners with fruit from some of the neighbouring "shambas" (small farms). He had been born at Kendu Bay, a village just a few miles from Homa Bay, across Lake Victoria in South Nyanza Province, where I was posted on a two year contract with the Kenyan Government on graduation.

My first visit to Homa Bay School became a dramatic introduction. The girlfriend of one of the teachers at the school lived in Kampala and she was going down to visit him for the weekend, so she invited me and James Duncan, who was also to be posted there, to come down with her, a couple of weeks in advance of our permanent move. We got there just after dark and the place was in pandemonium. There had been a powerful earthquake and the students had run off into the bush in panic. Ralph, the teacher we were staying with, was organizing cars to go after them and bring them back. There had been no earthquakes in the area in living memory although the neighbouring Lambwe Valley was obviously a rift valley and the landscape was dotted with volcanic cones, including Homa Mountain just out behind the school. There was a legend among the local Luo tribe that at one time in the distant past, the water had risen and drowned a village where nearby Lake Simbi was now to be found, a classic round volcanic crater lake. Apparently what had triggered the panic among the pupils was a rumour that this time it was Lake Victoria that was going to rise and flood the town. The search parties fanned out into the surrounding countryside and we managed to pick up a few frightened students and return them to their dormitories – they seemed to be reassured by the fact that the "Mzungus" (Europeans) hadn't fled.

The earthquakes continued for a few months after I moved permanently to Homa Bay. I was sharing a staff house with James Duncan. One afternoon we were both dozing in the living room after lunch when a particularly vicious one started and the windows began to rattle. We both made for the door at the same time and in true comic farce style got stuck in the opening. On another occasion some of us were out visiting a local village with some of the students on a Saturday afternoon when the rumbling started. There was an open grassy field stretching away from the huts outside which we were standing and you could see the ground rippling in waves towards us as the noise built up. It's a scary feeling when the earth moves under your feet. And then the shocks ended as suddenly as they had begun.

The year at Makerere ended in drama as well. Some freedom fighters had been hanged in Rhodesia which was in its UDA (Unilateral Declaration of Independence) phase under Ian Smith at the time and engaged in a civil war. The student council at Makerere had arranged a meeting to condemn the executions and show solidarity with the freedom fighters. For some reason best known to themselves James Duncan and another Scotsman on the Diploma course had gone along. When the meeting was asked to stand for a minute's silence for the executed men, they refused to do so. A riot broke out and the two Scots had to be rescued by the police before they were lynched. They were spirited away into hiding in one of the lecturer's houses but the rioting spread into town. Paul Theroux, the travel writer, was there with his wife, who was pregnant with their first child. Their car was attacked and they escaped with the skin of their teeth. I never met Paul, who was working in the Education Faculty at Makerere while I was there, but I remember somebody pointing him out as "Paul the yank" at some function on the campus. It was only later when I discovered his travel books and novels that I realized that our paths had crossed. After that, inter-racial relations on the campus were delicate to put it mildly and we were dispatched off to our postings as quickly as possible. James Duncan eventually turned up at Homa Bay, having narrowly escaped deportation.

Earthquakes weren't the only hazard in Homa Bay. "Homa" is the Kiswahili word for "fever", more specifically, malaria. Right on the edge of Lake Victoria, the mosquitos were rife but not as annoying as the lake flies which would swarm through any chink in the window netting or open door in the evenings. In my contract, Homa Bay was classified as an unhealthy station due to the malaria risk, entitling me to 5 months paid leave at the end of the contract as opposed to the standard 3 months. I managed to get away with one relatively mild attack but one of the other teachers had two young children who developed recurrent malaria – one attack following another – and the family had to return to Britain.

Homa Bay was quite close to the Masai Mara game reserve and I used to go down there camping some weekends. In the rainy season it was teeming with wildebeest and zebra following the migration north from the Serengeti. It was dangerous to get blasé about wild animals. One day I was driving casually along a narrow red dirt track when I spotted a rhino charging straight at me. I accelerated away and she passed behind me in a cloud of dust. Looking back in the rear view mirror I saw that I had got between her and her calf which had been on the other side of the track.

It was also dangerous to get blasé about driving through game parks. During the Christmas holidays, I decided to take a trip across Tanzania as far as the capital Dar es Salaam. The plan was to drive down the west side of Lake Victoria to Mwanza and then cut across the Serengeti game park to Arusha before heading south to Dodoma and then east to Dar. The Shell road map of East Africa had a nice fat red line across the Serengeti indicating a main road. One of the other teachers at Homa Bay had been coming with me but for some reason backed out at the last minute so I set out on my own. I wasn't far along the red line before I realized that it was a figment of Shell's imagination. The dirt road I had been following petered out and a fan of wheel tracks stretched into the distance before me. I took the freshest looking track and soldiered on. I was becoming increasingly agitated when I spotted a red object in the distance which gradually resolved itself into a Masai warrior in the traditional red cloak striding along carrying a spear. I stopped and asked him if there was a decent road anywhere near and he offered to come with me to show me the way. He climbed in, spear sticking out the window and off we set. We drove for miles before arriving at a large village where he got out, showing me a road of sorts which he said went to Arusha. Not for the first or last time, I thanked my lucky stars for the time I had spent learning Kiswahili at Makerere – I actually spoke it a lot better than the Masai tribesman. God knows how he got back to wherever he was going but the last I saw of him he was heading for the village bar with the fistful of notes I had given him for his trouble so I suspect that getting home was the least of his worries.

The headmaster had arranged a 6th form school trip to Nairobi to visit the parliament and meet the local MP, Tom Mboya, who was the Minister for Economic Development and the President, Jomo Kenyatta. One of the few African teachers in the school and I were to go with them. I was very impressed with both the politicians. Kenyatta had tremendous charisma; you could feel the power of his personality. He spoke to the boys about the value of a good education and the need for them to come out of school with the best exam results they could achieve. They were clearly over-awed in his presence. Every time I see Nelson Mandela on TV now, I am reminded of Kenyatta. While history's verdict on him is mixed, Kenya appeared to be relatively incorrupt and well run on his watch while I was there. Race relations between Africans and the remaining European colonialists were reasonably amicable – the Minister for Agriculture was European – and the economy was doing well.

There was however an undercurrent of inter-tribal unrest which came to a head when Tom Mboya was assassinated. The ruling party, The Kenyan African National Union (KANU), was dominated by Kenyatta's tribe, the Kikukuyu. The opposition, further to the left than KANU, had their power base among the Luo tribe and their neighbours the Luhia up around Lake Victoria. Mboya, a Luo, was exceptional in being among the leaders of KANU. Mboya's assassin was a Kikuyu and the suspicion was that it was related to a power struggle within KANU. Riots broke out in Homa Bay and a number of Kikuyu businesses in town were attacked. We had to rescue the few Kikuyu boys among the students, mostly sixth formers and give them refuge in the staff houses. The notorious General Services Unit of the Army appeared to restore order and gunfire was heard in town. We stayed within the school compound until things quietened down a couple of days later. After that, an uneasy peace developed but serious damage had been done to the political stability of the country and underlying tribal animosities remain to this day as demonstrated by the violence that erupted after the 2008 elections.

In the summer holiday of 1968 three of us from the school set off on a trip to the eastern Congo (Zaire) via Uganda and Rwanda. We went in Graham Rainbird's Peugeot which we thought would be more reliable than my Saab which had become notorious for its car-burettor problems. I think Graham was also relieved to be the main driver. I held the record time for the 90 miles (144km) trip from Homa Bay to Kisumu, averaging a mile a minute, a lot of that on dirt roads. Graham was the cautious type. Bob Greener, the third member of the party, was a Canadian, with the Canadian Universities Service Overseas (CUSO).

As we drove along Kampala Road, the main street of the city, I spotted my former girlfriend, Marita, standing at a bus stop. Kampala at that time had a population of well over 50,000 so I don't know what the odds were against seeing someone you knew on a drive along the main street. I had completely lost touch with her since moving to Kenya. Anyhow, we stopped and I arranged to meet her at the Susannah Club that evening. When we left the Club, Marita gave the taxi driver an address in Kololo, an up-market area of town where most of the European residents lived. "I've moved up in the world", she said. Her house turned out to be a smart bungalow set in a big garden with flame trees and bougainvillea. She went into a bedroom and I heard her talking in a low voice to a female. She emerged carrying a little blonde haired girl. "Meet our daughter" she said. "Her name is Cherie. She's just four months old." I had been away for a year.

It turned out that she was living with a Frenchman who was a sales representative for electrical appliances. "He's away in Mombasa selling washing machines" she said. She brought Cherie's cradle into the bedroom where we slept and I kept waking up during the night with her crying. Marita said that she hadn't been very well lately and that she was taking her to the doctor in the morning. That was the last I saw of my daughter.

We drove on down through Kigezi District in the South-West of Uganda and into Rwanda, switching from driving on the left to the right. Rwanda was vividly green and fertile, the hillsides terraced right to the summits, tea and coffee plantations, fields of maize and stands of bananas. We spent a night in Kigale, the capital, a small hill-top town at that time and then headed down towards the Congo (Zaire) border to a place called Shangugu where the river flowing out of the south end of Lake Kivu formed the border. We stayed the night on the Rwanda side in an old, run down hotel, with a mill wheel. It was run by an elderly French or Belgian lady who appeared to be completely on her own, with no sign of any staff, just a lot of cats. The meal she produced for us was superb. I got up during the night to go to the bathroom and heard the eerie sound of her voice coming from somewhere downstairs. She appeared to be talking to the cats.

In the morning, we crossed the bridge to the Zaire border post which we had seen from the hotel. Immediately we hit a problem. We didn't have visas. We had made enquiries about that in Kampala at the Zaire Embassy but the fee they quoted was exorbitant and we had decided to sort it out at the border. My school French lessons had been strong on grammar but abysmally weak on practising the spoken language, so we had some difficulty communicating with the border police. I thought Bob Greener would have been reasonably competent in French being Canadian but his was worse than mine and so was Graham's. However, we managed to persuade them that we weren't mercenaries, in spite of the beards and the French car and one of them jumped in a jeep to escort us into Bukavu to sort it out with their

Chief. When we arrived at police headquarters, the Chief was away until the following afternoon. For some reason we were released into the care of a Belgian who owned the local petrol service station and appeared to be one of the few Europeans left in the town. I never discovered what his link with the local security services was but he cooked us up a mean boeuf bourguignon in the evening with a couple of good bottles of French wine and provided comfortable beds.

In the morning we went to get breakfast at a local café. While we were eating, a drunken soldier came in brandishing a rifle in a menacing way and started demanding food from the proprietor who was an Asian. After he had left without paying, the Belgian shook his head and commented that the Army was completely out of control. Nothing much has changed since in that part of the world. We had come in during a brief lull in hostilities which had seen rebellions, civil war and atrocities in the Congo ever since independence in 1960. The last lot of white mercenaries involved in the conflict had left just the year before by the same route as we had come in so it was hardly surprising that the border police were suspicious of us. In the afternoon we went along to see the police chief. We were bumbling along in our school French trying to explain what we were doing there when all of a sudden the Chief broke into perfect English. He explained that unfortunately he did not have the powers to issue visas, which should have been obtained outside the country and that we would have to leave. To my surprise he got into the car with us to accompany us back to the border, a jeep load of heavily armed soldiers following up in the rear. If you're going to be deported, why not go out in style.

On another break from teaching, a group of six of us from the school went up to Lake Rudolph (now called Lake Turkana) in the semi-desert north. John Evans, a volunteer with CUSO (Canadian Universities Service Overseas) had an aunt who was working as a nurse in a mission station up on the lake. We loaded two land rovers with supplies including a vast amount of beer. John said his aunt had told him that with temperatures soaring away over 40C you had to drink at least 8 pints of liquid a day. I think she probably meant water: we took plenty of that as well in any case. We drove north through Eldoret and

Kitale, the views of Mt. Elgon bringing back memories of my teaching practice there. Further north, the inselbergs I had seen in Uganda on my previous visit to Karamoja, dominated the skyline - Kadam and Mt. Moroto, which rose to over 3,000 metres (10,000 feet). Cattle raiding across the border was still rife here between the Karamajong and the Turkana on the Kenyan side. Lodwar, the last place of any size before the lake, was a military post, located there to attempt to keep the peace. When we arrived at our destination, Lokwakangole on Ferguson's Gulf, John's aunt showed us to our quarters, an unoccupied staff house – a breeze-block bungalow with a corrugated iron roof and a wide veranda. The mission station was in a fishing village on the edge of the lake. There were some doum palms, thorn bushes and the occasional acacia tree but mostly just sand dunes. We saw some camels and donkeys: God knows what they survived on. The native's huts were just beehive-shaped conical mounds of leaves and reeds on a framework of branches, barely high enough to stand up in. Most of the men and boys were stark naked. The women wore nothing but tiny aprons hanging from strings around their waists but they were decorated with metal bangles around their upper arms, earrings and strings of beads around their necks. Naked children were milling round carrying large, flat fish on their heads, held by the tail. Columns of men were wading out into the shallow water, deploying nets. Dugout canoes were drawn up on the shore for use in deeper water. Further down the shoreline, some flamingos were feeding in the shallows. We went for a swim in the lake. Later back at the house, someone spotted a snake disappearing under a cupboard. We armed ourselves with brooms and tent poles; John Evans wielded an ornamental sword he had bought in Mombasa; we opened the doors to provide an escape route for the beast and started the chase. It was over a metre long and moved at incredible speed so we got nowhere near it as it took refuge under beds, other cupboards, sofas, arm chairs before eventually finding an escape door. When we told John's aunt about this later and described it to her, she said it sounded like a young black mamba, one of the deadliest snakes in Africa. I suspect she may have been having us on. When we told her we'd been swimming in the lake she screwed her eyes shut and then pointed at an island visible out in the lake. "See that island?" she said. "It's infested with crocodiles." The Leakey family of archaeologists had found some of the oldest fossils of early ancestors and relatives of man here around Lake Turkana, including one called Turkana Boy. It struck me that the people living at the lake now hadn't really advanced all that much since he had been around.

At the end of my contract we were advised that the gratuities paid by the British Government would be taxed if we got back to Britain before it was paid into our bank accounts. James Duncan, John Evans and I decided to make our way back through Ethiopia, the Sudan and Egypt. We flew with Ethiopian Airlines to Addis Ababa and got a certificate for crossing the equator. If I'd got one every time I did that at Maseno School, I could have papered the walls with them. We stayed in the Wabe Shabelle Hotel, one of the few high-rise buildings in the city at that time and a very up-market establishment by my previous standards, particularly the Bristol Hotel in Mombasa. We took a tour out to see the Blue Nile and visited a Coptic Christian monastery. Ethiopia was one of the first places to adopt Christianity. Earlier, Jews had migrated to Ethiopia as part of the Diaspora following defeat by the Romans and the faithful or perhaps that should be the benighted, were fully convinced that the Jewish Ark of the Covenant was hidden in one of their churches. Many Ethiopian Jews were emigrating to Israel. On the way back it started to snow, hail stones whitening the ground. A man on a white horse rode past looking miserable. I hadn't realized how high up the central plateau of Ethiopia was and that snow shower had the same jolting effect on my preconceptions of Africa as seeing the Coca Cola signs on the way into Kampala from Entebbe Airport when I first arrived.

There was an outbreak of cholera in the Sudan and we had to have vaccinations in Addis to enable us to get in. I hadn't had any adverse reactions to the inoculations that had been pumped into us before leaving for Uganda but this time I did. It seriously interfered with my drinking or rather vice-versa. This wasn't a big problem in Khartoum where it was difficult to find a bottle of beer but manifested itself later in Cairo. In Khartoum, we stayed in the Metro Hotel. This

Sahara Desert girt city was where General Gordon had been killed in 1885 by a rebellious army of Moslems led by the fanatical Mahdi who always reminds me of Osama Bin Laden (who was based in the Sudan for a time.) We saw the confluence of the Blue and White Niles where the two streams of water, one clear, one muddy, retained a neat seam as they flowed along together like a carefully poured Irish coffee.

In Cairo we stayed in the Windsor Hotel. Years later, I was watching Michael Palin's "Pole to Pole" trip on TV and he stayed in the same establishment. One of the joys of travelling is that you keep being reminded of familiar places long after you've been there. Egypt was still theoretically on a war footing with Israel after the 1967 Six Day War. There were sandbags in shop doorways and ostensibly a black-out at night, although bizarrely the bridges across the Nile were still lit up, which I would have thought would have been prime targets.

My first Wonder of the World, the pyramids at Giza, out on the southern outskirts of the city, lived up to expectations. For as often as I had seen pictures of them, nothing quite prepares you for the reality. The sheer size of the three pyramids was impressive, bearing in mind that they were built without the aid of machinery of any sort. The largest one, the Great Pyramid, the tomb of the Pharaoh Khufu (sometimes called Cheops, which is the Greek version of the name), was 138 metres (455 feet) high with each side of the base measuring 230 metres (755 feet). Some of the estimated 2.3 million limestone blocks from which it was built weighed 16 tons. The granite blocks used to line the burial chamber, some 8,000 tons in all, weighed from 25 to 80 tons each. The limestone appeared to have been quarried quite close to the Pyramids, where traces of ancient quarries still remained but the granite blocks were transported from Aswan, 500 miles away up the Nile. The Great Pyramid had remained the tallest man-made structure in the world for over 3,800 years until the spire on Lincoln Cathedral in England was completed around 1300AD. The original structure was some 8m (25 feet) higher as it was surfaced with smooth, white, polished limestone slabs, quarried from the opposite side of the Nile. These were dislodged in a massive earthquake in 1300 AD and subsequently scavenged to build mosques and fortresses in Cairo, where they could still be seen. The original Pyramid must have been an even more magnificent sight, shimmering white in the desert sun.

Archaeologists and historians have dated the completion of the Great Pyramid to around 2560 BC and estimated that it took from 14 to 20 years to complete. This was around the same time that Stonehenge was built in England. As for Stonehenge, there has been academic speculation over the years about how the Pyramids were built. The Greeks believed that slave labour was used but more recent theories suggest that the work force was housed in a nearby workers' settlement called the "Lost City" which has been excavated by archaeologists and dated to the period when the Pyramids were built. From the artefacts found, they appear to have been well looked after. It would make sense that there would have been no need to press-gang the workforce. The Pharaohs were considered to be Gods and the Pyramids were designed to carry them to the after-world. The workers probably considered it to be a privilege to be involved in such a project. On a subsequent trip to Cairo, I visited the National Museum and discovered that the Ancient Egyptians had very clear beliefs about what happened in the after-life, all set out in diagrammatical form.

One thing is clear, the manpower involved must have been huge, possibly in the order of 100,000. The consensus is that the Pyramids were built using earth ramps, the building blocks being hauled up using ropes and rollers. It has been estimated that to complete the job in 20 years, about 800 tons of rock would have had to be put in place each day. No doubt the fertile Nile Valley would have been able to support surplus manpower not needed to grow food. For three months of the year, the arable land would have been covered in the Nile's floodwaters and no work on the land would have been possible in any case. For those three months in particular, a massive work force could have been available.

Just below the Pyramids sat the Sphinx, the body of a lion with a human face, believed to represent the Sun God, Ra. It was much bigger than I had expected, 73 metres (241 feet) long, 20 metres (66 feet) high and 6 metres (20 feet) wide. The sight of a security guard seated on a camel brought back to mind a scurrilous poem I had once heard:

The sexual life of the camel is stranger than anyone thinks.
At the height of the mating season, it tries to bugger the sphinx.
But the Sphinx's posterior passage is blocked by the sands of the Nile,
Which accounts for the hump on the camel's back,
And the Sphinx's inscrutable smile.

Its legendary inscrutable smile probably had less to do with where the sands of the desert had got to than the fact that its metre-wide nose was missing, allegedly at the hands of a fanatical Sufi Muslim armed with a hammer and a hatred of idolatry who had found some peasants making offerings to it in the hope of boosting their crops. It was carved from a limestone outcrop and is the largest monolithic statue in the world as well as the oldest known monumental sculpture. It is generally believed to have been sculpted around 2500 BC during the reign of the Pharaoh Khafra, the builder of the second Pyramid at Giza, but some scholars think it may be much older based on evidence of weathering by rainwater – North Africa and the Sahara had been much wetter during the Ice Age and gradually dried out as the world emerged from it.

We flew on to London with Swissair via Athens and Geneva. I remember seeing the Parthenon (a runner-up in the New 7 Wonders competition) as we landed in Athens. This was the era of the "Colonels'" dictatorship in Greece and armed soldiers patrolled the airport. As we came into Geneva, there was a beautiful view of the snow clad peak of Mont Blanc off to the right. Shortly afterwards, I watched the drama unfold on TV of the PLO's (Palestine Liberation Movement) hi-jacking of three planes to the Lebanon, where they eventually blew them up. I realized that the Swissair flight involved was the same one we had travelled on a few days previously, probably the same aircraft. I had narrowly missed a very dramatic end to my African adventure.

Back in the Shetland Islands with five months paid leave, I had plenty of time to consider my future. I had caught the travel bug and started looking for other job opportunities overseas. Oil had been dis- covered in the North Sea east of Shetland but at that time I had no idea that it was to change the course of my life later on.

JUNE 1986: RETURN TO EAST AFRICA

In June, 1986, I made a return trip to East Africa. By this time, I was back in the Shetland Islands working as Deputy Director of Planning with the Shetland Islands Council, trying to cope with the workload brought on by the rapid development following on from the construction of the massive Sullom Voe Oil Terminal on the Islands, the terminus of the oil pipelines coming in from the Brent and other North Sea oilfields.

Since leaving East Africa, I had kept myself up to date with events unfolding there – the rise of General Amin, the escalation of terror under his regime, his expulsion of the Asians, his deposition by the Tanzanian army, President Obote's return to power with savage reprisals against the people who had supported Amin, and finally Museveni's successful rebellion against Obote, returning some stability to the battered country. A million people were estimated to have been killed in Uganda since I had left. The thought that I had a daughter there caught up in this gnawed at my conscience. In Kenya, Nairobi's reputation as "Nairobbery" was already developing. I felt drawn to go back and see the situation for myself.

As I boarded the Kenya Airways flight to Mombasa, they were playing the Kiswahili song "Malaika" (Angel) over the intercom. This had been the signature tune of the South African band which had played at the Susannah Club during my time in Kampala and it immediately brought back a rush of nostalgia. I stayed at the beachfront Whispering Palms Hotel, a few miles up the coast from Mombasa. All the familiar landmarks were still there in Mombasa, bringing back memories – the huge imitation elephant tusks forming an Arc de Triomphe on the main road, Fort Jesus built by the Portuguese after they had captured the city from the Arabs. The Bristol Hotel was still there but now seemed to be a much more sedate establishment.

I took the overnight train from Mombasa heading for Nairobi. I shared the sleeping compartment with a Chinese man Mr. Da, who worked for the China Road and Bridge Engineering Company and was involved in various development projects in Kenya being carried out by the Chinese government – "Plojects are load and blidge" he said, spitting into the wash hand basin. The bridge was a major one across the Tana River in northern Kenya; the roads were in the Kinangop area, President Arap Moi's home area, an indicator of how nepotism, cronyism and tribalism were now the underlying principles of government in Kenya. Since then, Chinese involvement in economic development in Africa has grown dramatically. Mr. Da was a strange, nervous, restless character, wearing a white, Filipino style Panama hat, muttering "Only one beddings here; no, is two beddings" as he struggled to make up his bunk and when the train stopped, rushing out into the corridor, screeching "Why is tlain stopping?" He told me that he had been working in Kenya for 4 years without a break and hadn't wanted to come in the first place. Before that, he had spent 4 years in the Middle East – he'd only spent 3 months in China in 8 years. As the train snaked up the escarpment forming the edge of the plateau land beyond, I watched a huge silvery full moon swinging in and out of sight behind us. The magic of Africa was starting to get hold of me again.

Nairobi was noticeably bigger and busier, the high-rise skyline now resembling the profile of the CBD (Central Business District) of an American city. The New Stanley Hotel and Thorn Tree restaurant were still there but the El Sombrero nightclub which I had frequented on trips to the city was gone. There was a rawer, edgier feel to life on the streets and I took taxis at night between restaurants and bars. But it was good to speak Kiswahili again to some girls in a bar where I noticed I had the only white face.

I hired a car to visit my old school at Homa Bay. The traffic getting out of the city was horrendous, overloaded trucks grinding up the hill towards the edge of the Rift Valley escarpment, overtaking and lane-changing with total disregard for human life and limb, belching pungent diesel fumes and pumping out roaring noise from burst exhaust pipes and silencers. But it was a thrill to arrive at the edge of the Rift Valley again and take in the wide vista of plain and lakes. On the other side, I drove through the familiar bright green tea plantations near Kericho. When I got to Homa Bay, it was barely recognisable. What had been a small, sleepy, compact town, scarcely bigger than a village, had grown and spread out immensely. In the evening down by the lakeside in the old main street the smell of dried fish was still in the air and fishing dhows from the rugged volcanic island of Mfangano, visible to the west out in Lake Victoria, were in port as in the old days. But this was not the peaceful little town I had known.

In the morning, I went along to the school. I called in to see the Headmaster, who was still in the same old office but of course after fifteen years a new incumbent. I explained who I was and asked if it was O.K. for me to take a walk around. He was not friendly and expressed no interest in me or my past experience in the school. He said the pupils were on strike in a couldn't care less tone of voice. As I walked around I was appalled to see the scale of dilapidation of the buildings, broken doors and windows, weeds everywhere (in my day, the boys had kept the grounds immaculate with pangas). When I was there, the buildings had been brand new, the school expanding rapidly under the patronage of Tom Mboya, the local Member of Parliament and Minister for Economic Development, whom I had met and who had subsequently been assassinated. It looked as if little had been done in the way of maintenance since. I saw some of the pupils sitting outside one of the classrooms so I walked across to talk to them. It turned out that the strike was closely related to the neglect I saw around me. They said the school was being starved of resources through corruption at government level and teaching standards had fallen, reflected in deteriorating exam results. "Why don't you come back, Sir?" one of them said.

The condition of the staff houses didn't seem to be much better. They had also been brand new in my day, finished just in time for us to move into. The previously neat, open gardens were now a mass of vegetation, tall trees and shrubs, with the houses buried among it. The paw paw tree which had provided countless breakfasts when I was living there till stood by the gable of my old house. I saw no sign of the pot plant (marihuana) which had mysteriously appeared outside my bedroom window and given hours of pleasure to an old Kenya African Rifles World War II veteran who came around regularly in his old khaki army greatcoat to pick a few leaves until Were, the student who looked after our garden in return for us paying his school fees, told us what it was and suggested that we should perhaps get rid of it before the police got wind of it. Growing and smoking marihuana had been illegal, but the old women smoked it in pipes quite openly. Oddly enough, the younger generation didn't seem to use it. There didn't seem to be anyone at home in my old house so I just walked away, saddened by what I had seen.

Back in Nairobi, I headed for the airport for my flight to Entebbe. On the taxi drive out there, the sky was as blue and high as ever and I saw an ostrich loping across the plain. I was looking forward to seeing Uganda again but with a certain amount of trepidation about what I might find. There was only one other white face on the flight who turned out to be an Italian Roman Catholic missionary. Marita, my former girlfriend, had claimed to have Italian ancestry, which was quite possible from her colouring and facial features. It had occurred to me that the only Italians her forebears would have been likely to come into contact with were priests like my flight companion.

Coming into Entebbe Airport, I spotted some damaged fighter planes huddled behind a hangar. It occurred to me that these must be the result of the Israeli attack during Idi Amin's time when they had rescued hostages held there by PLO guerrillas. The Arrivals area was in a large hangar. As we were passing through Customs, the power went off and we were plunged into darkness. Dim lights came on again as an emergency supply kicked in. A Customs officer was taking great interest in my bag. He held up my travelling alarm clock. "This is nice," he said. "Yes, it's from Woolworths," I replied. "Would you like it?" "Oh, yes. Thank you," he said, zipping up the bag. My camera had been buried at the bottom of the bag and I didn't want him getting there.

On the way in from the Airport, we were stopped at a roadblock manned by soldiers. A boy, who couldn't have been more than 12 years old, lugging a Kalashnikov over his shoulder, came across and demanded to see my passport. I spoke to him in Swahili and told him that I used to live in Uganda. He smiled and said "Welcome back." The road from the airport into Kampala had been reconstructed by the Israelis during my time there with an immaculate tarmac surface.

It now looked as if giant rodents had been gnawing away at the edges, leaving just a narrow, jagged strip down the middle, barely wide enough for one vehicle, so that approaching vehicles played chicken with each other before pulling off in clouds of red murram dust.

In Kampala, I was booked into the Speke Hotel. This had been the plushest hotel in town in my time there. The intervening years had not been kind to it, signs of neglect everywhere – broken fittings and faded paintwork. The restaurant had been outstanding; now it was basic to say the least. There was a large, illustrated poster on the wall at the foot of the stairs warning about the dangers of Aids and some prostitutes in the bar and out on the terrace. During the night I awoke to the sound of gunfire. Peace had obviously not broken out just yet. A couple of hours later I was wakened by the sound of the Muezzin calling the Moslems to prayer, a reminder that Idi Amin had promoted the growth of Islam in the country. He was now in political asylum in Saudi Arabia.

In the morning, I walked down to the main street. The old familiar Asian shop names had gone along with their former owners and the spicy smells of the bazaar. The shops now were dilapidated and there were hardly any goods on display behind the heavy metal grills in the grimy windows. Hawkers were selling poorly printed newspapers on the cracked pavement. It was a depressing sight. A row of sinister looking Maribou storks were sitting on a telephone wire strung between two high buildings. They had earned a macabre reputation for feeding on human corpses left lying around during Amin's nightmare rule. I walked up the hill to the University. I noticed quite a few double-takes followed by broad smiles from the people I met. They were still not used to seeing white faces on the street again after the years of turmoil. The University was in an equally bad state of repair. The Quonset huts were still there but now occupied by African families, chickens wandering in and out of the doors. A woman was sweeping the concrete area outside the hut where I had stayed, some little children playing in the dust nearby. I walked over and greeted her in Swahili and told her that I used to live in her house. We chatted for a while in Swahili, mostly about my time at Makerere. After a while she shook her head, tears in her eyes. "These have been terrible years" she said in perfect English. I gave her some money "to buy something for the children". She hesitated but then took it; pride has no place where abject poverty rules.

I soon discovered that all the normal urban amenities and services were only partly functioning in the city. The electricity supply was intermittent and the public water supply patchy. The roads were potholed; telephones worked sometimes. I had been meaning to try to track down Marita and my daughter but it soon became obvious that it would be an impossible task. Over a million people had died and society had pretty much broken down. I visited both her old house and the one at Kololo where she had lived with the Frenchman but the new owners had no knowledge of her. Telephone directories and a badly out of date voters' role at the city council office had nothing under her own name – I didn't know the name of the Frenchman, if she had taken his name. If she had stayed with him, they would have got out of Uganda during the Amin terror years. I gave up.

MAY 2006: RETURN TO CAIRO

In May 2006, I had a return visit to Cairo. By this time I was back living in New Zealand. On a trip back to visit my mother in Shetland, I had booked a tour through Israel and to Petra in Jordan. I flew with Emirates to Dubai but it wasn't possible to get a flight directly to Israel from there so I was routed through Cairo. This time I stayed in the Hilton Hotel, down by the Nile – I had moved up in the world. The old security problems were still there, this time not Israel but the enemy within – the extreme Islamist groups. There was a security cordon around the hotel, manned by armed policemen and my taxi couldn't get within about 100 metres of the entrance. That evening, I took a taxi to visit the Windsor Hotel, where I had stayed previously. The décor was familiar; it hadn't changed much since I'd been there last. The grand old hotel had clearly seen better days. I had a drink in the bar but sometimes it doesn't pay to go back to places you've enjoyed – better to remember them as they were.

That philosophy didn't apply to the Pyramids, however, where I went next day as part of an organized tour of the city, escorted by my trusty guide Shady Maurice. They were as impressive as ever and the Sphinx still had its inscrutable smile. It helped that I had picked up some knowledge about the Ancient Egyptians and their culture in the intervening years. On the tour we had gone out to see the prototype pyramid at Saqqara and seen the site of the ancient city of Memphis which helped to set the Giza Pyramids in context. We had also visited the National Museum with its vast display of Ancient Egyptian artefacts including the treasure found in Tutankhamen's tomb. I now felt that I had done justice to the world's oldest Wonder.

2

MACHU PICCHU, PERU
OCTOBER 1975

IN 1973, MY older brother, Gilbert, was killed in a car accident in Malawi. He had been working there for the government as a vet. On his way home from work he swerved to avoid a bus suddenly pulling out in front of him, went off the road, hit a tree, and that was it. He was a much more careful character than me. I drove like a maniac for three years in East Africa and got away with it. Life isn't always fair. I got the news in a telegram in New Zealand where I had gone in early 1971 on a teaching contract and moved into town planning. After that my sister started suggesting in letters that I should try to get home to see my parents who were pretty cut up about my brother's death. I was beginning to feel the need for a change of scenery anyway. New Zealand in those days was fairly isolated from the outside world and I felt that I was missing out on something. I finally decided to return to Shetland in 1975.

I decided to make my way back through South America and complete a circuit of the globe. I had a friend, Peter Allan, who had worked in the Ruakura Agricultural Institute in Hamilton and was now involved in an agricultural development programme in Puno, up on Lake Titicaca in Peru. I wrote to him and arranged to visit him there.

My first stop was Tahiti. I had seen photographs of the island, read about Captain Cook's voyages there and seen "Mutiny on the Bounty" and "South Pacific", which I associated with Tahiti, even though it was filmed on the island of Kauai in Hawaii. Perhaps it was the fictional island Bali Ha'i and the song extolling its virtues that confused me. There was plenty of confusion all round. James A. Michener's book "Tales of the South Pacific" on which Rodgers and Hammerstein's musical and the subsequent film were based was set in what is now Vanuatu and the Solomon Islands. To confuse matters further, years later, on a visit to Bora Bora in the Leeward group of the Society Islands to the west of Tahiti, I had a meal in a restaurant called Bloody Mary's. She had been a central character in the book/musical/film but as far as I know was never supposed to have gone anywhere near Bora Bora. This was all typical of the romantic myths that had grown up around Tahiti ever since Captain Cook had spent three months there in 1769 observing the transit of Venus across the sun so that some boffin back in Blighty could work out how far the sun was away from the earth. The tales the crew of his ship the "Endeavour" brought back about gorgeous women who would shag for the price of a rusty nail (Cook had had to put an end to this trade in case the ship fell apart) got Europe very excited. Cook himself wrote that the girls would "dance a very indecent dance while singing most indecent songs" and that they liked telling dirty stories. And of course when Captain Bligh in his ship the "Bounty" arrived ten years later to pick up a cargo of breadfruit to ship to the West Indies to feed slaves, his crew became so besotted with the local talent during a five month stay that they mutinied shortly after they left, set him and the non-participants in the mutiny adrift in a small boat off Tonga and eventually sailed away with their Tahitian girlfriends to Pitcairn Island where they ended up mostly killing each other apart from John Adams who survived to father a race of incestuous paedophiles now serving time in a specially built island jail. It was going to be difficult for Tahiti to live up to its reputation. I knew that the missionaries had got into the act later and spoiled the sort of parties that Cook and Bligh's men had had so I hadn't bothered to bring a packet of six inch nails in my check-in luggage (in those days I could probably have put them in my carry-on bag). But I was hopeful that under French control (or rather the lack of it) a bit of "je ne sais quoi" or "Ooh, la, la" would have survived the troublesome priests.

My first view of the island at Faaa Airport on the north-west corner was every bit as exotic as I had imagined it to be. The soaring, craggy, volcanic mountain peaks rising to 2,241 metres (7,283 feet) in Mount Orohena and the deep valleys carved by swift flowing streams took the breath away. The jagged outline of the neighbouring island of Moorea, lying just to the west, reminded me of Bali Ha'i: I could almost hear "Some Enchanted Evening" playing in my head. The dense, lush, green vegetation with coconut and pandanus palms, breadfruit, flamboyant and papaya trees and groves of bananas was everyone's image of a tropical paradise. I had booked a room in the capital Papeete in the Kon Tiki Hotel at the far north-eastern end of Boulevard Pomare which ran along the waterfront past the tourist office and yachts moored in the harbour. The first European to discover Tahiti had been the Englishman Captain Samuel Wallace in 1767, followed by the Frenchman Bougainville the next year. Walking around town, I saw Bougainville's impressive statue in the park named after him and plenty of the beautiful flowering vine which also bore his name. Whaling ships started calling in the early 1790s spreading diseases including venereal ones and introducing alcohol. The population of at least 40,000 in Cook's time (Cook thought it might have been as much as 200,000 but this is now believed to be a considerable over-estimate) fell to 6,000 in the 1820s. (Things were even worse in the Marquesas Islands to the north where a population of 80,000 at the time of first European contact was reduced to 2,000 in a century.) Further irrevocable damage to the culture was done by the missionaries. In 1797, 25 of them from the protestant LMS (London Missionary Society) arrived in the ship "Duff" and eventually managed to ingratiate themselves with the Pomare family which gained control of the islands and set itself up as the royal family in 1815. Soon singing and dancing were forbidden, cover-up clothing required and sex outside marriage outlawed. In 1836, two French Roman Catholic missionaries landed clandestinely but were caught and deported. This intensely annoyed the French who were already in the process of annexing the Marquesas Islands and they landed a military force in 1842. After some bitter fighting they annexed Tahiti in 1846. I visited the Catholic Cathedral of Notre Dame with its tall, narrow, red-tipped spire, looking like the Virgin Mary's lipstick. Further west, along Rue du General de Gaulle, just inland from Bougainville Park, the French government buildings were grouped around Place Tarahoi, where the royal palace had stood until brought down by termites (how the mighty had fallen.) I had a look around the market with its vast array of Pacific tropical produce. In the afternoon, I caught "le truck" out to Point Venus on Matavai Bay where Captain Cook had based himself. These do-it-yourself buses were wooden trailers mounted behind lorry cabins, open at the back and with sliding windows to provide natural air conditioning and bench seats running down both sides. With its picturesque red lighthouse and little black-sand swimming beach, Point Venus was a pleasant spot to imagine what it had been like in Cook's day. From there, the forested central mountains looked very close. Mt. Aorai rose to 2,066 metres (6,715 feet). Years later, when I returned to New Zealand and discovered that Mount Cook had been returned to Maori as part of a settlement under the Treaty of Waitangi and given back its old name of Aorangi (Cloud-breaker), I realized that the two mountain's names were the same. There couldn't be much doubt where the New Zealand Maori had originated. The basic Tahitian greeting "Ia orana" had its equivalent in Maori "kia ora"; in Tahitian a house was a "fare", in Maori "whare" but pronounced exactly the same.

In the evening, I strolled along to where the "roulottes" were parked on the seaward side of Boulevard Pomare near the tourist office. These vans with side-flaps lowered to provide serving counters and with tables and chairs grouped around them had a wide variety of food on offer from the humble croque-monsieur (toasted ham and cheese sandwich – croque-madame with a fried egg on top) to steak-frites and delicious crepes. A number of roulottes were manned by "Tinito" (Chinese) offering a range of Chinese food. Their ancestors had arrived from 1864 to work on cotton plantations which had mushroomed to meet the shortfall produced by the American Civil War.

(The locals had been reluctant plantation labourers.) I discovered a number of excellent French restaurants in Papeete. France has tended to have a deeper impact on its colonies than Britain, not least through its influence on local food. At that time, I was not familiar with French food and some of the delights I discovered from breakfast croissants and French bread to confit of duck became firm favourites of mine. Some of the local Polynesian dishes were excellent as well: "poisson cru" (raw fish), marinated in lime juice and garlic with coconut milk added and a variety of vegetable ingredients including tomatoes, capsicum and green onions; and suckling pig (traditionally cooked in underground ovens using heated stones, like the Maori "uma") and accompanied by breadfruit, kumara (sweet potatoes) or taro. The game-fish "mahi mahi" was another discovery, delicious with vanilla sauce: I came across it again later in Hawaii and now very occasionally in New Zealand fish shops. After a steak-frites, followed by a vanilla ice cream filled crepe at the roulottes, I went to look for a drink and some nightlife. Things seemed to be fairly quiet (it was mid-week) until I strayed up Rue des Ecoles and found a bar which was busy, mostly French sailors and Foreign Legionnaires and some rather hard-faced women. France was still carrying out nuclear tests on Mururoa Atoll and the French military presence was everywhere. It soon dawned on me that the women were not what they seemed: they were all transvestites. What had these missionaries done? I later discovered that they were called "rae rae". Somebody wrote that the British navy had been built on "rum, sodomy and the lash" and it looked as if the French navy were carrying on the tradition, assuming that the "ladies" were prepared to throw in a bit of bondage. I finished my Hinano beer quickly and moved on, eventually finding a convivial small pub called the Café de la Gare but I couldn't find anything resembling a nightclub. The missionaries had obviously done their job – there was going to be no indecent singing and dancing or dirty stories for me that night.

The following day I took a tour around the island. The guide said that the coastal road measured 114 kilometres (71 miles) which made for an easy day trip. We set off clockwise, past Point Venus and on through Papenoo where there was a surf beach. I hadn't realized how poorly served Tahiti was with beaches. There were none worth speaking about near Papeete apart from the scrap of black sand at Point Venus and I was to find that the same went for the rest of the island. It was fringed by a lagoon inside a protecting coral reef but there were none of the stretches of white sand that a Pacific island conjures up in the mind. At Faarumai we detoured inland for about a kilometre to see a waterfall, the road lined with coconut palms, breadfruit trees and banana plantations. Further on, towards Tiarei, the coastline became rugged, with black basalt cliffs and steep headlands. We stopped where a blowhole at the base of the cliff was sending showers of spray across the road. Beyond that, the coastal plain widened and we passed through villages, each with its picturesque little church (those damn missionaries again). We crossed crystal clear river estuaries separated by mountain spurs. The little village of Hitaa was where Bougainville had landed. The little town and military base of Taravao stood at the isthmus connecting the off-shoot of Tahiti Iti (Small) to the main part of the island Tahiti Nui (Big) – the words "iti" and "nui" were identical in Maori. About half-way round the island on the south coast, we stopped to visit the Gaugin Museum and the botanical gardens and have some lunch in the restaurant at the museum. The museum was disappointing because all his great paintings had been spirited away to galleries in Europe and America. The museum dealt mainly with his life story but there were some reproductions of his paintings. I was to see some of his original work in the Louvre in Paris a few years later and later still his grave in Hiva Oa in the Marqueses Islands, 500 km to the north, where I also briefly met his grandson. Gaugin had first arrived in Tahiti in 1891 and after a brief return to Paris returned for good in 1895. He had died in the Marquesas in 1903 at the age of 54, riddled with syphilis. His liaisons with pre-pubescent local girls didn't amuse the missionaries and he fell out with the French colonial authorities as well. I had read Somerset Maugham's novel "The Moon and Sixpence" based on his life story. While the central character in the story, Charles Strickland, had been English, like Gaugin he had been a former stockbroker who abandoned his family to move first to Paris and then Tahiti to pursue a career in art. I had always associated

Maugham's short story "Rain" with Tahiti as well, although it had actually been set in Pago Pago in American Samoa. This story about the San Francisco prostitute Sadie Thompson who had moved to Pago Pago to start a new life and fell foul of the hypocritical missionary Mr. Davidson who ended up shagging her and then drowning himself in the sea in the throes of guilt pangs, ticked all the boxes in my character profile of a typical Pacific island missionary. We walked through the botanic gardens. Many of the most colourful plants in Tahiti – bougainvillea, frangipani, hibiscus – originate elsewhere such as South America. But the Tahitian Gardenia, the beautiful snow white tiare flower which the girls wear in their hair, was first discovered in Tahiti, although it may have originated in Melanesia. Further along the coast at Vaipahi there was a waterfall right beside the road. Then the coastal plain widened out along the more sheltered west coast with plantation crops and the distinctive taro plants with leaves like elephants' ears. We stopped to visit the overgrown ruins of what had been the largest marae (temple) on the island in Captain Cook's day, Mahaiatea Marae, with the remains of the "ahu" (altar) where sacrifices had been performed. In Cook's time, a cult associated with the War God Oro had been developing, leading to a period of warfare during which the Pomare family wrestled control of the whole group of the Society Islands. The missionaries of course had soon put an end to all that nonsense and the old religion had been obliterated, the old temples and idols destroyed.

I flew on to Lima, the capital of Peru. On the way in to the centre from the airport, out near the city's port at Callao, I saw hoardings advertising Inca Cola and some appalling slums. I was staying in a small Spanish colonial style hotel, the Hostal del Sol, opposite the Municipal Theatre and a couple of blocks from the city centre, the Plaza de Armas. The wide Plaza with palm trees, colourful flower beds and a bronze fountain dating from 1650 in the centre was surrounded by impressive colonial style buildings. The city had been founded in 1535 by Pizarro, the Spanish conquistador, shortly after he had overthrown the Inca rulers. The Incan capital, Cuzco, was well inland in the Andes Mountains and Pizarro needed a new one with direct access to the sea for his new empire. I was fascinated by the story of the conquest of the Incas in 1532 by Pizarro with only 168 men. Pizarro epitomised the Spanish Conquistadors of the 16th century. He was born into a military family in the poverty stricken region of Extremadura in central Spain. In 1502 he sailed to Hispaniola (now the Dominican Republic and Haiti) with the new Governor in a fleet of 30 ships. In 1513 he accompanied Balboa on his expedition across the Isthmus of Panama and they were the first Europeans to see the Pacific. After a couple of expeditions in the 1520s from Panama City down the west coast of South America, where he learned of the wealth of the Inca Empire, in 1532 Pizarro led a third expedition with the aim of conquering the territory for Spain. He only had 168 men of whom 62 were horsemen. They were helped by the fact that the Incas had been weakened by a recent bloody five year long civil war in which the Emperor Atahuallpa's brother, Huascar, had been deposed. They had also been weakened by European diseases, including smallpox, which had killed the previous Inca Emperor and his heir apparent. Diseases had spread into South America since the 1520s from the Caribbean where the native people had first been in contact with Europeans. Pizarro found Atahuallpa at Cajamarca, which he had recently made his capital. (He had been based in Quito in the north of the Empire and the Inca capital Cuzco had been his rival Huascar's stronghold.) Atahuallpa agreed to meet Pizarro formally and appeared in ceremonial mode with a contingent of about 6,000 unarmed or lightly armed men from his army of 80,000 which was camped outside the city. After an altercation with a Roman Catholic priest travelling with Pizarro, during which the Inca threw down a bible he had been given, the Spaniards made a surprise attack, opening up with cannon and musket fire. The combination of horsemen, cannon and muskets was decisive. The Inca's party was all but wiped out and Atahuallpa taken prisoner. After negotiations, the Inca agreed to fill a room with gold and twice with silver by way of ransom for his release. However, the Spaniards welched on the agreement and the following year, Atahuallpa was garrotted. Pizarro then went on to conquer Cuzco, the Inca capital, and take over the whole Empire. The Inca Empire had been a conglomeration of relatively recently conquered peoples, some of whom were glad to see the end of it and supported the Spaniards, so Pizarro was able to employ the same divide and rule tactics as had worked so well for Cortez against the Aztecs in Mexico a decade earlier. Atahuallpa's army from Quito, which was with him at Cajamarca, were seen as much as foreign invaders as the Spanish by Huascar's former supporters in the civil war from Cuzco. There is an interesting discussion of Pizarro's conquest of the Inca Empire in Jared Diamond's book "Guns, Germs and Steel".

None of the buildings surrounding the Plaza de Armas were as old as they looked. Lima was seriously earthquake prone and they had all had to be restored or rebuilt several times. The Cathedral with its imposing twin bell towers was on the site of the original church founded by Pizarro but its ornamental baroque style façade had last been rebuilt as recently as 1940 following an earthquake. The baroque model for the rebuild had been completed in 1758 following a disastrous earthquake in 1746 which had destroyed much of the city. Inside, the ornate carved wooden choir stalls had been sculpted in the 17th century. Pizarro's remains lay in a chapel by the main door. (It was an impostor: Pizarro's real remains were found in the crypt a couple of years later.) The Archbishop's Palace with its carved wooden Moorish-style balconies had been restored in 1924 in colonial style and stood alongside the Cathedral. The Palacio de Gobierno, the President's residence, occupied the north-east side of the square. It had been restored in grandiose baroque style in 1937. The Presidential Guards in their technicolour blue and red uniforms were on duty outside, performing an amusing, suspiciously camp, goose-stepping changing of the guard at midday. The creamy-yellow town hall, with its graceful, arched "cloisters" at ground and first floor levels faced the cathedral across the Plaza. I went to the elegant main post office just off the Plaza to get some stamps. In the next block to the west was the pink Church and Convent of Santo Domingo originally built in the 16th century but again rebuilt several times. The convent was laid out around a cloistered courtyard decorated with colourful mosaic tiles from Seville in Spain. Inside, the skulls of various saints were on display in glass cases. Next door, the light-blue painted Casa de Oquendo mansion, built in the early 1800s, with its four stories and a lookout tower, had been the tallest building in Lima for a while. There were several other impressive colonial style buildings in the immediate vicinity of the Plaza. The 1735 Palacio Torre Tagle featured an ornate baroque stone-carved portico and a beautifully carved wooden balcony in the Moorish Mudejar style. Just north of the Plaza de Armas, the virtually dry bed of the Rimac River cut through the city, channelled between concrete walls. Beyond that, the shanty town slums knocked together from corrugated iron and cardboard were appalling. To the north, the 409 metres (1,330 feet) Cerro (Hill) San Cristobal, with a huge cross on its summit, was just visible through the smog, the slightly higher Cerro El Agostino rising to the east. The climate of Lima was oppressive. The cold Humboldt Current which swept up the coast created an incessant sea fog known as the "garua", a grey pall hanging over the city from morning to night, with leaden, ashen skies hiding the sun. A dry, acrid heat, coupled with the traffic fumes, made my eyes water and dried out my mouth and throat.

From the Plaza de Armas, I walked down the pedestrianised Jiron de la Union, lined with neo-colonial and art deco buildings, to the Plaza San Martin, named for the "liberator" who had declared independence for Peru from Spain in 1821. There was a statue of him sitting astride his horse in the centre of the park-like square. He had been born in Argentina but went to study in Malaga in Spain at the age of seven. He fought for Spain in the Peninsular Wars against Napoleon and then returned to Argentina to take part in the war of liberation against the Spanish. After Argentina had won independence in 1814 he led the Army of the Andes over the mountains into Chile which was liberated by 1818 after several major battles. He then invaded Peru by sea with the newly formed Chilean navy under the command of the English Admiral Cochrane, one of Nelson's former officers. He declared independence in Peru in 1821 before the Spanish royalists had been fully defeated. In 1822 in Guayaquil, Ecuador, he had met with fellow "liberator" Simon Bolivar who had won independence for Venezuela, Columbia and Ecuador. It was agreed that Bolivar would take over the job of completing the liberation of Peru. Bolivar then went on to free Bolivia, which was called after him. San Martin went back to Argentina and then Europe after his wife died. He died in France in 1850. The two of them were big heroes throughout Latin America. Bolivar had a plaza named after him as well in Lima but as a liberator, he would probably not be too happy to see that the Museum of the Spanish Inquisition was located on it. The north-west side of the Plaza San Martin was taken up by another reminder of his fellow liberator, the opulent Gran Hotel Bolivar, built in 1924. The Bolivarcito Bar in the hotel was famous for its "pisco sours." Pisco was a strong, clear, "aguardiente" (grape brandy), named for the port in the arid south of Peru where grapes were grown under irrigation and from where the brandy had been exported. It was made "sour" by mixing it with lime juice, sugar syrup, egg white and angostura bitters over ice cubes. The huge doubles served in the Bolivarcito were called "catedrales". I had one and it was so good that I had another one and then one for the road. The hotel claimed as former guests Clark Gable, Robert Kennedy and Mick Jagger. I suspect that they all went on the piscos there too, especially Mick. In the evening I went for dinner at the El Cordano Restaurant, just across the street from the Presidential Palace. The potato (called "papa" in Spanish) originated in Peru, with over 1,000 varieties grown there in Inca times and it had become Peru's gift to the world. Something which hadn't caught on outside Peru was the roast guinea pig which I had. It tasted like guinea pig. Unfortunately, it also looked like guinea pig which was a bit off-putting.

The following morning I took a taxi out to the wealthy, sea-side suburb of Miraflores ("Look at the flowers!" in Spanish) which overlooked the Pacific across low, crumbling, brown, dusty cliffs above a gritty, boulder strewn beach – not at all inviting especially in October when summer was still a couple of months away. There was good surf running, but compared to the beaches in New Zealand it was no contest. Miraflores was the place for up-market restaurants and nightclubs. I went for a meal in the evening and discovered "ceviche" - raw fish and shellfish marinated in lime juice, onions and chillies. There were allegedly over 400 variations on the basic recipe. I followed it up with "papas rellenas" – potato croquettes filled with meat, egg, olives, tomatoes, onions and paprika. After the meal, I walked along to a night club. Like everything else in Miraflores, the girls were pretty up-market too compared to the ones I had seen lurking in the shadows around the Plaza de Armas the previous night.

I flew up to Cuzco, nestled high in the Andes and stayed in the El Virrey Hotel in the central square, yet another Plaza de Armas. The colonial style buildings surrounding the square were colonnaded, many with ornately carved wooden balconies. The cathedral with its flanking chapels occupied the north-east side of the square, opposite the hotel, with the domed Iglesia (Church) de la Compania de Jesus on the south-east side. A fountain played in the centre of the Plaza. Cuzco lay in a basin surrounded by mountains at 3,330m (10,900 feet) above sea level and the air was crisp, cool and clear seeming to bring the snow-capped peaks of the Andes closer to the city than they actually were. The sun appeared weak but the faces of the local Quechua Indians showed its power while the red, chapped faces of the children reflected the dryness of the air. The lack of oxygen at that altitude made moving around an effort. The Spanish city was built over the Inca one so that the buildings incorporated Inca stonework in their lower walls. In these drystone walls, each block fitted against the next so that you couldn't insert the blade of a knife between them.

Cuzco had been founded in the 12th century by Quechua speaking people who according to their traditions had moved north from Lake Titicaca. The city's name meant "navel of the earth". The name "Inca" was originally just applied to the Emperor but later came to represent the people and the culture as well.

There had been other advanced cultures in the area before them and at first they just established control over a limited territory around the city. In 1428 they defeated the powerful neighbouring Chanka kingdom and began a rapid military expansion which within 50 years had won them an empire stretching from what is now Columbia to Chile and extending into Argentina and Bolivia. As well as military action, they used treaties, including marriage alliances, to incorporate territories into their Empire. The subjugated peoples had to worship Inti, the Inca Sun God, adopt the Quechua language and pay homage to the new rulers. The Inca absorbed technology from the conquered territories in the fields of textiles, architecture, metallurgy (especially gold working), irrigation, pottery and medicine. They applied these lessons to develop Cuzco into a magnificent city with stone built palaces and temples and to increase agricultural output by terracing hillsides and constructing sophisticated irrigation systems. Corn (maize) was the staple crop and potatoes, beans and quinoa (a plant related to sugar beet but grown for its seeds and used like a grain crop) were also plentiful. Llamas and alpacas were domesticated for food and as pack animals. Food surpluses were stored and redistributed to the people in an early example of a welfare state. There was no private property, everything was organised communally. However, it was no communist state: society was very hierarchical with the Inca at the apex of the pyramid and several layers of nobility. The Inca was considered to be divine, a direct descendent of the Sun God. Earlier Incas were mummified and worshipped. The food surpluses enabled a large army to be maintained and a vast network of roads to be built, around 4,000 kilometres (2,500 miles) in all, stone paved and about a metre (3.25 feet) wide. Rivers and ravines were crossed by rope suspension bridges. Every 10 kilometres (6 miles) along the road system, "tambos" were built – roadhouses or caravanserai with storehouses for goods in transit and accommodation for travellers. There were also food storage depots for armies on the move and huts serving as relay stations for the relay message runners who could carry a message from Cuzco to Quito in 10 days. Labour for public works was provided through the "mita" system, a sort of community tax whereby each village contributed able bodied representatives in a form of "national service" scheme. The Inca never developed the wheel for practical use although they were aware of the principle as toys with wheels have been excavated. The steep terrain, extensive forests and lack of powerful domestic animals to haul wheeled vehicles probably made its application impractical. They also never developed writing although cords with colour-coded knotted strings attached (called "quipus") were used as an accountancy system in trading to record quantities of goods and may also have been able to transmit basic messages with different knots representing different syllables. As well as the sun and the Incas, they also worshipped the moon and physical features like waterfalls and mountains in an animistic way. The condor and puma were sacred animals. Animal sacrifices were common but human ones only made on special occasions when children from the aristocracy were the chosen victims. Divination was important in the culture: high priestesses fuelled up with "ayahuasca" (an infusion of coca leaves) making predictions. Calendars based on the sun and moon provided timing for planting and harvesting. It was a very sophisticated culture, in many ways superior to that of the Spaniards who overthrew it.

I set out from the hotel to explore the city. The Cathedral, with its twin bell towers had been started in 1559 but had taken 100 years to complete. It was on the site of a temple dedicated to a former Inca, Viracocha, and built from reddish granite blocks taken from the massive Sacsayhuaman fortress which stood on a hill above the city. According to Inca legend, Viracocha had "gone away" to the west. This was one of the straws that Thor Heyerdahl had clutched at to justify his theory that Easter Island had been colonised from South America. Inside the Cathedral there was a collection of colonial art including a painting of The Last Supper by the Quechuan artist Marcos Zapata – the feast featured roast "cuy" (guinea pig), legs in the air in the missionary position. A crucifix with a blackened figure of Christ on it known as "The Lord of the Earthquakes" was believed to have brought an end to the disastrous earthquake of 1650 after it was paraded through the streets by the terrified citizens. Christ's heavy tan which had led to the effigy being known as "El Negrito" was believed to have been due to candle smoke. It occurred to me that it may have got too close to the fire when the Spanish Inquisition was busy burning heretics at the stake in the Plaza outside. It was still paraded through the streets in an annual festival on Easter Monday. The cathedral had an ornate carved wooden choir and side chapels were decorated in gold and silver leaf. The adjacent Iglesia de la Compania de Jesus had originally been built by the Jesuits and completed in 1571 but had to be rebuilt after the 1650 earthquake. Its flamboyant baroque façade and towering dome threatened to upstage the cathedral. I walked down the pedestrian alleyway known as the Loreto, lined with the massive stone blocks of Inca walls. At the end was Santo Domingo Church, built on the site of the Incan Temple of the Sun where the mummified bodies of deceased Inca Emperors had been kept, lavishly dressed and seated on thrones of gold. They had been worshipped with offerings of food and drink. A huge gold disk representing the sun had covered one wall; a similar silver one on another wall simulated the moon. Other walls were covered in sheets of gold studded with emeralds and turquoise. In the patio, there had been life-size gold and silver statues of llamas. Many of these treasures had been used to meet Pizarro's ransom for Atahuallpa and taken away to Spain to be melted down. The main commercial street, the Avenida El Sol, ran back to the Plaza de Armas, parallel to the Loreto. North-east of the Plaza was a mainly residential area with narrow, twisting, steep, cobbled streets, the houses huddled around cobbled courtyards. I met coca-chewing women leading llamas with packs on their backs. They wore the traditional dress – wide, layered, brightly embroidered skirts, knotted shawls and cardigans over embroidered waistcoats, reds, blues and black the predominant colour scheme. They wore black bowler or stovepipe hats or upside-down red berets like soup plates and their hair in long plaits. A two kilometres walk uphill to the north on cobbled roads took me to the fortress of Sacsayhuaman. Only about 20% of the original structure remained – the Spanish had robbed it for building material for their churches, palaces and mansions, but it was still impressive. It comprised three terraces faced with massive blocks weighing as much as 350 tons and some standing over 5 metres (16 feet) high. It stretched for 300 metres (nearly 1,000 feet). The terraces were built in a zigzag, saw tooth pattern with salients and re-entrants which would have exposed the flanks of attackers. It must have taken a prodigious amount of labour to construct it. In the evening, I went into a bar to sample the local chicha beer. I wasn't very impressed with the pungent taste of the dirty looking, opaque, milky liquid and the dark, smoky atmosphere in the dimly lit bar room, with its morose, all male clientele didn't appeal to me so I headed for a restaurant I had seen nearby and had the "anticucho" – kebabs of pieces of beef heart with a potato skewered on the end.

I took the 80km (50 miles) three and a half hour train trip north-west to Machu Picchu, (which was later voted as one of the New 7 Wonders of the World from the short-list.) From the railway station, a bus took us up the steep, zig-zagging road to the 2,430m (7,970 feet) saddle between the two mountains, Machu Picchu (Old Peak) and Huayna Picchu (Young Peak), where the ancient city stood within a loop of the Urubamba River, one of the tributaries of the Amazon. Machu Picchu remains the most impressive archaeological site I have ever seen. The buildings were amazingly well preserved with gables still standing and window openings just waiting for a passing double-glazing salesman. Perhaps it was the mountain setting and the way the exquisite stonework sat so naturally in such an inaccessible place with the neat stone-faced agricultural terraces falling away below but the composite picture left an indelible imprint on my memory. The sur-rounding mountains held high religious importance in the Inca cul-ture and perhaps the knowledge of this creates a sort of aura around the place affecting even non-believers. Machu Picchu is believed to have been a sacred city, built for the Inca Emperor Pachacuti round about 1450AD and abandoned in 1572, possibly as a result of a small-pox epidemic introduced to Peru by the Spanish. As part of its reli-gious role various buildings had obviously been used for astronomical observations. It may also have served as a "summer palace" for the Inca, his country retreat from the pressures of Cuzco and as an admin-istrative centre for the surrounding area. The Spanish Conquistadors never discovered it. It was re-discovered in 1911 by the American his-torian Hiram Bingham, who called it "The Lost City of the Incas". My awe of the place was further heightened by the sight of a majestic con-dor circling the summit of Huayna Picchu. Perhaps it was the spirit of Pachacuti coming back to survey his lost city. The 1983 UNESCO designation of the city as a World Heritage Site described it as "an absolute masterpiece of architecture and a unique testimony to the Inca civilization."

Like the remains of the Inca buildings in Cuzco, Machu Picchu was constructed with polished dry stone walls in which blocks of stone were cut to fit together tightly without mortar. Without the wheel, the city must have been built using inclined planes and massive man-power to move the huge blocks of stone. The entrance was at the open fronted House of the Terrace Caretakers, with a view of the city across a strip of agricultural terraces immediately in front. I marvelled at the neat emerald green stone faced terraces and the remains of the ancient irrigation system, fed by springs on the mountainside. It has been estimated that enough agricultural land was created to feed four times the maximum population of the city, which from the number of houses would have been around 1,000. A shallow moat marked the edge of the city proper. Just beyond, a chain of 16 little ceremonial baths were known as the Fountains, fed by a canal from a mountain spring. The Temple of the Sun showed the most perfect stonework in the whole complex, melded seamlessly onto a smooth rock outcrop. A semi-circular tower had windows aligned to where the sun rose at the summer and winter solstices. The heavy stone lintel over the entrance door fitted perfectly. Beyond lay the Sacred Precinct with the Temple of the Three Windows, the neat openings trapezoidal in shape, the House of the High Priest, the Principal Temple and beyond on a sum-mit up a stone stairway, Intihuatana – the Hitching Post of the Sun. This cylindrical stub of rock, a squat pillar like the fat foresight of a rifle, had been used for solar observations but quite how hadn't been figured out. It was too fat for a sundial but it was leaning at an angle of 13 degrees, the latitude of Machu Picchu and at the June 21st solstice cast no shadow. Another stone staircase led down from Intihuatana, across the Central Plaza to the residential and "industrial" areas of the city on its east side. Further on, back towards the entrance, the Temple of the Condor appeared to be shaped like the sacred bird with outstretched wings.

I returned to Cuzco and the following morning caught a collec-tivo taxi down the Urubamba Valley to Puno on Lake Titicaca. These vehicles were notorious for over-crowding and suicidal driving. There were the expected baskets of chickens and red faced, snotty nosed children piled on top of each other but I had a reasonable amount of room among the mainly female passengers and the driver appeared to value his life. We passed herds of llamas and alpacas and men digging in fields with the primitive spade known as a chaqui takla, others working with wooden ploughs pulled by two oxen yoked together. The Urubamba River burbled merrily along beside us in the sparkling sunshine. The Urubamba Valley had been known as the Sacred Valley in Inca times. Abandoned stone-faced Inca agricultural terraces could be seen along the valley sides: civilization here had gone backwards since their time. We passed through stone-built villages, the inhabitants brightly clad, predominately in red, the men wearing triangular caps, the women in black bowler hats and long skirts, the children in helmets with ear flaps.

I arrived safely in Puno and Peter Allan met me at the bus station where the collectivo terminated. Puno had been founded in 1668 near rich silver mines from which it had grown wealthy. There were few signs of that wealth now but it remained the main city for the bleak Altiplano (the Andean Plateau) and the main port on Lake Titicaca. Titicaca was the highest navigable lake in the world at 3,856 metres (12,725 feet) above sea level and measured 194 kilometres (120 miles) long by 80 kilometres (50 miles) wide, with a maximum depth of 280 metres (920 feet). With its intense dark deep blue water shimmering in the high altitude sun, it was an impressive sight. The city was less so: the centre was yet another Plaza de Armas with a baroque style Cathedral dating to 1757 on the west side: the main street, Jiron Lima ran from north to south from the corners of the east side of the Plaza. In the hilltop Parque Huajsapata, stood a larger than life statue of Manco Copac, the legendary first Inca, who was supposed in Inca mythology to have emerged with his sister-wife, Mama Ocllo, from Lake Titicaca. Peter took me around in his land rover to see some of the agricultural projects he was involved in and we saw the remains of a pre-Inca culture that I had previously been unaware of at the Chullpas (cylindrical burial towers) at Sillustani, about 35 kilometres (20 miles) from Puno on the shores of beautiful Lago (Lake) Umayo where we saw flocks of waterfowl. Peter said that there was a herd of the endangered vicuna on an island in the lake, a wild relative of the llama. These chullpas had been built as tombs for the nobility of the Aymara speaking Colla civilization which had dominated the area before the

Incas absorbed them. They were up to 12 metres (39 feet) high and slightly wider at the top than the bottom. The stonework could rival that of the Incas. On the south side of Lake Titicaca, the Tihuanaca civilization had flourished from 200 AD to 900 AD so the Incas were just the last in a succession of sophisticated cultures in this part of the world. Down at the lake we saw the floating villages known as the Islas de los Uros, made from totara reeds, where fishermen lived with their reed and bolsa wood boats with llama figureheads. There were over 40 of those islands some with meeting halls and schools on them. New reeds had to be added continuously to replace those rotting away at the bottom. The original Uros people who had developed the islands had now been absorbed into the local Aymara people and spoke their language. In the twilight at the harbour we watched a ferry unload passengers from Bolivia across the lake to the south. Peter had organized a party, mainly local people attending. I had taken evening classes in Spanish at Waikato University in Hamilton but I soon discovered that I had a long way to go to become fluent or even reasonably competent in the language. I think it was then that I realized how much more you appreciate foreign countries if you can speak the language and made it my business over the ensuing years to bring my Spanish, French and German up to a level where I could hold an intelligent conversation if not discuss Einstein's theory of relativity. I also developed the habit of giving myself a crash course in the languages of countries I was going to visit, covering basics like greetings, ordering a beer, counting, and asking the way. This would disappear within a few weeks of leaving the country but for countries which I visited several times like Thailand, the basics became embedded on the hard disk of my brain as opposed to the disposable floppy disk where the crash courses stayed.

I caught a train back to Cuzco, changing trains at the grimy looking city of Juliaca and then flew down to Lima. I don't recall having any worries about travelling alone in Peru. I have since discovered that Abimael Guzman had formed his Sendero Luminoso (Shining Path) Maoist guerrilla group in the late 1960s but as far as I am aware they were not yet operating on any scale when I was in Peru. They went on to become one of the most ruthless and feared terrorist groups in the world rendering parts of rural Peru no-go areas in the 1980s until Guzman was arrested in 1992. Blissful ignorance of political and security problems seems to have been the general rule at this stage of my foreign travels and was to crop up again on this trip in Columbia and Jamaica.

I flew on to Quito, the capital of Ecuador. Nestling in a narrow valley up in the Andes, the elongated city sprawled along the valley floor between flanking mountains. (I bought a city map which had to be rolled up like a sheet of wallpaper.) In the taxi from the airport, it struck me as an attractive city, much cleaner and better maintained than Lima and as far as I saw, without the disfiguring slums. The mountain air was refreshing at 2,800 metres (9,200 feet) above sea level. Although the equator was just 25 kilometres (16 miles) north of the city, the altitude kept the temperature year round like an English spring. I was staying in the Old City, founded in 1534. This was where Atahuallpa had been born and his power base in the Inca civil war against his brother Huascar. Walking along to the centre, the Plaza de la Independencia, I was impressed with the state of preservation of the old colonial houses painted in pastel colours. (It was declared a World Cultural Heritage Site by UNESCO in 1978.) The Plaza was dominated by the Cathedral, built between 1550 and 1562, the Archbishop's Palace opposite it and the Town Hall and Government Palace facing each other on the other two sides. A block to the south, the Jesuit Church of La Compania had a richly sculptured façade and just to the west, on the Plaza de San Francisco, the church and monastery which gave it its name was the oldest in the city, built in 1553. Standing on a terrace, with a flight of steps leading up to it, the ornate portico of the church in brown stone contrasted with the twin bell towers and long two-storey wings painted white. The inside was beautifully decorated with a carved wooden choir and ceiling and a golden high altar. It was also full of art treasures, including the painting "La Virgen de Quito" depicting the Virgin Mary with silver wings. I walked up to the tall statue modelled on the painting on the Panecillo (Little Bread Loaf), a hill at the south end of the city with excellent views out across it. I walked back through the narrow, cobbled, Calle Morales, one of the oldest streets in the city, the buildings decorated with wrought iron balconies. The following day, I arranged a tour at the hotel reception desk to see the active volcano, Cotapaxi, 28 kilometres (17 miles) to the south down the Pan American Highway. With its impressive snow-capped, symmetrical cone rising to 5,897 metres (19,347 feet), it looked serene in the sunshine but concealed a hidden menace – it had erupted as recently as 1942 with a major event in 1903-04 and over 50 times since 1738. A massive eruption would threaten the suburbs of Quito.

The flight across the Andes to Bogata, the capital of Columbia, with the Avianca Airline started off routinely enough. Just above the summit ridge we hit an electrical storm. The cabin lights went out and we started to buck and shudder as if riding in a rodeo. Without seat belts people would have been bouncing off the ceiling. I looked out the window and saw the rivets in the wing jumping. I was holding on to the seat arm rest and the Mexican lady sitting next to me was stringing on to the back of my hand. Her finger nail marks were still visible a week later. People were screaming and praying and children crying. It seemed to go on for ever. The story of a charter plane, carrying a Uruguayan rugby team, which had crashed in the Andes, the survivors eating the bodies of those killed in the crash, came into my head. The crash had happened on Friday the 13th October, 1972, just three years earlier, and its aftermath had made sensational world-wide news headlines because of the cannibalism involved. Uruguayan Airforce Flight 571 had been carrying the Old Christians rugby union team and their family and friends from Montivideo, Uruguay to Santiago, Chile to play a match. Over the Andes they hit bad weather and in dense cloud flew into a mountain. Miraculously, 27 of the 45 passengers initially survived the crash but in the middle of the Andes at an altitude of 3,600 metres (11,800 feet) and with little food their situation was desperate. Eventually they agreed to eat the bodies of the casualties from the crash in order to stay alive. They heard on a transistor radio rescued from the wreck that the search for them had been called off and eventually two of them, Roberto Canessa and Fernando Parrado set off across the mountains in a desperate attempt to seek help. After ten days they came across a Chilean herdsman on horseback on the other side of a river they couldn't get across and on December 23rd, more than two months after the crash, the last sixteen survivors were rescued. These weren't the happiest of thoughts bearing in mind the situation we were in but I remained remarkably calm; after all there isn't a hell of a lot you can do about it in situations like that. A sort of fatalism took hold of me. And then we were out of it as suddenly as it had started. The lights came on. There had been no messages from the pilot during all this. I wondered if it was just business as usual for him or if he was as terrified as the rest of us and too busy trying to keep the plane in the air to offer words of comfort to the passengers.

Bogota lay in a highland basin in the Andes at 2,625 metres (8,612 feet) above sea level, with the towering peaks of Monserrate and Guadeloupe flanking it on the east. I stayed in the Ile de France Hotel in Calle (Street) 18, near the central business area. The city had been founded in 1534 and the old colonial "barrio" with its 300 years old buildings in various states of preservation and cobbled streets was by a long way the most attractive part of the city that I saw. The Plaza de Bolivar was the centre of the old city, with a bronze statue of the great "liberator". The buildings surrounding the Plaza were a mixture of styles and ages, reflecting Columbia's turbulent political history. The only survivor from colonial times was the baroque Capilla (Chapel) del Sagrario. The bulky neo-classical Cathedral had been completed in 1823. The Supreme Court was a new building, its predecessor having been burned down by a mob during a civil disturbance in 1948. (It, in turn, was later burned down again in 1985 when it was occupied by guerrillas from the M-19 revolutionary group and a fire broke out when the army moved in to reclaim it.) The Mayor's Office had been finished in 1905. The Capitolio Nacional on the south side of the Plaza, the seat of the National Congress, had been begun in 1847 but due to numerous political uprisings, not finished until 1926. Political unrest was still obviously the order of the day. The next day when I walked down to the Plaza, I found it full of tanks, crawling with military personnel and sealed off to the public. I didn't hang about to find out what was happening and caught a taxi to the funicular which went up Cerro de Monserrate. The view out across the city and surrounding mountains from the 3,152 metres (10,244 feet) peak with a white church on top was stupendous. In the late afternoon, I went along to see the changing of the guard outside the President's Palace, the early 20th century Casa de Narino. In the evening I had a crawl through some bars and was making my way unsteadily on foot back to the hotel around midnight when I met a well dressed man. He stopped and asked where I was going. Initially I was suspicious, but something in the alarmed look on his face made me take him seriously and when I told him the name of my hotel he said "This is a very dangerous area. Strangers shouldn't walk alone here." He came with me all the way to the hotel. He explained that he was a city councillor and said "I feel responsible for the safety of visitors to our city." I understand that Bogata is a much safer city now.

From Bogota, I flew down to Barranquilla on the Columbian coast. It wasn't a particularly attractive place, a major port and industrial centre on the Magdalena River and the humid heat was uncomfortable after the cool mountain air of Quito and Bogota. But the nightlife was lively. I went to a nightclub and picked up a girl who came back to the hotel with me. When we emerged in the afternoon she suggested going to the cinema. The film she chose was called "The Erotic Adventures of Zorro", an incongruous genre best described as pornographic comedy. It was hilariously funny in parts and judging by Rosita's peals of laughter, would have been even funnier if I had been able to follow all the Spanish dialogue. The following morning I took a bus down the coast to Cartagena, an old colonial city defended by an impressive fortress. I went for a swim at the beach and exhausted after a couple of nights of debauchery in Barranquilla, fell asleep on the sand. I still have freckles all over my body from the resulting sun burn.

My flight to Jamaica was via Panama City. We flew in over the Panama Canal and I saw ships making their way through the enormous locks. In Kingston, I stayed in the Indies Hotel in the upper part of the city, New Kingston. The receptionist turned out to have lived on the Shetland island of Unst for a while – her father had been a Church of Scotland Minister there. After dinner, I decided to walk down to the town centre and the harbour. As I walked downhill, the buildings lining the street were getting more and more ramshackle and the surroundings seedier and seedier. A tall Rastafarian fell into step beside me. "Want a girl?" he inquired. I declined politely. "Want a boy, then?" Again I declined, slightly less politely. "Want some ganja (pot), man?" By this time I was getting alarmed. I reached a small square where I spotted a taxi. I jumped in and retreated back to the hotel. In the morning I took a taxi down to the town centre. It looked as run-down and decrepit in daylight as it had in the darkness, with an air of menace. I later discovered that Jamaica was in the grip of a virtual civil war during an election campaign. The murder rate was higher than New York. Again I had been blissfully unaware of all this. Kingston at that time was the most dangerous place I have ever been.

And so I returned to Shetland after an absence of nearly five years. I had very little money saved and only the possessions I could carry but I had seen a lot of the world and been right round it. I decided that I would stay in Britain this time and look for work there.

3

THE STATUE OF CHRIST THE REDEEMER, RIO DE JANEIRO, BRASIL APRIL 1985

BACK IN BRITAIN, I worked for a couple of years in Shrewsbury as a Town Planner with Shropshire County Council and then in late 1978 moved back to Shetland as the Deputy Director of Planning with the local Council. Oil had been discovered offshore in the North Sea and was to be brought ashore to the massive Sullom Voe Oil Terminal in pipelines from the Brent and Ninian fields. The Shetland economy boomed and my professional life was pretty hectic so I got into the habit of taking all my holidays overseas to get away from it for a while. Initially, I stuck to Europe but I had taught myself some Portuguese from a TV/Radio series and a Linguaphone course and got in some practice on a couple of holidays in Portugal, so the idea of a trip to Brazil took root in my mind. I booked a flight and accommodation in Rio de Janeiro through Kuoni, the Swiss specialists in long haul tourist travel and in April 1985 set off.

I switched on the TV in my hotel room and for a moment I thought the wires must be crossed with the Rio Royal Infirmary. On the screen was an X-ray picture of someone's stomach and the commentator was going on at great length about what was wrong with it – quite a lot it seemed, even with my limited knowledge of Portuguese. All was revealed eventually: it was the entrails of the new Brazilian President, Tancredo Neves, which I had been privileged to examine. It was only about a fortnight since his inauguration and already he'd had three operations. It was obviously tough at the top in Brazil. I was staying in the four star 20 storey Luxor Continental Hotel in Leme, at the north-eastern end of Copacabana Beach, with private bathroom, mini-bar and coloured TV – hourly medical bulletins thrown in – unbelievable luxury for the price. Brazil's economy at the time was in almost as bad a way as the President. Inflation was at an astronomical figure with so many zeros on the bank notes that they looked like the results of Ronald Regan's IQ test. Before leaving for the trip, I had contacted a Town Planning Consultancy firm operating in Brazil (I was thinking of a move overseas again) and they had sent me some information about themselves. The package was literally covered in stamps – 34 at 500 cruzeiros each, a total of 17,000 cruzeiros to post a letter to Britain. No wonder the President had a bad stomach.

I'd pre-booked some tours through Kuoni including an introductory city tour of Rio to help me get my bearings. The setting of Rio was the most spectacular I had seen anywhere in the world. Enclosed by smoothly weathered, steep-sided granite mountains, including O Corcovado (The Hunchback) on which the statue of Christ the Redeemer was perched and the iconic Sugar Loaf Mountain, Rio looked out on the enclosed Guanabara Bay, the city of Niteroi shining white in the distance across the bay at the end of a 15 kilometres (10 miles) long cross-harbour bridge. Ocean beaches with golden sand fringed the coastline from Copacabana through Ipanema and Leblon and then again in Sao Conrado, over the spur created by the Dos Irmaos (Two Brothers) mountains, and continued west in Barra de Tijuca and beyond. There were smaller beaches in towards the city centre at Botofogo and Flamengo. Inland from Ipanema and Leblon and ringed with mountains, the large Lagoa (Lake) Rodrigo de Freitas was surrounded by top bracket residential development, restaurants, cafes and bars. You had to look for the poverty. The slums (favelas) were perched on mountain sides off the main drags, but very close. Two of the most notorious, Vidigal and Rocinha, lay above Sao Conrado, perilously close to the luxurious Sheraton Hotel, making this one of the most dangerous areas of the city.

The first Europeans to visit Rio were in a Portuguese expedition under Gonsalo Coelho in January 1502. His chief pilot, Amerigo Vespucci, who gave his name to America, allegedly named what is now Guanabara Bay, Rio de Janeiro – "rio" meant bay as well as river in 16th century Portuguese. However it was the French who first founded a settlement there in 1555 to trade in brazilwood and other forest products. They had been preceded some 9,500 years earlier by so-called Indian groups. In 1567 the Portuguese drove out both the French and the local Indians and set up a fortified town. At first it grew slowly, exporting brasilwood and sugar cane. The local Indians, forced to work on plantations, suffered heavy losses from European diseases and maltreatment: in 1580 a shipment of 2,000 black slaves arrived from West Africa, the first of some 4 million over the next 300 years, forming the basis of Brazil's mixed-race population. In the 1690s gold was discovered in Minas Gerais inland from Rio and the city became the main port serving the goldfields – shipping in the hordes of gold diggers who arrived from Europe and shipping out the gold they dug up. Rio's population mushroomed and it grew wealthy. In 1763 the capital of Brazil was transferred from Salvador in the North-East to Rio.

The Kuoni city tour mini-bus took us south along Avenida Atlantica which backed the wide Copacabana Beach, with its palm trees and the occasional refreshment stall. The broad pavement was decorated with mosaic patterns: multi-storey hotels and apartment blocks lined the landward side. Some steep-sided islands glinting white in the sun lay offshore. Up ahead in the distance the soaring twin peaks of the Dois Irmaos Mountains had taken on a reddish tinge. Beyond the Arpoador headland we swung west and were in Ipanema, more up-market than Copacabana but the name meant "dangerous waters" from the rips affecting the beach. The shops, restaurants and clubs here were classier than in Copacabana and so were the girls on the beach. We detoured inland a block to see the café-bar A Garota (Girl) de Ipanema where two old perverts used to ogle a girl who passed by regularly and penned the famous song the "The Girl From Ipanema." Bearing in mind that she was a schoolgirl, they would now probably be classed as paedophiles and placed on the Sex Offenders Register. We called in at the H. Stern Museum, housed in the headquarters of the famous jeweller, for a demonstration of the process of transforming rough precious stones into jewels which were way beyond my price range never mind a favela-dweller. The window displays in the boutique shops in this area were opulent beyond anything seen other than in the very smartest shopping streets in Western Europe. It illustrated the enormous gap between rich and poor in this society and why it was such a dangerous place. Disparities like this can only breed resentment, envy and an eye for helping yourself to some of the goodies whenever the opportunity presents itself. H. Stern was as burglar proof as Fort Knox; but tourists weren't, as I was to discover.

We turned north for a drive around the Lagoa Rodrigo de Freitas, which I was surprised to learn from the Guide, was a saltwater lagoon, as it was some distance from the beach. Here there were some very expensive looking residential areas, smart lake-front restaurants and bars, the horse racing track and the botanic gardens all in a magnificent setting beneath the surrounding forested mountains with Christ the Redeemer on Corcovado looking down on it all.

We continued round to the Botafogo district to visit the Pao de Acucar (Sugar Loaf Mountain). From near the attractive little Praia de Vermelha beach we caught a cable car up to the Moro de Urca and then another to the summit of the peak at 365 metres (1,186 feet) above sea level. The views were superb. Back at Moro de Urca on the way down, a girl held up a plate with a photo of me against a backdrop of the mountain on it. I hadn't come across this magic trick before and bought it without haggling – a mug shot of a mug. We carried on towards the city centre. The Guide pointed out the Sol-e-Mar seafood restaurant down by the shore which she recommended and added that Bateaux Mouches (pleasure boats) left from there for harbour cruises and trips to Paqueta Island. We continued on, passing Flamengo Park on the seaward side with its variety of trees and the attractive little 18th century Gloria Church perched on a hill to our left. We stopped at Cinelandia which with the adjacent Praca Floriano was the modern centre of the city although it all looked a bit run-down and threatening, not an area that I would have felt safe walking round in at night. The main public buildings were here: the City Council offices; the Municipal Theatre, built in 1905 in the style of the Paris Opera; the National Library; and the National Museum of Fine Arts. The main street, Avenida Rio Branco ran north from here. Just to the west, beyond the tall arches of a former aqueduct, the Arcos de Lapa, which now carried the "bonde" (tram) up to the Santa Teresa neighbourhood, was the brand new Municipal Cathedral. It bore no resemblance to a traditional church, its conical shape looking like a cross between a loofah and a Mayan temple with hints of a beehive and honeycombs. The architect must have been on the same stuff as the designers of Brasilia.

In 1989, I took a "Brazilian Contrasts" tour, with Kuoni again, which included Brasilia. Brasilia had been created from scratch as a new capital to promote the development of the interior. A competition had been launched for the design of the new city and it had been won by the Urban Planner Lucio Costa. Work had started in 1956 and by 1960 enough had been built to transfer the capital there from Rio. Government officials had to be bribed to go there with subsidised accommodation and higher wages. This came as no surprise to me as I disliked it as much as its clone Canberra which I had visited in 1974. Laid out to look from the air like an aeroplane about to nose dive into a huge boomerang shaped lake, the residential and commercial areas formed the wings sweeping round the concave side of the lake, the public buildings strung out along the fuselage. Like Canberra, the distances between individual buildings were immense, a nightmare for pedestrians, a city designed for cars. And like Canberra, it seemed to me to have no soul, none of the vivacity which characterised Rio. To me, there is the same difference between these artificially created cities and ones which have grown organically as between a robot and a human being.

But the architecture of the individual buildings was often spectacular, many of them designed by Oscar Niemeyer, a protégé of the French architect Le Corbusier. This has since been recognized by UNESCO which has included Brasilia in its register of World Heritage Sites. The cathedral, like the new one in Rio, was a completely new concept in church design and very striking: the roof design, looking a bit like a pineapple top, was intended to represent hands raised towards heaven in prayer – cynically, I thought they might be praying on behalf of the congregation to get the hell back to Rio. The glass roof allowed soft light to fall on the altar and the stained glass was beautiful. The J.K. Memorial was a museum of Brasilia dedicated to President Juscelino Kubitschek who had pushed through its construction: a huge stone bust of his head stood outside it. The group of buildings around the Plaza of the Three Powers – the President's Palace; the National Congress buildings; and the Federal Supreme Court – was particularly impressive. The two 28 storey towers of the Congress building were linked half way up like Siamese twins, the Senate and House of Representatives like two soup plates, the latter upside down. Outside the Supreme Court, a sculpture of a seated female wearing a blindfold represented blind justice and perhaps a desire to blot out the city. A statue of two skeletal Lowry-like figures represented the workers who had built the city. They had obviously not been very well fed. The Palacio do Itamaraty, which housed the Foreign Ministry, was an architectural gem, its ornamental arches reflected in a pool with floating gardens. Curtains of water cascaded down the outside of the Ministry of Justice. While we were standing admiring this complex, I heard the strains of a George Michael song coming from a manhole. I remarked to a member of the group: "I wonder what George Michael is doing down there?" "It isn't the first manhole he's been down" he replied. It occurred to me later that this was remarkably prescient on the part of my fellow traveller as it was years before George came out and had his unfortunate "zip me up before you go go" incident following careless whispers to an undercover cop in a public toilet in Los Angeles.

Our Rio tour moved on to the old city centre at the Praca de XV Noviembre, named for the date when Brazil declared independence from Portugal in 1822. Here stood the former Royal Palace which had started life as the Governor's residence in the 18th century. The royal family had been deposed in 1889 and Brazil had been a republic ever since. Just north of the square, through the Arcos de Teles archway, the narrow Travessa do Comercio was lined with bars and restaurants in the original colonial style buildings. Just beyond, on an island in the wide Avenida Presidente Vargas, was the Candelabria Church, work on which had started in 1775. Its interior was lavishly decorated in the over-the-top rococo style. We drove up to the Santa Teresa district. The Guide laid warnings on us not to use the tram if we fancied coming back to spend more time here as it was infested with thieves. I was beginning to wonder if there was anywhere in Rio that wasn't. The whole central area had struck me as decidedly dodgy. I later learned that Ronnie Biggs, the escaped Great Train Robber, lived in Santa Teresa. Santa Teresa was an attractive area of gabled Victorian era mansions, with narrow cobbled streets, wrought iron fixtures, stained glass windows and flowers and trees in the streets and gardens. There were a number of restaurants and bars around the central square, Largo dos Guimaraes. But like the rest of the old part of the city it had seen better days.

That evening, I had dinner in the Moenda Restaurant in the Trocadero Hotel on Avenida Atlantica with a superb view of the lights of Copacabana and out across Guanabara Bay. The restaurant specialized in Bahian food from the North-East of Brazil and the waitresses were dressed in traditional Bahian style – white, off- the- shoulder lace blouses, long, full-skirt dresses in white or bright floral prints, turbans in white or green and brightly coloured beads and bangles. I started with vatapa, a mixture of fresh and dried shrimp, fish, ground peanuts, coconut milk, dende oil (from a palm tree of African origin) and seasonings, thickened with bread crumbs to a creamy mush; followed by xinxim de galinha – chicken fricassee with the obligatory dende oil, dried shrimp paste and ground peanuts. I couldn't resist topping the meal off with quindim – little sticky cakes made from eggs and coconut. Bahian food was heavily influenced by the African slaves who were brought to the area and tended to be spicy – often accompanied by a dish of red hot malagueta (red or green chilli pepper) sauce.

I visited Salvador, the capital of Bahia, on my "Brazilian Contrasts" tour in 1989. The Portuguese first discovered Brazil in 1500 when Pedro Alves Cabral landed at Porto Seguro further down the coast of Bahia from Salvador. In 1548 Salvador became Brazil's first capital. The local economy was heavily based on plantation agriculture of tobacco and sugar cane, hence the huge influx of African slaves. We stayed in the Praia Salvador Hotel on Avenida Presidente Vargas which skirted the white sandy Ondina Beach lined with palm trees. The beaches around Salvador were some of the most beautiful I have seen anywhere, particularly a little further up the coast at Itapua with its lighthouse, palm trees, statue of Iemanja (the Goddess of the Sea) in the form of a mermaid and snow white sand dunes surrounding the Lagoa (Lagoon) de Abaete. The old city was badly run-down but its 17th and 18th century glory could still be clearly seen. It was built on two levels: the port, commercial areas and the market (with handicrafts and artwork as well as food and drink) down at sea level; the upper town, accessed by the Lacerda Elevator (or steep alleyways and stone stairs), with the public buildings, churches, museums and residential districts. At the top of the elevator was the Praca Municipal, the administrative centre with the Town Hall and Mayor's Office in restored colonial buildings. To the north past the Archbishop's Palace, on the Praca da Se, was the 17th century cathedral, built by the Jesuits, the altar decorated with gold leaf. Nearby, on the Terreiro de Jesus, were the Dominican and St. Peter's Churches. In the adjacent Praca Anchieta the 18th century Church of St. Francis had been built from stone imported from Portugal. According to the tour guide, it was one of the most opulent baroque churches in the world. The interior was indeed stunning, covered with intricate carvings smothered with gold leaf. This had once been a very wealthy parish.

Down Rua Alfredo Brito, we reached the Largo do Pelourinho (Pillory), the centre of Salvador's best preserved area of colonial buildings, some of them dating back to the 16th century. While badly rundown, the narrow cobblestone streets of faded pastel coloured houses – turquoise, blue, cream, green, and pink – with wrought-iron balconies and red-tiled roofs, readily conjured up a past era of opulence when this area had housed the aristocracy: now, it had a reputation for prostitutes and petty thieves. The square took its name from the whipping post where slaves and thieves had been punished; slave auctions had also been held here. Just past the square was the Church of our Lady of the Rosary of Black Men which slaves had built for themselves as they were not allowed to worship in other churches: its site was just beyond where the former city wall had stood as they were not allowed to build within the walls. On the square was a museum and library dedicated to Jorge Amado, Brazil's most famous author, who was a native of Salvador. Next door was the tiny City Museum with displays of Afro-Brazilian folklore including, on the top floor, mannequins dressed as Orixas (Gods) of the candomble religion, which was still widely practiced in Brazil in parallel with Catholicism. It was based on the ancestral Yoruba religion from West Africa: the slaves had seamlessly matched their old Yoruba Gods with Christian Saints when they had forcibly been converted to Christianity. Outside in the street, a donkey was laden with drinking coconuts for sale and a woman in traditional Bahian dress was selling acaraje (shrimp and bean fritters) from a tray on her head. There were little shops selling lacework – blouses, dresses, tablecloths. In the evening, the tour guide took us back to the Senac Restaurant on the square for a Capoeira performance. This had originated as a form of martial art among the slaves and when it was banned by the colonialists they had converted it to a balletic dance. It was no longer a contact sport but the flying, thrusting legs and arms often didn't miss their mark by much in the cart-wheeling moves between pairs of dancers. The display was accompanied by rhythmic drumming and tuneful plonking on the berimbau, a musical instrument made from a hollowed out gourd with a bent bow attached and a single metal string stretched between the two, which was played with a coin.

I had heard about the nightclubs in Rio but the reality was even wilder than anything I had imagined. There were some respectable places with lavish floorshows where you could even have taken the wife over in Ipanema and Leblon, such as the Lido and Plataforma 1 and plenty of discothèques for the younger generation such as Mikonos and Hippopotamus. But the more notorious places known as "Boites" (pronounced Bwatshays) were in Copacabana, centred on Praca do Lido and lying between Rua Duvivier and Avenida Princesa Isabel – Boite Lido, Boite Holiday, Boite Erotika, Don Juan, Frank's Bar. In these, the entertainment usually started off fairly tamely with dances by samba troupes and go-go dancers, followed by striptease acts and as the night wore on erotic shows including live sex acts. I didn't see any performances involving donkeys which urban legends about Rio had featured but it was still pretty full on. And of course there were plenty of female drinking partners available including take-away services. Apart from the nightclubs there were also establishments describing themselves as Saunas which were open during the day in case anyone couldn't wait until nightfall. In the interests of research, I visited one called Oasis 123 in Botafogo. The list of services available included shows, thermal pools, sauna, massage, manicure, pedicure, bar, live music and satellite TV. I very much doubt if many men came there to watch TV because the main business was covered by the phrase "e muito mas" (and much more). The staff were called "Receptionists" and dressed in black stockings and suspenders they appeared to be very receptive to any requests the clientele might have for services covered by the "muinto mas" category.

One night in Frank's Bar, I met a samba dancer called Michely. When she had finished her last show, I invited her back to my hotel. "No," she said, "they might think I'm a prostitute. We could go to a Love Hotel. I've got a car." There were apparently a number of these motel-style places where you could rent rooms by the hour. Michely led me out to a smart yellow Volkswagen and we set off: as soon as the engine started and she accelerated away, I could hear and feel that this was no ordinary machine; someone had seriously souped it up. I was hoping that there weren't too many police around as she had a cavalier approach to traffic signals and speed limits. "Did you take driving lessons from Fitipaldi? (The famous Brazilian Formula 1 racing driver)" I asked. "No," she said. "He used to ask me for advice." After that, I just called her Fitipaldi. The hotel she took me to was far from a doss house: it was almost of equivalent standard to my four star hotel, only the décor was Victorian brothel style with lots of red velour and mock-gilt mirrors, even in the ceiling and there was a Jacuzzi in the bathroom. Fitipaldi had been brought up in a favela but there was no slumming it that night.

I got up early one morning and went for a walk along the beach. I came across what looked like a little altar built from sand at the edge of the sea. There was a straw effigy on it dressed in a black coat and red trousers with a black top hat, some candles in a little ceramic holder, some chicken bones, a wreath of flowers and some dried up entrails – I knew they weren't the President's ones as I had just seen them earlier on breakfast TV. I asked Fitipaldi about this later and she confirmed my suspicion that this was an offering to Iemanja, the Goddess of the Sea in the condomble religion, akin to Voodoo in Haiti and still widely practised in Brazil. The sun was already getting hot so I decided to take a quick swim. I scrambled down a steep bank cut in the sand by the sea in the previous night's gale and cooled off in the surf. When I got out and my head emerged above the bank again I saw my clothes scattered up the beach like a paper-chase trail and I knew I could say goodbye to the nice watch I had bought in Fiji years ago. Fortunately, I had headed the warnings issued by the tour guide and not taken any money with me but I'd forgotten to consign my watch to a hotel safety box with the rest of my valuables as advised by the guide.

I visited Brazil twice more in later years and got robbed each time, with increasing degrees of aggravation. After my "Brazilian Contrasts" tour in 1989, I stayed an extra week in Rio. One night I took a taxi to try to find a nightclub I had seen in passing from another taxi that day but couldn't remember exactly where it was. I asked   the taxi driver to let me out in the vicinity of the club. It was raining but I knew I wasn't far away from the club. I wasn't paying attention, concentrating on trying to remember where I had seen the place, when I became aware of a group of favela types running across the road towards me. At first I thought they were just running to get out of the rain but suddenly I was surrounded, five or six of them, demanding money. I didn't argue and took out my wallet. They snatched it and were off. Fortunately my credit card was in a separate little holder and I hadn't been carrying a lot of money but it was a sobering experience.

The third robbery was a much more serious affair. I went back to Brazil in 1993, splitting my time between Rio and Sao Paulo. We had visited Sao Paulo on my "Brazilian Contrasts" tour but had only spent one night there and not had time to see much of it other than the Butantan Snake Farm where we watched staff milking venom from the fangs of a variety of evil looking serpents for dispatch all over the world as anti-dotes to snake bites. There was also an exhibition of snakes, scorpions and spiders – not everyone's cup of venom – one member of the group said later that she had kept her eyes shut during the entire visit. We also visited Ibirapuera Park and saw the huge granite Monument to the Bandeirantes (flag or banner carriers), 37 early pioneers who had been massacred by the local Indians. On my return visit in 1993, I had more time to get to know the city. I stayed in the Brasilton Hotel, just off Rua Augusta, where there were a number of very lively nightclubs including the Kilt, Puma and Chalet which if anything were even more full-on than the Rio clubs. Sao Paulo had started life as a mission station founded by two Jesuit priests in 1554. The site was marked by a replica built in the 1950s with a museum containing a collection of original relics dating back to these early days. Other than that, there was little left of old Sao Paulo – the nearby cathedral was a 20th century building. The rapid growth of the city was built on the 19th century coffee boom which generated considerable wealth for the area. The city was now an ugly, sprawling industrial and commercial centre of over 10 million people, producing cars, electronics and chemicals, with chronic traffic, crime and pollution problems – it was located in a basin in the plateau, ringed by mountains, which created ideal conditions for smog arising from traffic fumes and industrial emissions. The main drag was the Avenida Paulista but there was no real city centre, no grandiose master plan a la Brasilia here. But it was lively, bustling, with a character which had been lacking in Brasilia. Much of this character came from the ethnic mix. Unlike most of Brazil, only 10% of the population were of negro and mulatto descent. It had the largest concentration of Japanese immigrants anywhere in the world, with 600,000 descendents. In their heartland, Liberdade, a red-painted traditional Japanese Torii Gate straddled the main street. The Bon Retiro area around Rua 25 de Marco was a Lebanese enclave, with a million people tracing their roots back there. The Italian area was Bela Vista (colloquially known as "Bixiga" after a former tripe factory) centred on Rua 13 de Maio. Here, in a row of red and green cantinas and two storey houses, I found some of the best Italian restaurants I've eaten in anywhere, including Italy. I visited the Ipiranga Museum housed in an attractive palace with a colonnaded portico flanked by two storey arched wings, set in a park modelled on the gardens at Versailles. There was an equestrian statue of Emperor Dom Pedro I commemorating his declaration of independence from Portugal near here in 1822. The museum had sections on Pedro I, the local Indians, the pioneer aviator Alberto Santos Dumont and the colonial period, with furnishings and farm equipment.

I flew back from Sao Paulo to Rio to spend my last week there. A few days before I was due to return to Britain I was walking down Avenida Atlantica from the Olinda Hotel where I was staying, heading for a bar with tables out on the wide pavement which I could see up ahead, when I felt an arm round my neck from behind and glancing down could see a short knife being held to my neck. This was around ten o'clock at night and there were still plenty of people around – a woman in Bahian dress, accompanied by a toddler, had a pavement stall set up about twenty metres away with a fire in a brazier where she was cooking acaraje for sale. My assailant had appeared silently behind me from a side street. With a knife at my throat I couldn't risk struggling or making any noise to attract attention so I just let him help himself to my wallet and credit card sleeve. He was trembling so much I was afraid the knife was going to end up in my neck anyway. He let go of me and I just caught sight of him briefly as he careered back around the corner from which he had emerged – young, emaciated, and from a brief eye contact he looked high on drugs. I found a policeman in a booth back towards the hotel and reported the robbery. Apart from the money in my wallet the mugger had got away with one of my credit cards. When I got back to the hotel, I phoned the credit card company and got the card stopped. It was just as well I did because the thief had started using it almost immediately – when the next statement arrived it showed that the first purchase by the new owner had been an enormous amount of meat: he must have been intending to feed the whole favela. Amazingly, a few weeks later, the credit card company contacted me. The thief had been caught and did I want him prosecuted? Silly question.

The following morning, I was walking along the main shopping street in Copacabana when I noticed a gob of something disgusting on the upper of my shoe. A young shoe-shine boy about eleven or twelve years old appeared alongside me, offering to clean my shoes. I had read about this scam: they would splatter your shoes with something gooey while you weren't looking and then appear at your side like a white knight. I was in a seriously bad mood after the previous night's robbery. I grabbed a cloth from his box and wiped off the gob, then seeing a large refuse container just ahead, grabbed him and stuffed him headfirst into it, closing the lid. Not strictly politically correct, I know, but I had had enough. For as much as I liked Brazil, scammers like him and thieves like the knife wielder from the night before and his fellow professionals from my previous trips had finally convinced me that it was not a place I would ever come back to.

One Saturday lunchtime, I went with Fitipaldi to meet a group of her friends for a feijoada, the national dish, traditionally eaten at that time so that you had the rest of Saturday and Sunday to recover from it. When Fitipaldi introduced me to her friends she said: "He speaks very good Castilhana" (Spanish). I had tried very hard to learn Portuguese and had bought a book by the Bahian author Jorge Amado which I could read quite easily with a bit of help from my pocket dictionary but when speaking Portuguese I would keep slipping into Spanish. Linguists have a technical term for this – "interference" – the two languages are so similar that there is a natural tendency to mix them up especially when you are much more fluent in one than the other. The feijoada had originated as a slave dish: its basic ingredient was black beans and traditionally the remainder of the stew was anything that the masters wouldn't eat – pigs' ears, feet, tail and snout for example – but the modern version contained a variety of dried, salted and smoked meats including salt pork, dried beef, tongue, pork loin and ribs, sausage and bacon. This was all cooked for hours in large metal pots with onions, garlic and bay leaves.

This was just the main dish, served in earthenware casseroles. The waitresses littered the table with a daunting array of accompaniments: rice; bright green kale; orange slices; crisp bacon; and farofa – manioc flour sautéed in butter with onion, egg and raisins mixed in. There was a dish of fiery hot bean sauce with onions and hot pepper and a pile of tiny malagueta chilli peppers called pimenta which brought tears to your eyes. And then of course there was the drink – ice cold draught beer called chopp (pronounced shop) and the lethal caiparinhas. Caiparinha became my favourite drink although I haven't found anywhere else in the world where they are made as well as in Rio or as strong. Limes are mashed with a pestle, crushed ice added and then cachaca – fiery cane-sugar spirit – added with sugar or syrup. I lost count of how many we had. The meal lasted virtually all afternoon and I could hardly stand up at the end of it. Fortunately the hotel wasn't far away and Fitipaldi didn't have her car or we would have ended up wrapped around a lamp-post. Back at the hotel, I switched on the TV and there was the President's pancreas, looking like a prime candidate for inclusion in a feijoada: I made a bee-line for the bathroom.

Fitipaldi also introduced me to the rodizio style churrascarias – meat restaurants where waiters came round continuously with skewers of different cuts of barbecued beef, pork, chicken and sausage for as long as you were able to eat. We went to Mariu's on the Avenida Atlantica in Leme, just near my hotel. You could regulate the flow of meat using a little wooden block, green on one side, red on the other. You turned up the green side when you wanted more meat and the red side while you were clearing the backlog and when you were finally capitulating. Again there was a vast choice of accompaniments – a salad bar, chips, rice, fried bananas, hearts of palm, farofa and a variety of sauces. Rio was no place for vegetarians.

One morning, Fitipaldi took me up in the yellow VW to see the statue of Christ the Redeemer up close and personal. She called him "O Corcovado", the Hunchback, which was actually the name of the 700 metres (2,300 feet) high mountain on which he was perched, arms outstretched in the peace symbol or perhaps to allow himself to be frisked by a mugger from one of the favelas spread out below. If you've been crucified once already the last thing you want is a knife in the back for refusing to cooperate with an armed robber. The drive up through a roller-coaster of hairpin bends had been hair-raising: speed limits were a foreign concept to Fitipaldi but she was actually a very good driver, grinning as she gunned the powerful little souped-up machine through the bends. We hadn't picked the best of days for our pilgrimage as low cloud swirled around the peak at times descending to obscure the Saviour completely. When he did emerge from the cloud, his size was impressive, 39.6 metres (130 feet) tall including his pedestal, the outstretched arms 30 meters (98 feet) wide. Taking nine years to construct from 1922 to 1931 (substantially longer than God took to make the world but then this was laid-back Brazil) the statue was erected to commemorate the 100th anniversary of Brazil's independence from Portugal in 1822. Made of reinforced concrete with a soapstone outer layer he was crucifixion proof and metal lightning-rods protected him from thunderbolts – not always successfully.

In spite of being called the hunchback, there was nothing wrong with his back as far as I could see but he appeared to have some sort of a congenital disfiguration in the chin department. "He looks like Bruce Forsythe or Jimmy Hill" I said. "Who are they?" Fitipaldi asked. "Bruce is a game show host on TV in Britain. The contestants have to try to remember the prizes they've seen going past on a conveyor belt so that they can win them. Jimmy Hill's an ex-footballer who comments on football on TV. What they both

have in common, apart from big heads, is big chins – long ones, like the Redeemer here." Fitipaldi squinted up at the statue as it briefly emerged from the cloud. "That's not just his chin," she said. "He's got a beard." I looked a bit closer. "Could have fooled me," I muttered. I couldn't get the images of Bruce and Jimmy out of my head. For the life of me I couldn't imagine the Redeemer looking down on the hordes of thieves and muggers streaming out of their mountain-side favelas down onto the streets and beaches of Copacabana to rob tourists and saying something messianic like: "Forgive them, for they know not what they do – to the Brazilian tourist economy." All I could envisage was him with a manic, toothy grin, babbling "Cuddly toy, cuddly toy"; or commenting on a football match between Liverpool and a Spanish team with a divinely named goalkeeper, getting excited at the sound of his own voice, and shouting: "Jesus saves, but Dalgliesh nets the rebound." I had been waiting to get a photograph but the low cloud kept swirling down around his head just as I was about to push the shutter button. Suddenly, as if by a miracle, it lifted and there he was clearly revealed, resurrected above me as if on his way up to heaven or back down again for the second coming. Brucie's catchphrase came to mind. "Nice to see you," I muttered, clicking away, "to see you, nice."

When I was writing this chapter, I discovered from the internet Wikipedia web site that there had been some very un-Redeemer-like goings on in the voting for the New Seven Wonders. Apparently after supporting the Swiss-based Foundation which had undertaken the exercise, UNESCO had distanced itself from it. Votes could be cast through the internet or by telephone and there was no mechanism for weeding out multiple votes. The web site had the following to say about the elevation of the Redeemer to the top seven in the voting:-

"In Brazil, there was a campaign "Voto no Cristo" (Vote for the Christ) which had the support of private companies, namely telecommunications operators that stopped charging voters to make telephone calls and SMS messages to vote. Additionally, leading corporate sponsors including Banco Bradesco and Rede Globo [a TV Channel] spent millions of reais [the new currency] in the effort to have the statue voted into the top seven. Newsweek reports the campaign was so pervasive that:

One morning in June, Rio de Janeiro residents awoke to a beeping text message on their cell phones: "Press 4916 and vote for Christ. It's free!" The same pitch had been popping up all over the city since late January – flashing across an electronic screen every time city-dwellers swiped their transit cards on city buses and echoing on TV infomercials that featured a reality-show celebrity posing next to the city's trademark Christ the Redeemer statue."

So it looks like there's an impostor among the New Seven Wonders, a great big re-enforced concrete one at that, with a chin like Bruce Forsythe, who didn't get there by divine intervention or a miracle of any sort, just good old Brazilian dishonesty. I'm sorry, Christ, but I'm with UNESCO on this one: I don't think you belong in the top seven.

We drove from Corcovado through the Tijuca National Park heading for Sao Conrado. There were spectacular views across the city from the lookout points at Vista Chinesa and Mesa do Imperador. At Alto da Boa Vista, we entered the main area of forest, the Floresta da Tijuca surrounding the highest peak, Pico da Tijuca, at 1,012 metres (3,289 feet). This remnant was all that was left of the Atlantic tropical rainforest which had once enveloped Rio. The smooth granite mountain peaks were clothed in lush emerald green forest; there were swift flowing streams and waterfalls. We stopped to photograph the Cascatinha de Taunay, a 30metre (100 feet) waterfall just inside the entrance to the forest. I had seen Murchison Falls on the Nile in

Uganda and the falls on the Blue Nile in Ethiopia so this one was not particularly striking in comparison.

However, four years later, on my "Brasilian Contrasts" tour, we visited Foz do Iguacu in the south of the country on the border with Argentina and Paraguay and that was by a long way the most stunning waterfall I have seen anywhere, making Niagara Falls look like a burst pipe by comparison. The Iguacu River flowed from the east into the mighty Parana and, just before the confluence, plunged over an array of 275 individual falls, nearly 3 kilometres (1.8 miles) wide and 100 metres (330 feet) high, much higher and wider than Victoria Falls; 20 metres (66 feet) higher and twice as wide as Niagara Falls. We went out on a walkway under the falls towards the middle of the river. The roar of the plunging water was deafening, the spray creating a permanent rainbow. At one point we could see right up the river to the Devil's Throat where fourteen falls combined to produce a torrent of falling water that was frightening in its power. An elevator took us up to the top of the falls where we could look down on them as they plunged over the precipice. The water had a reddish tinge, caused by erosion of the red tropical soils upstream; the foam was like soap suds in a giant Jacuzzi. The name of the falls meant "large waters" in the language of the local Guarani Indians, an understatement in any language. We were taken up for a helicopter ride over the falls with Helisul Taxi Aereo, the most thrilling taxi ride I've ever had, the pilot performing low-level manoeuvres that would have given Health and Safety Inspectors in most parts of the world nightmares. We went around to the Argentinian side for a different view of the falls. I saw a blue sign outside a café cum petrol station where we stopped saying "Las Malvinas Son Argentinas" (The Falkland Islands Belong to Argentina.) I was glad for the sake of the proprietor that Maggie Thatcher wasn't on the tour armed with her famous handbag. We moved on to see the giant hydroelectric dam at Itaipu, 14 kilometres (9 miles) to the north on the Parana River, the largest plant of its kind in the world, supplying

22% of Brazil's electricity requirements and 90% of Paraguay's. At 185 metres (600 feet) the dam was the height of a 62 storey skyscraper. The Ponte (Bridge) da Amazidaje (Friendship) crossed the Parana River into Paraguay where we paid a visit to the contraband city of Puerto Stroessner (called after the infamous Dictator but since re-named Ciudad del Este after his demise). This tawdry, duty-free smugglers' paradise was crammed with shops spilling out onto the side-walks selling imported Japanese electronic goods (Sony and Nissei adverts everywhere), fake designer label clothing and counterfeit watches. A busy emporium called Casa Hua Fung suggested that the Chinese were in on the action here too. Street vendors were as busy as the shops, including local Indian women in black bowler hats, with brightly coloured cloth and rugs draped over themselves for sale. Wandering around, I didn't feel the sense of danger from muggers and petty thieves that I did in similar places in Brazil, perhaps due to the presence of a lot of armed police in the streets. Dictatorships tend to provide better public security than democracies, albeit at the expense of some personal freedom of action. In November, 2011, Foz do Iguacu was voted one of the Seven Natural Wonders of the World, a follow-up exercise by the same Foundation as administered the New Seven (man-made) Wonders initiative. No doubt there was some manipulation of the voting again but this time I wouldn't disagree with the ranking: the falls would be in my personal top seven natural wonders.

Still in Tijuca National Park, Fitipaldi and I had lunch at the Restaurante a Floresta and then carried on towards Sao Conrado, past the soaring flat-topped, anvil shaped, granite peak of Pedra da Gavea and the nearby Pedra Bonita from where hang-gliders took off at 510 metres (1,658 feet) to soar down to Sao Conrado Beach. The drive back into Leblon along the sweeping curves of Avenida Niemeyer was exhilarating, snaking around the end of the Dos Irmaos Mountains, past the Sheraton Hotel, the Vidigal and Rocinha favelas lurking above, hugging the cliffs, with steep falls to the sea – Fitipaldi in her element.

Kuoni organised a tour to see a football match at the Maracana stadium. It was in a dodgy part of the city, north of the central area, so I was glad of the security provided by a tour guide who knew the ropes. We saw the local side Flamengo beaten 2 – 1 by the out-of-town team Guarani in a downpour which made the pitch more suitable for growing rice than playing football. The din of the 60,000 plus crowd, the incessant beat of drums, the crackle of fire crackers when Flamengo scored, created an atmosphere more like a Billy Graham rally than a game of football – but then football is a religion in Brazil. When we left the ground, the crowd seemed remarkably good-humoured in spite of the home side losing, unlike the post-match atmosphere in Britain after a home set-back.

On my "Brazilian Contrasts" tour in 1989, I went back to Maracana to watch Brazil play Chile in a World Cup qualifying match. This time the massive stadium was near its 180,000 capacity, the largest football ground in the world. Brazil was leading 2 – 0 when a flare was fired from the crowd, landing near the Chilean goalkeeper. He went down as if shot by an elephant gun, writhing around on the ground, clutching his face. The referee went across and had a look at him and then held up a yellow card for play acting; the   Chilean team crowded around him, jostling him and gesticulating and then led by their captain, walked off. The following day the newspapers were full of the story. It was clear from the published photographs that the flare had landed several metres away from the goalie. Brazil had been awarded the game. A local Carioca girl (native of Rio) had been arrested for firing off the flare. There's never a dull moment at a Brazilian football match.

I took a tour down to the "Green Coast" south of Rio. The bus drive from Leblon through to Sao Conrado on the Avenida Niemeyer was even more spectacular in this direction than coming the opposite way with Fitipaldi had been and this time I didn't have to close my eyes in terror so often. As we plunged down towards Sao Conrado, the vista spread out ahead of white, surf fringed, ocean beaches and flat-topped Gavea Mountain was awe inspiring. It was a two and a half hour scenic drive down the Rio-Santos Coastal Highway to Angra dos Reis, the road rising high up mountainsides with wide panoramic views, then dropping in tight bends to the shoreline, passing cattle ranches and fishing villages, through luxuriant, bright green vegetation bristling with flowers. In Angra dos Reis we took a schooner trip out into Sepitiba Bay for a ninety minute trip to Ilha Grande, a large offshore island, where we anchored off a golden sand beach. The tour guide said that anyone who wanted could swim ashore to the beach. I noticed on the swim in that there was a very strong current running parallel to the beach: I allowed for this on the way back but had to swim hard against it at the end to make the ladder. An elderly man and a Japanese girl were not so lucky and were being carried past the stern: a crew member leapt in with a couple of life belts and stayed with them till the boat manoeuvred back to pick them up. Another Health and Safety Inspector's nightmare.

I took another tour up to Petropolis, a mountain retreat in the Serra Fluminense range, the drive taking just over an hour from Rio. The road was a major engineering feat, rising 840 metres (2,750 feet) from sea level in 65 kilometres (40 miles), curving around mountains, concrete bridges soaring above green valleys. There were spectacular views of the Serra dos Orgaos, weirdly shaped mountains resembling organ pipes, the highest peak, Pedra do Sino rising to 2,260 metres (7,410 feet); the rocky spike of O Dedo de Deus (The Finger of God) pointing at the sky. Emperor Dom Pedro II had built a summer palace in Petropolis in the early 1840s, sparking off a planned town, where he was joined by other members of the aristocracy. The palace was a rose coloured neo-classical building, relatively modest in size, the central part two stories high, with single storey wings. It was now a museum, the exhibits including the crown jewels and a cape of bright Amazon toucan feathers. There were a number of fine buildings in the town, the Quintadinha Hotel looking even more impressive than the palace. It was cool after the heat and humidity of Rio.

A few days before I left Rio, the President died. I spent my last day in bed with Fitipaldi watching his funeral. It was like seeing an old friend being buried, so familiar had I become with what made him tick – the inner man. It was as if he'd been the star in a TV hospital drama series – called "Down in Rio with the President's Pancreas" perhaps – and had now been written out of the script. He had put up a magnificent fight. He'd had guts.

4

THE COLOSSEUM, ROME, ITALY OCTOBER 1988

In October 1988, I took a seven night city break in Rome, flying over from Gatwick on a cheap flight. By this time I was taking two overseas holidays a year to get away from the frustrations and pressures of trying to cope with the overheated planning system in Shetland. I had been appointed Director of Planning the previous year so the salary had gone up but I had just bought and furnished my first house so funds were low and this was a low budget trip – I was booked into the two stars Hotel Embassy, which I later came to regret.

I had been in Italy once before in June 1980, based in Naples for a week and then in Sorrento for five days. That was a much better planned and organised trip than the Rome one. I wrote to the Italian Tourist Office in London and got a lot of brochures from them including hotel lists. In those days, you couldn't go on the Internet and find details of virtually every hotel in a town. The range of tourist guide books was much more limited too. I made bookings for hotels and transport through CIT which was effectively a branch of the Italian National Tourist Organization. I had also been preparing for a trip to

Italy for some time by learning the language. I had watched an amusing 25 programme TV series called "Avventura" with an accompanying book and two LPs (Long Playing records.) (Technology has come a long way since then.)

In Naples, I was booked into the Royal Hotel, a first class establishment on the Via Parthenope, right on the waterfront with views out across the Bay of Naples. It was an excellent choice and drove home the lesson that when you're travelling, it pays to do your homework in advance. On Pizzofalcone Hill behind the hotel, the ancient Greeks had established a colony in the 7th or 8th century BC. They called it Parthenope after the Siren that Odysseus allegedly threw overboard and who swam ashore here. This of course was a load of bollocks but it still appeared in the tourist literature as if it was gospel, aptly enough since the gospel is a load of bollocks too. A new Greek city, Neapolis, was later developed a little to the east. So Naples went back a long way.

Just around the corner from the hotel was the picturesque Castel Dell'Ovo, originally built in the 9th century AD but rebuilt after 1503 when it was almost destroyed in a siege by the Spanish. Its imposing yellow walls rose straight from the sea, constructed from the local tufa rock, a form of consolidated volcanic ash. You didn't have to look far for the source of the rock: the menacing twin volcanic peaks of Mount Vesuvius loomed worryingly close to the east. It didn't bear thinking about what might happen to Naples in a future Pompeii-burying scale eruption. It had sent out warning smoke signals as recently as 1944. The castle had been undergoing restoration work since 1975 as a tourist attraction. Beneath the walls, the little settlement of Borgo Marinero had been built for fishermen from nearby Santa Lucia in the late 19th century and was now a lively café and restaurant scene. The castle had originally been built on the offshore islet of Megaris but was now connected to the mainland by an arm of a little harbour crammed with small boats, yachts and fishing craft.

Back on Via Parthenope, the traffic roared past in never ending waves. I was reminded of a spoof advert for Italian cars in a British TV comedy show. It showed gleaming new cars flowing smoothly off an automated production line followed by footage of spectacular traffic pile ups resulting in piles of twisted, smoking metal. The punch-line was: "Made by robots: driven by Italians." Crossing the street, even on zebra crossings – perhaps especially on zebra crossings – was a suicide mission. In spite of the traffic, the walk along the waterfront esplanade known as the Lungomare to the little harbour of Mergellina was a pleasant experience with views out across the Bay of Naples to the south. On the inland side the extensive gardens of the late 18th century Villa Comunale (formerly Villa Reale) was now a public park with pine, eucalyptus, palm and monkey-puzzle trees, sculptures and fountains and the oldest aquarium in Europe specialising in species from the Mediterranean. Mergellina had originally been a fishermen's settlement and the harbour was still busy with their boats, pleasure craft and ferries to the offshore islands. The cafes and restaurants were busy. I had become reasonably familiar with Italian food when living in England but its range beyond the basic pastas and pizzas was an eye opener, especially the seafood and fish in these waterfront locations. They seemed to be able to do things with squid and octopus which defied the native toughness and rubbery-ness of these creatures. I became a fan of several pasta dishes as well – fettuccine alle vongole (clams) and the spicy penne all' arrabbiata among them. Naples was of course the home of the Pizza Napoletana and also the Pizza Margherita, with its tomato, mozzarella and basil topping.

The centre of Naples lay around the Castel Nuovo and Palazzio Reale (Royal Palace) and the main artery, Via Toledo, which ran northwards, inland. The busy port lay on the seaward side of this area. Construction of the Castel Nuovo had begun in 1279 during the reign of King Charles I of Anjou but it had been rebuilt completely from 1443 by King Alfonso V of Aragon. Until the unification of Italy in 1861, Naples had been a separate duchy or kingdom, sometimes independent, sometimes part of wider empires. From its Greek origins it had become part of the Roman Empire, then over-run by barbarians before being re-occupied by the Byzantine arm of the former Roman Empire when it briefly re-occupied Italy in the 6th century AD. A Norman king had followed in the 12th century, succeeded by dynasties from

Anjou in France and Aragon in Spain, Naples remaining independent. However, in 1503 it became a colony of Spain, ruled by a Viceroy. In 1707, following the War of the Spanish Succession, it passed to Austria. In a final twist in 1734, the throne passed to the Bourbon King Charles III, and Naples once more became an independent kingdom. Perhaps all these changes of ownership is what has produced the predominant trait in the modern Neapolitan character – a total disregard for authority in any shape or form.

The Castel Nuovo was a massive structure shaped like a trapeze with two sturdy, cylindrical, crenellated towers on the wider seaward side and three on the inland side. An ornate triumphal arch between two of the inland side towers formed the entrance, its white marble contrasting with the dark volcanic rock used for the rest of the fortress. Inside, the Barons' Hall was a magnificent room now used for meetings of the city council and there was a civic museum with paintings, sculptures and other art objects. Work on the adjacent Palazzo Reale had started in 1600 but it had not been completed until 1843. The main three storey façade on Piazza Plebiscito had statues of the kings of Naples in alcoves at ground level. It now housed a museum and the National Library. The decoration and furnishing were exquisite as might be expected in Italy, the former court theatre particularly ornate. Naples had obviously once been a very wealthy place, at least for the rulers.

In the Piazza Trieste e Trento, in front of the 1737 Teatro San Carlo opera house, I spotted a very attractive girl in a short skirt sitting side-saddle on a parked Vespa scooter. I was enjoying the view when I saw a well-dressed man approach her hesitantly and say something to her. She suddenly erupted, slapped his face and shouted "Non sono prostituta!" followed by a torrent of abuse that I couldn't understand except that I recognized the name "Pulcinella". The man was backing away, apologising profusely: "Scuzi, Signorina, scuzi." Whata mistaka to maka, I thought. Pulcinella was a stock comic figure or clown in the local comedy tradition – stupid, cunning, dogged by bad luck and always hungry. Mr. Punch of Punch and Judy fame was modelled on him. The scooter girl's clip on the ear was straight out of a "That's the way to do it" script. As I passed the girl, she had seen the funny side of it all and was laughing. She gestured towards the retreating Pulcinella and said in my direction "E pazzo!" (He's nuts.) "Certo" I replied. (He certainly is.) But perhaps it was worth a try. You never know your luck. And of course I had been wondering if she was a prostitute myself.

Just off the Piazza Trieste e Trento were two Naples institutions, the elegant late 19th century shopping centre Galleria Umberto I and the Caffe Gambrinus, dating back to 1860 and once frequented by artists and writers including Guy de Maupassant and Oscar Wilde. Monsieur de Maupassant was presumably relieved that he couldn't see the hated Eiffel Tower from the cafe. The adjacent Piazza Plebiscito was enclosed in smothering arms created by the curved wings of the Neo-Classical, early 19th century Church of San Francisco di Paola.

North of the modern city centre, the heart of Naples, going back to Greco-Roman times, had been around the long street commonly known as Spaccanapoli. This area was like an open air museum of old multi-storey houses and palaces with a plethora of old churches – Gesu Nuova, San Domenico Maggiore, Santa Chiara – there seemed to be one in every block: Italy must be one of the most priest-ridden countries in the world. The main street was lively with plenty of cafes and restaurants, shops and craft workshops. Narrow streets led off on both sides with washing lines strung across them up to five storeys high. I marvelled at the logistics of getting washing in and out. I took a detour into one of these streets. I had seen and heard a group of American tourists earlier and now spotted them up ahead again. All of a sudden two teenage boys on a scooter whizzed past them, the pillion passenger neatly grabbing a handbag off one of the women, the driver accelerating away. "God damn thieving Spicks!" one of the American men bellowed after them, waving his fist but it was too late, they were well away. Petty theft was endemic here, practically the national sport and tourists were sitting ducks.

A block further north, parallel to Spaccanapoli, the Via dei Tribunali was another historic street dating back to Greco-Roman times. In Piazza Belini, a lively square at the western end, the remains of the Greek city walls could still be seen. In a side street, the via

San Gregorio Armeno, craftsmen were producing high quality wood carvings and terracotta ware, mainly with religious themes such as the nativity, saints and shepherds; and there was a lavishly decorated monastery. The Duomo (Cathedral) dated back to the late 1200s but there had been Christian churches on the site from as early as the 4th century AD. A crypt housed the relics of San Gennaro, the Patron Saint of Naples, who was credited with having protected the city from the 1631 eruption of Mount Vesuvius. Every May and September a ritual was held where his alleged congealed blood, contained in two phials, liquefied. Tradition held that if this miracle did not happen, the city would suffer catastrophes. A picture formed in my cynical mind of a Mafioso, brandishing a sub-machine gun, standing over a perspiring priest who was waiting for the chemicals he had surreptitiously added to the phials to work, growling: "So da Sainta don'ta wanta bleeda? Perhaps you wanta bleeda on his behalf? We don'ta wanta no catastrophes – issa bad for business! Capisce?" (Unnerstanna?).

The Mafia or Camorra as they were known in Naples had had a stranglehold on sections of the local economy (including essentials like the milk and fishing industries, the coffee trade and bakeries) in addition to their purely criminal activities of drug pushing, prostitution, illegal gambling, extortion of protection money and robbery since their origin in the 18th century and indeed a stranglehold on Italy as a whole (along with the Sicilian Cosa Nostra and other Southern Italian criminal organizations) since unification in 1861. Political patronage was one of their strategies. In 1901 a judicial review had found a rapport between the central government and the Camorra. In 1995 Giulio Andreotti, who had been Prime Minister of Italy several times, was put on trial for association with the Mafia including the murder of a journalist who had published allegations that he had such links - including with the kidnapping and subsequent murder of Aldo Moro, a former Prime Minister. He was acquitted in 1999 but convicted in 2002 following an appeal by the prosecution and sentenced to 24 years in prison. He appealed that conviction and was again acquitted of the murder charge. Another Court later acquitted him of the Mafia association charges but only on a technicality relating to a time bar:

the Court found that Andreotti had indeed had strong ties to the Mafia until 1980 and had used them to further his political career to such an extent as for him to be considered part of the Mafia itself. It has recently been estimated that there are about 111 Camorra clans in and around Naples with over 6,700 members. They are organised as a loose confederation of independent family groups giving them a horizontal structure as opposed to the Cosa Nostra which has a pyramidal command structure. This makes them more resilient to arrests of "Capos" (Chiefs) on the odd occasion when the police can get past the wall of corrupt politicians and officials and the "omerta" (vow of silence) which protects them. At the time I was writing this chapter, pictures appeared on TV of rubbish piling up in the streets of Naples. The Camorra had taken control of garbage disposal in the Campania Region since the mid 1990s and illegal dumping and burning of waste including heavy metals and industrial waste had been widespread. Since June 2007 no legal dumping sites were in operation in the Region and no alternatives had been found. Naples was disappearing under a mountain of toxic garbage. With the economy and political scene in turmoil under Prime Minister Berlusconi you could say much the same about Italy as a whole. Thirty years earlier things had not looked nearly as bleak.

In an alleyway out behind the Duomo, a statue of San Gennaro was perched at the top of a tall, ornately carved spire known as the Guglia di San Gennaro. It had been erected to thank the Saint for saving the city from Mount Vesuvius. Since my visit to the Louvre in Paris, I had become a bit less of a Philistine when it came to art. I had seen in my guidebook that a charitable organization called the Pio Monte della Misericordia had a famous painting by Caravaggio, "The Seven Acts of Mercy", in their premises just across the street from San Gennaro's statue. It formed the altarpiece in the church within the complex. With its use of light and shade and the realism of the figures it almost came to life. For a Philistine, I was impressed.

I paid a visit to the National Archaeological Museum in a 16th century building which had later been rebuilt to house the University of Naples for a time. Its exhibits had mostly been excavated from the cities buried by the 79AD eruption of Mount Vesuvius such as Pompeii and Herculaneum but there was also an Egyptian collection and one of my favourite pieces was the 200 BC "Faranese Bull" sculpture, a group of people trying to control an enraged bull, which had been excavated from the Baths of Caracalla in Rome. The collection included frescos (watercolour paintings done on fresh plaster) from the walls of villas, including the "Sacrifice of Iphigenia" from Pompeii. There was also an eye-catching mosaic "The Battle of Alexander" depicting Alexander the Great's victory over the Persian Emperor, Darius, whose chariot could be seen retreating in the distance. It had been found in the House of the Faun in Pompeii. In some rooms, whole floors paved in mosaics had been reproduced. On the upper floor, a beautiful large blue glass vase covered with decorative white motifs caught my eye. It was apparently a wine vessel found in a grave in Pompeii. There was a room dedicated to erotic works from Pompeii and Herculaneum. When I wandered in there, I got such a dirty look from the elderly female attendant that I felt as if I was sneaking into a Porn shop – which as it turned out, wasn't so far from the truth.

I took a trip out to see Mount Vesuvius. The Circumvesuviana railway took me to Ercolano (Herculaneum) station from where I caught a bus up to the chairlift. A funicular railway had been built in 1880 taking visitors up to 1,180 metres (3,870 feet) above sea level (this had inspired the popular song "Funiculi Funicula") but the service had been discontinued in 1944 following a series of accidents. A hike from the top of the chairlift with a compulsory guide took a group of us round the impressive crater which was 200 metres (655 feet) deep and 600 metres (1970 feet) in diameter. Vesuvius was dormant now but as recently as 1944 it had spat out lava which poured down the slopes and it had showered Naples and surrounding towns with cinders and ash. San Gennaro had obviously taken his eye off the ball.

The following day I took the Circumvesuviana again to Pompeii, which had felt the brunt of Vesuvius's wrath in 79 AD. It had been a thriving market town of 20,000 people. A strong earthquake in 62 AD had done a lot of damage, including knocking out an aqueduct which brought water from the Sarno River and some of the people had left.

But life had been returning to normal when out of the blue Vesuvius blew its top. The people didn't have time to get away from the shower of cinders and ash and the more deadly cloud of poisonous gas which spewed down the mountain side at a speed no one could outrun. These toxic fumes killed many people in the course of carrying out everyday tasks and then buried them under metres of volcanic ash and cinders. There they lay among the ruins of their city until somebody accidentally came across some remains in the 17th century. Systematic archaeological excavation had started in 1754.

As I entered the site through the Porta Marina, passing the Temples of Venus and Apollo and the Basilica, which had been the Law Courts and into the Forum, the commercial centre, I was amazed at how well it was all preserved. Roofs had obviously collapsed under the weight of volcanic debris but many walls remained to roof height and the layout of the buildings could be clearly seen. The nearby Teatro Grande had been able to seat 5,000 people: the adjacent Little Theatre had been used for musical performances. I walked out to the Amphitheatre at the extreme east of the site: it had been used for gladiatorial spectacles. Next to it was the Gymnasium, with a swimming pool in the centre. I walked back along the Via dell' Abbondanza. This had been the liveliest street in the city with a mixture of shops, houses and inns. There had been a bakery, laundry and a leather workshop. The most famous of the inns had belonged to Asellina. The Gladiators had been billeted in the inns. From graffiti on the walls of Asellina's establishment, depicting the foreign waitresses and maids who worked there, they clearly not only made the beds but also helped the guests to rumple them. In an alleyway behind the Stabian Baths, was the best preserved of Pompeii's many brothels, known as "lupanare". I had leered at the erotic paintings rescued from here in the Archaeological Museum in Naples, under the jaundiced eye of the caretaker.

The best preserved houses were in the north-west sector of the site off the Via di Mercurio. These houses had been very high quality buildings, constructed of stone, brick or concrete. I was amazed to learn that the Romans had invented concrete: I had thought it was a modern material. They were generally rectangular in shape, built round an atrium (courtyard): the spacious gardens were surrounded by a colonnaded peristyle, Greek style, with an "impluvium" (pond) in the middle. This inward looking layout meant that few windows were needed on the outside to ensure privacy, an essential commodity if the goings on in the erotic wall paintings were an everyday occurrence. They were serviced with a public water supply and sewage disposal. The House of the Vettii had been fully restored, its inner walls adorned with paintings, a small room off the kitchen dedicated to erotic ones. The House of the Faun had a bronze statue which gave it its name in the middle of the impluvium in an atrium. I had seen the original in the Archaeological Museum in Naples along with the "Battle of Alexander" mosaic which had also come from here. The Via dei Sepolcri led off to the west beyond the city walls, lined with monumental tombs. Out this road was the large Villa of the Mysteries which had been restored. Its walls were decorated with frescoes of brightly coloured, life-size figures set against a vivid red background. Compared to the house I had been born in, these houses were like palaces.

The Finals of the European Championship were being held in Italy and Naples was bursting at the seams with football fans. Scotland was in a group with Germany and I managed to pick a bar full of Germans to watch them play each other on TV. When Scotland scored first, I couldn't avoid giving myself away. Sons and daughters of SS men and Gestapo turned their steely eyes on me and I expected to see beer glasses flying in my direction in a re-enactment of Kristallnacht. But it all ended well: Germany won; I was offered condolences, bought beer and escaped with my life. It's not often I'm pleased to see Scotland lose a football match but sometimes it's better to concede to superior forces and live to fight another day, as Machiavelli used to say.

I caught a hydrofoil out to the island of Ischia, lying 30 kilometers (18 miles) west of Naples in the Tyrrhenian Sea. It was green and rugged with the extinct volcano of Mount Epomeo rising to 788 metres (2,585 feet). Just 10 kilometres (6 miles) long by 7 kilometres (5 miles) wide, it was small enough to explore much of it on foot. We arrived in the main town, Porto d'Ischia. I walked along the seafront to the fortress island of Castello Aragonese, approached by a causeway. It had been built as early as the 5th century BC and sheltered churches, convents and houses. I took the cable car up to the Belvedere on Mount Epomeo from where the views were spectacular across the pine clad ridges of the island itself with villages nestling in bays all around the coast and across to the neighbouring island of Procida. I walked round to the spa town of Casamicciola: the island was famous for its hot springs. The Norweigian writer Ibsen had written Peer Gynt while living here. It had a pleasant little beach and I settled down for some lunch at a restaurant looking out across the harbour. I ordered a bottle of the local Epomeo wine: I had picked up some tourist literature and one leaflet waxed eloquent about the virtues of the local wines: "made from juicy grapes growing on vines nurtured by the rich volcanic soils of Mount Epomeo." As I was waiting for the meal to arrive, I found myself embellishing the hype a bit – "plucked by the nimble fingers of Neapolitan pickpockets; trampled by the feet of retreating Italian troops." I mused that the reputation of modern Italian armies for military incompetence was well deserved. The Fascist Dictator, Benito Mussolini, had seized power in 1922. He had delusions of grandeur with ideas of setting up a new Roman Empire. He had some initial success using airpower against Ethiopians mostly armed with spears. But when World War II broke out and things got serious his armies in North Africa were quickly routed by the British and only saved when General Rommel rode to the rescue with the Panzer equivalent of the US cavalry; likewise, when he invaded Greece, his forces were losing heavily on points until the Germans stepped in to pull his chestnuts out of the fire. And yet in the days of the Roman Empire, their legions had been some of the finest soldiers the world has ever produced. It occurred to me that Italy was not alone in Europe in having seen better days in the military field. Lithuania had been a major power in the early middle ages; Spain and Portugal had set up world-wide empires in the 16th century; Sweden had regularly knocked hell out of the Russians during the 17th century but had been parked in neutral since. It was as if nearly every country had its fifteen minutes of fame when it was top dog; then tired itself out defending its territory and crawled back into its kennel and dozed off.

I had booked a transfer by car down to Sorrento on the Peninsula of the same name which formed the southern crab's pincer enclosing the Bay of Naples, a drive of about 50 kilometres (31 miles) from Naples. The siting of Sorrento was spectacular, perched at the edge of a low cliff. It was unashamedly a tourist resort but at that time a reasonably sophisticated one, catering as much for Italians as foreigners. My hotel, the Europa Palace Grand Hotel, was another good choice and fully lived up to its rather grandiose name. It stood at the edge of the cliff above the Marina Piccola, the town's deep water harbour, where the ferries left for Capri, Naples and around the Amalfi Coast. A path and steps led down to a private pier and stretch of foreshore where you could swim. Sorrento had originally been a Greek settlement and the pattern of the narrow streets in the town centre still followed the Roman layout. The hub of activity was the Piazza Tasso around which the evening "passegiatta" took place, when families and the golden youth of the town turned out to see and be seen, mostly the latter since they were Italians and fond of their own appearance. There were some attractive buildings: the Duomo (Cathedral) had ancient origins but had been rebuilt in the 1400s and remodelled since. The choir stalls were decorated with inlaid wood, a craft for which, along with lacework, Sorrento was famous. The Church of San Francesco had bougainvillea flowers tumbling down its cloisters. There was a lot of greenery in parks and gardens and orange and lemon groves – the sizeable Cataldo Lemon Orchard was near the centre of town just minutes away from my hotel. The tasty limoncello liqueur was a local speciality. A strip of tree lined park, the Villa Comunale, overlooked Marina Piccola. Fruit and vegetable stalls lent colour to the narrow streets. At Marina Grande, there was room at the foot of the cliff for a picturesque group of houses, mostly four storeys high and painted in pastel colours. The little harbour was crowded with fishing boats and pleasure craft. I saw fishermen mending nets.

I hired a car with a driver for a tour around the Peninsula taking in the Amalfi Coast on the south side. I had thought about hiring a self-drive car but I was soon thanking my lucky stars and all the Saints I had come across so far, including San Gennaro, for not doing so.

Once we had arrived on the south coast, State Highway 163 became a vertiginous roller coaster of twists and turns, in places cut into the cliff face with rocky crags towering above us and a sheer drop to the sea below. The thought of driving an unfamiliar car on the wrong side of the road, while meeting vehicles made by robots and driven by Italians coming the other way, brought me out in a cold sweat. Luigi, the driver, seemed quite unperturbed, looking very Mafioso in his designer shades and I soon relaxed and began to enjoy the spectacular scenery, stunning views around every bend. This must be one of the great drives of the world, as long as somebody else is driving. We explored Positano, its jumble of pastel coloured houses clambering up the hillside in steps and then stopped in Amalfi for lunch. Steps led up from the Piazza Duomo to the Cathedral, its 13th century Campanile (bell tower) decorated with Arab style inter-locking arches giving it almost an oriental appearance.

I took a ferry from Marina Piccola out to the Isle of Capri which lay 13 kilometres (8 miles) to the west beyond the end of the Peninsula, a forty minute trip through sparkling water past soaring cliffs. It was much smaller than Ischia, just 10 square kilometres (4 square miles) in area and was a limestone island, not volcanic like Ischia. As we approached the port at Marina Grande, a sheer, chalky-white cliff could be seen running diagonally across the island. Monte Solaro, the highest point, rose to 589 metres (1,932 feet). I had a look around Marina Grande and then took the funicular up to the main town which was unimaginatively just called Capri, like the island. Where had the famous Italian flair been when early settlers were founding and naming their town? Capri was a bit too twee and touristy for my liking, full of boutique shops. The Baroque façade of the Church of San Stefano formed one side of the central square, the Piazzetta, its dome and bell tower rising above it. I walked round to the Certosa di San Giacomo, a former Carthusian Monastery, founded in the late 14th century and fortified in the 16th century. One of its twin cloisters was lined with marble columns. It now housed a museum and a school. I carried on down to Marina Piccola from where there was a breathtaking view out along the cliffs to the Faraglione sea-stacks, rising 109 metres (360 feet) out of the sea.

Back in Capri town, I found an outdoor table in one of the restaurants in the Piazzetta for lunch. I ordered a bottle of one of the island's highly praised wines and settled down to browse through the tourist literature I had accumulated. Capri had had a lot of distinguished residents and visitors over the years. The Roman Emperor Augustus had had a villa here and his successor Tiberius had run the Empire from the island from 27 AD to 37 AD: the ruins of his villa had been excavated. Lenin had been here, Oscar Wilde, Somerset Maugham, Graham Greene and the Lancashire singer Gracie Fields had seen out her days here. The service was a bit slow and the wine was ebbing fast. My mind started to wander: a picture emerged of Gracie Fields out in the centre of the square where a busker was singing "O Sole Mio". Gracie was singing a raunchy version of her 1934 hit song "The Isle of Capri":-

"'Twas on the Isle of Capri that I met her.

She was naked and tied to a tree.

I could not resist the temptation,"

A waiter appeared with the Linguini alla Pizzaiola. By the time my mind wandered back to my reverie, Gracie had been joined by Vera Lynn in a duet and they were high kicking and belting out the punch-line in fine voice:

"And now she's the mother of three."

The meal had dragged on a bit – I'd had a Limoncello and then a Strega – a fiery green liqueur I had discovered in Naples - with the coffee. I realized that I wouldn't have time to see both the famous Blue Grotto (a sea cave in the limestone cliffs, which would involve a boat trip from Marina Grande) and Anacapri, the fractionally more imaginatively named second town, perched high above the cross-island cliff. I settled for Anacapri and caught a taxi up there, the driver pointing out the Villa San Michele, built by the Swedish author and physician, Axel Munthe, on the site of a Roman Villa. I took the cable car up to the summit of Monte Solaro from where there was a spectacular view of the island spread out below – pine forests, vineyards, orchards – just the sort of place I'd have chosen to rule the Roman Empire from.

Back in Italy, in Rome this time, eight years later, I was less than impressed with the Hotel Embassy. The tour company's brochure claimed that "the recently refurbished rooms feature private shower and W.C." This was indeed the case but the public areas were dark and dingy, one of these places where corridor lights switched themselves off to save power, just as you were trying to find the keyhole. And the recently refurbished bathroom smelled as if a wounded gladiator had crawled in and died in it and never been discovered. The brochure went on to claim that "Travelscene guests have the added bonus of colour TV and mini bar." Again this was true but the TV picture was so poor it was barely watchable and the mini bar was empty. Landing in a Fawlty Towers facsimile doesn't necessarily spoil a holiday but it undoubtedly colours your impression of a place.

I had booked a half-day guided tour of Rome as work pressure had hindered me from putting in much time to prepare for the trip, other than brushing up on my Italian. I thought a short tour would help me to orientate myself and identify the places to spend more time later. Up until now, I had avoided this type of tour, never feeling the need to be herded around by a flag waving robot, programmed to churn out the same banalities and misinformation to successive groups of what must eventually come to resemble sheep more than individual human beings in their eyes. However, when arriving in a new city now, I invariably take one of these tours to get my bearings. The tour started at the Spanish Steps which led up to the twin bell-towers of the Trinita dei Monti Church founded in 1495. The steps had been completed in 1726 to improve access to the Church and were now one of Rome's main tourist traps. Already, this early, there was a crowd of people sitting on the steps and some vendors of tourist souvenirs trying to relieve them of their lira. The Guide pointed out a dingy building to the right of the steps which he said was where John Keats, the English poet, had died of TB in 1821 and was now the Keats-Shelley Museum. There was a fountain by the famous 17th century sculptor and architect Bernini in the Piazza di Spagna at the foot of the steps called the Fountain of the Old Boat. To me it looked more like a misshapen mushroom but then Bernini was a genius so who was I to criticise him? The Via Condotti led off the Piazza, one of Rome's most exclusive shopping streets, home to Gucci leather goods and Bulgari jewellery: Versace was in the parallel street next to it. It led into the Via del Corso, another shopper's Mecca, running north-south from the Piazza del Popolo to the Piazza Venezia.

I had seen Anita Ekberg cooling off in the Trevi Fountain in Federico Fellini's 1960 film "La Dolce Vita" but the Guide told us that bathing in it was now strictly forbidden in case anyone was tempted. He regurgitated the old legend that if you stood with your back to the fountain and lobbed a coin back over your shoulder into it you would come back to Rome. A group member who I'd heard earlier loudly telling someone he was from Texas didn't have any coins so he balled up a 1,000 lira note and launched it into the water. The Guide looked as if he hoped the Texan's wish wouldn't come true. The fountain had been designed in 1762 in the over-the-top rococo style with a statue of the Sea God Neptune, flanked by two Tritons leading winged horses. One of the horses was acting up – supposed to represent stormy seas according to the Guide. The Triton with the peaceable horse was blowing into a conch shell – I didn't know if he was experiencing sea-fog or shark- calling.

The original Pantheon, a temple to all the Roman Gods and God knows there were plenty of them; had been built in 27 BC but so seriously damaged in one of Rome's periodic fires in 80AD that Emperor Hadrian had it completely rebuilt early in the second century. The triangular portico was supported by sixteen massive Corinthian columns, each made from a single block of Egyptian granite. The original bronze doors were 8 meters (24 feet) high and weighed 20 tons. The walls were 6 meters (20 feet) thick. But the most striking feature was the dome, its height, 43 meters (142 feet) exactly matching its diameter, with a 9 meter (30 feet) wide oculus (hole) in the centre the only source of light, which streamed down into the building. The construction of the dome showed all the genius of Roman engineering. To keep down the weight of the huge structure the concrete from which it was cast over a temporary wooden framework was mixed with light volcanic tufa and pumice and it was composed of hollow coffers (panels). The marble floor preserved the original design. It had been converted to a Christian church early in the 7th century but now served as a mausoleum for the painter Rafael and more recently the first two kings of a united Italy.

The rectangular Piazza Novona was on the site of Emperor Domitian's Stadium where sporting events, including horse racing, had been held in the days of the Empire. Now it was full of people posing and eating ice cream at outdoor cafes, bars and restaurants, street entertainers and artists pretending to be Michelangelo. There were ornate fountains at either end and in the centre Bernini's 17th century Baroque masterpiece "The Fountain of the Four Rivers" surrounding an Egyptian obelisk. The figures represented the Nile, Ganges, Plate and Danube, one river from each continent according to the Guide. The west side of the square was dominated by the Baroque Church of St. Agnes by the 17th century architect Borromini. The Guide told us that it had been built on the site of the brothel where a young Saint Agnes had been paraded around naked in the early 4th century AD to try to persuade her to renounce her Christian faith. Miraculously her hair had sprouted to cover her modesty but she had been martyred regardless. This of course was more bollocks but it made a good story. The nearby Piazza Campo de' Fiori held a colourful open-air street market with fruit, vegetable, meat, fish and the flower stalls after which it was named. In the middle ages it had been used for public executions. A statue to one of the victims, a philosopher burned alive at the stake in 1600 as a heretic, stood in the Square. I wondered what he thought about that.

We moved on to the Vatican City to see St Peter's Basilica and the Sistine Chapel. St. Peter's Square was another Bernini masterpiece, keyhole shaped to represent St. Peter's key to the door of Heaven. The Vatican had been an independent, sovereign state with its own currency, stamps and police force (in the shape of the Swiss Guards) since the Lateran Treaty between the Pope and Mussolini in 1929. At just over 42 hectares (108 acres) it was by a long way the smallest territory entitled to send a representative to the United Nations if it so wished. The boundary was enclosed by a medieval wall, except at the entrance to the Square. The round, key-ring end of the Piazza, immediately in front of St. Peter's Basilica, was surrounded by a colonnade of travertine pillars, four deep and there was a 26 metre (84 feet) high obelisk in the centre, brought to Rome from Egypt by Caligula in 37AD. The obelisk had been the central feature of the Circus developed on the site by Nero, where many early Christians had been put to death, blamed for the fire of 64 AD which destroyed much of Rome. Among the victims it was believed had been St. Peter. The original St. Peter's Basilica was built in the 4th century on what was claimed to be his grave. By the 16th century it had fallen into serious disrepair and the present day replacement was started in 1506 and finally consecrated in 1626. A number of architects were involved including Michelangelo who designed the magnificent dome. Bernini had laid out the Piazza between 1656 and 1667.

St. Peter's was the largest Catholic Church ever built, 187 meters (615 feet) long, Michelangelo's cupola soaring to 136 meters (448 feet) with a diameter of 43 meters (139 feet). Just inside the door was Michelangelo's sculpture called the Pieta, with the Virgin Mary cradling the body of Christ across her lap. Up near the main altar was a 13th century bronze statue of St. Peter. Bernini's spectacular Baldacchino, a gilded bronze canopy supported on columns 20 meters (66 feet) high, overhung the altar. Next door, the Sistine Chapel lived up to its reputation. Even a non-believer and erstwhile Philistine like me could only look up at Michelangelo's frescoed ceiling depicting the creation of the world and the fall of man according to Genesis with an open mouth. It had taken him four years (1508 to 1512) working from special scaffolding. Recent restoration work had brought out the original colours. It was a magnificent piece of work. The walls had also been frescoed by a variety of artists including Botticelli with scenes from the lives of Moses and Christ and Michelangelo had capped it all with his "Last Judgement" on the altar wall, taking him seven years late in life and illustrating the end of the world and its rebirth.

The tour ended in the Piazza Venezia in front of the huge white marble Victor Emmanuel Memorial which has been accurately described as an iced wedding cake. The low towers at either end of the colonnaded façade were topped by chariots carrying winged figures each drawn by four horses. It had been completed in 1911 to celebrate the unification of Italy and honour her first king: his equestrian statue stood out in front with the Tomb of the Unknown Soldier underneath him. Cynically, it occurred to me that it was no wonder he was unknown if he'd thrown away his dog tags in order to desert. The Guide announced the end of the tour but pointed out that they had another tour which covered Ancient Rome which lay just beyond the monument to the east. I had to admire this example of Italian salesmanship but decided to leave the best bit of Rome for another day and to tackle it on my own.

In the evening, I went for dinner at the Ristorante Da Pancrazio on Piazza del Biscione, just off the Piazza Campo de' Fiori. The underground dining area had once been the Theatre of Pompey on the steps of which Julius Caesar had been murdered. I had a small serving of spaghetti all' amatriciana as a starter followed by roast abbacchio (lamb), which was superb, washed down with a bottle of Chianti and followed by a Strega with the coffee. I caught a taxi over to the Via Veneto which wasn't far from my hotel. The street was busy with plenty of cafes, bars, restaurants and hotels but a bit seedy: it appeared to have come down in the world since La Dolce Vita days. I had a drink in the open-air terrace bar on the top floor of the Eden Hotel, with spectacular, all-round views of the city skyline and then moved on to the renowned Harry's Bar.

I got back to the hotel just after midnight. The front door was locked so I rang the bell. I waited a while and then banged on the door in case the bell wasn't working. Eventually it opened. The same two men who had been on Reception when I had arrived the day before and who were the only staff I had seen were hovering there. "It's very late" one of them said truculently. I made a show of consulting my watch. "People would still be having dinner in Spain at this time," I said. "This is Italy, not Spain," the other one pointed out. I'd had a fair bit to drink and my fuse was shorter than usual. I said that I'd been under the impression that this was a hotel, not a boarding school and that if there was no one on duty at night they should have given me an outside door key. They continued to mutter and grumble about inconsiderate guests disturbing other guests in the middle of the night: I expressed surprise that anybody else would be stupid enough to stay in a dump like this. They made a drama out of finding my room key. They were strangely alike and I had wondered earlier if they were brothers. But now, with their mannerisms and tendency to tantrums and hissy fits, it dawned on me that what these two drama queens had in common wasn't blood but other bodily fluids which they had been exchanging, probably for years – they were like an old married couple. My parting shot was "Why don't you go away and fuck yourselves." Which they probably did.

On Sunday, it seemed appropriate to head for the headquarters of one of the world's great religions again to see a bit more of the Vatican City area than we had had time for on the city tour. On the way, I called in at the Castel Sant'Angelo. I crossed the Tiber over the Ponte Sant' Angelo, a pedestrian bridge lined with statues of Saint Peter and Saint Paul and ten angels sculpted by Bernini in the 1660s. Part of the original bridge was incorporated in the structure: it had been built by Emperor Hadrian in 136 AD to link the Castel, which had been built as his mausoleum, to the city. The bulky, round, citadel was surmounted by a huge bronze statue of the Archangel Michael with wings spread as if about to launch himself into a sky dive or a bungy jump. As usual, there was a religious legend attached to this. In 590 AD Pope Gregory allegedly saw a vision of an angel alighting on the turret, following which a plague which was ravishing the city miraculously disappeared. Presumably it never occurred to anyone at the time that the old bugger was probably short-sighted and it was more likely to have been a bird of prey after some carrion from the plague victims and that the plague had run its course anyway. (What is it with these Italians? They'll believe anything, even Berlusconi's promises of economic reform.) During the time of a later Emperor, the mausoleum was converted into a fortress which was subsequently used by successive Popes as a bolt hole when under attack – a passageway still connected it to the Vatican Palace. From the Renaissance period to the early 20th century it had been a prison: the cells could still be seen, in one of which a Cardinal had been strangled. (His sermons can't have been bad enough to warrant that.) Inside, a spiral ramp led up past the papal chambers to the terrace inside the battlements from where there was a good view out across the Vatican and the city. Assorted military equipment was on display in the museum along with Renaissance period furnishings: some of the rooms had their walls decorated with colourful fresco paintings. Piles of stone cannonballs were stockpiled in the courtyard, perhaps in case Italy's military capability was reduced to the stage where they became needed again.

I walked around to Saint Peter's Square. At midday, a figure in what looked like a nightie, appeared at an upper window of one of the buildings flanking the Piazza in front of the Basilica. This was the Pope himself, presumably just having got up. I knew everybody was entitled to a lie in on a Sunday morning but in a profession where Sunday was the only day you did any work this seemed a bit self-indulgent. But then again, he was infallible and who was I to preach? Loudspeakers crackled and from among the static the Pontiff's voice emerged bestowing his blessing on the multitude assembled below in the Square. I had forgotten all the Latin I'd learned at school so the message went over my head but the rest of the audience seemed to be impressed.

I've never been able to get my head around religion. My parents had sent me to Sunday school during my Primary School days and in the boarding school I attended from age eleven we were supposed to attend a church service in the town every Sunday morning, with a religious service again on Sunday night in the Hostel. So I had been pretty well indoctrinated. But I never developed what Believers call "faith": perhaps my mind is too logical – I can't for the life of me see how virgins can give birth; Gods can have earthly children; men can rise from the grave and float up to heaven; archangels can settle on the turrets of castles. And if there is a heaven somewhere up there, why haven't the telescopes at Jodrell Bank picked it up? If it exists in some parallel universe is it any better than earth? If we think that our planet is getting a bit overcrowded with 7 billion people what must heaven be like with everyone who has ever lived crammed in there like winged sardines? I can see why people need religion. It's a bit hard to take the prospect that when the fat lady sings it's all over, there's no life after death. Personally, I think unscrupulous Priests over the ages have taken advantage of people's fear of death to build up their own power and prestige. I can envisage Moses leading the Israelites out of Egypt and having all sorts of problems trying to control the unruly bunch with adultery, incest, buggery and coveting neighbours' wives rife. A priest comes up to him and hands him a tablet with a lot of hieroglyphics on it numbered one to ten. "Here, take this," he says, "stuff it up your robe and go up that mountain. Bring it back down and tell them that God gave it to you and that they'll all go to hell in a hand cart if they don't obey every word of it. The only way to get this mob to behave is to scare them shitless." Gazing up at the Pope and listening to his meaningless monotone chant, I thought: "I'm sorry, Your Holiness, but I just can't buy it."

Christianity was declared the official religion of the Roman Empire in 380 AD by Emperor Theodosius. The Christians had been persecuted, thrown to the lions in grisly spectacles in the arenas built to keep the masses amused and quiet, ever since they had arrived in Rome but especially after the great fire of 64 AD which they were accused of starting. But then in 312 AD Constantine had a vision of a cross in the sky the night before the Battle of Milvian Bridge. (Not another bloody vision!) Diocletian had divided the Empire into West and East sectors in 284 AD, deciding it was too big for one man to manage. On his death, war had broken out between the two halves and Constantine was trying to re-unite them. He took his victory in the battle as a sign that the Christian God was top dog, converted to Christianity himself and issued an edict granting freedom of worship to Christians in 313 AD; in 324 AD it became to all intents and purposes the state religion, a status later officially confirmed by Theodosius.

When things started going seriously pear-shaped for the Empire with the sacking of Rome by the barbarian Goths in 410 AD, Civil rule broke down and the leader of the Christian Church, the Bishop of Rome, stepped into the political vacuum. Pope Leo I managed to buy off another sacking by Attila the Hun in 452 AD but was unable to stop the Vandals in 455 AD. The Empire limped on until 476 AD when the last Emperor was deposed, Italy coming under the rule of the Germanic Ostrogoth King Theodoric, who ruled from Ravenna on the Adriatic coast, not Rome. By 600 AD Rome was a shadow of its former self. The city of over a million people at the height of the Empire had shrunk to 20,000 living among ruins down by the Tiber: the barbarian invasions had knocked out the aqueduct system supplying water to the seven hills which now became uninhabitable by large numbers of people. The Papacy survived this period of anarchy and under Gregory the Great (590 – 604 AD) sent out missionaries all over Western Europe to spread the religion and assert Papal authority. The Frankish King Charlemagne conquered Italy in 778 AD: in 800 AD the Pope crowned him Holy Roman Emperor to provide the Church with a secular wing as well as a spiritual one. This didn't work too well, as the two wings ended up at loggerheads. This, plus constant feuding between the various families vying for the Papacy meant that Rome degenerated into the chaos which Dante described in his "Divine Comedy". Things got so bad that the Papacy moved to Avignon in France in 1309 where it stayed until 1377. On its return to Rome, the Papacy got its act together again. This was much needed; during the absence of the Papacy the Black Death had further decimated the population; wolves roamed in the vicinity of St. Peter's at night; goats grazed on the Capitoline Hill; and the Forum, the former city centre in the days of the Empire, was used to pasture cattle. With revenues again flooding in from churches all across Europe, successive Popes financed the Renaissance flowering of art and architecture which I had seen throughout the city.

With all this wealth, moral standards in the Church deteriorated. The Vatican became worldly, known for its love of luxury and sexual peccadilloes. Popes fathered children. The political intrigue was described in Machiavelli's 1513 book "The Prince". The Papacy built up an army and became involved in the struggle for secular power in Italy between the patchwork of independent states; open warfare broke out with the Holy Roman Empire resulting in the "Sack of Rome" in 1527 by Emperor Charles V. This behaviour also led to the Protestant Reformation. A German priest, Martin Luther, incensed by the corruption of the Church, particularly the sale of "Indulgences" – essentially passports to heaven – allegedly nailed the equivalent of a hard copy of his Facebook page to the door of his church in Worms, tweeting and twittering about the state of the Church. This caught on and the Catholic Church was faced with a major rebellion. Their fight back in the Counter Reformation after 1545 coupled with the need to re-build the damage inflicted by the sacking in 1527 led to another phase of city building and beautification during the Baroque period characterised by the work of Bernini and the completion of the rebuilding of St. Peter's Basilica. In recent times, the unmasking of hundreds of paedophile priests has seriously damaged the Church; and with the world's population spiralling out of control and food and water shortages developing, it is difficult to see how Papal bullshit condemning contraception can be divinely inspired.

That night I had dinner in Da Giggetto in the Portico d'Ottavia in the old Jewish ghetto area down near the Tiber, which specialised in traditional Roman cuisine. I had the carciofi alla giudia (Jewish style artichokes) as a starter and the Roman version of oxtail stew, coda alla vaccinara. It was an old-fashioned, family-style restaurant with excellent service and tables outside; and for the best meal I had in Rome, it was remarkably cheap.

I had left my exploration of Ancient Rome till last. I started on the Capitoline Hill where legend had it Rome had started. In the Palazzo dei Conservatori, the first of the matching pair of Capitoline museums facing each other across Michelangelo's Piazza del Campidoglio, I found the famous statue of Romulus and Remus being suckled by a bronze she-wolf. The legend was that the twin boys were sons of the War God Mars who had impregnated a Vestal Virgin. They were to be drowned in the Tiber but were rescued by a she-wolf which carried them up to a cave in the adjacent Palatine Hill and fed them until they were rescued by a shepherd who brought them up. They later quarrelled about who should give his name to the city and Romulus killed Remus, founding the city on April 21st 753 BC. April 21st was still celebrated as the anniversary of the founding of the city. This of course was all bollocks and got me going again. I imagined little Romulus saying: "I feel a right tit sucking this wolf" and his twin replying; "Cheer up, Bro". I hear they're going to name a city after you. All I'm going to be remembered by is a bloody Edinburgh detective." Romulus laughs, almost choking on a mouthful of wolf's milk: "That's Rebus, not Remus, you daft little bugger." There was another famous bronze sculpture of a boy trying to remove a thorn from his foot and a homo-erotic painting of St. John the Baptist by Caravaggio. Down in the courtyard stood a huge stone head of Emperor Constantine. The complete statue must have been massive: these old Emperors were certainly big-headed.

Across the Piazza was the other Capitoline Museum, the Palazzo Nuovo, specialising in ancient Roman statuary. I admired the marble Capitoline Venus, modestly covering her private parts with one hand but not quite managing to hide her tits with the other one. Further on was the Dying Gaul, sitting on his shield, his hand resting on his broken sword. It is estimated that over a million Gauls were slaughtered during the Roman conquest of Gaul. Building empires doesn't come cheap. Out in the courtyard was a fountain with a statue of a River God called Marforio.

The Capitoline Hill had been the religious and political centre of ancient Rome with the Temple of Jupiter where the consuls were inaugurated every New Years Day. Now it was dominated by Michelangelo's Piazza del Campidoglio approached up his magnificent stairway, the Cordonata, guarded by statues of the twin Gods Castor and Pollux. Facing the stairs was the Palazzo Senatorio with its clock tower and a copy of an equestrian statue of Emperor Marcus Aurelius out in front – the original was in the adjacent museum. The Palazzo now housed the office of the Mayor, re-echoing the ancient role of the hill.

From the Tabularium, accessed from the Palazzo dei Cosevatori and where ancient Rome's archives were kept, there was an excellent view out across the Forum, the heart of ancient Rome, to the Colosseum. The real story of the origins of Rome had been un-earthed by archaeologists and its meteoric rise to dominate the known world was well documented historically. It had started as a cluster of Iron Age villages on the low hills above the valley of the River Tiber in the 8th or 9th centuries BC occupied by the Latin and Sabine tribes. Cattle and vegetable markets had developed down by the river, opposite the island in the Tiber called the Isola Tiberina, to trade with the Etruscan civilization across the river to the west. The Etruscans had eventually absorbed these villages into their kingdom and it was them who drained the marshes and developed the first Forum down on the flat land around 600 BC. This was a common space for meetings, buying, selling, and settling disputes and later the site of a temple where Vestal Virgins guarded the Sacred Flame which ensured Rome's survival. In 509 BC the Romans rebelled and drove out the Etruscans, setting up a Republic governed by the system of consuls and senate which was to last until Augustus became Emperor in 27 BC. The Romans went on to conquer the Etruscan territories and despite a setback when the city was sacked by the Gauls in 390 BC, went on to gain control over the whole Italian peninsula. The city grew, spreading onto the famous seven hills. They went to war with the powerful Cathaginian state based in North Africa across the Mediterranean, eventually defeating them and destroying their capital Carthage in 146 BC, making Rome the dominant power in the Mediterranean. They had defeated the Greeks in the Macedonian Wars in 168 BC giving them control over the Greek territories. The former Carthaginian and Greek colonies in the Iberian Peninsula fell to Rome with these victories and they went on to absorb the whole Peninsula into their Empire. The Middle East, including the territories of the Jews, became theirs. Julius Caesar later vanquished the Gauls between 58 and 51 BC, taking in what is now France as far as the River Rhine. England was absorbed in the 1st century AD. Emperor Trajan (98-117 AD) conquered Dacia in present day Romania, crossing the Dunube, which had been the previous boundary. He also extended the Empire to Persia and Arabia. This was the peak of the Empire. It contained nearly 60 million people and Rome itself had swollen to over a million. Trajan's successor, Hadrian, decided that enough was enough and built walls to defend the frontiers from the barbarians beyond, including the one which took his name on England's northern boundary. Defending an Empire this size was an enormous strain on resources. In Diocletian's time around 300 AD the army consisted of 28 legions, 400,000 soldiers. The subsequent decline and fall was almost inevitable.

The city itself underwent constant change during this time, often as a result of the periodic fires which destroyed parts of it and as successive emperors sought to leave their mark for posterity. The streets were paved, stone bridges were built across the Tiber and aqueducts were built to provide a water supply. Julius Caesar had the Forum extended. Augustus, the first Emperor (27 BC -14 AD) vowed to transform Rome from "a city of bricks to a city of marble" – which he did. Large public buildings were built including basilicas where legal cases were heard, a new Forum, theatres, heated baths and temples mushroomed all served with running water and piped sewage disposal. Claudius had the port of Ostia built at the mouth of the Tiber to enable direct grain shipments from North Africa to feed the growing population. Nero re-built a large area of the city destroyed by the fire of 64 AD including his enormous, ostentatious palace, the Golden House. The Colosseum was completed in 80 AD. Trajan (98-117 AD) built a new Forum and his Markets, a huge complex of shops, public baths, libraries and meeting halls. Emperors erected triumphal arches and columns to celebrate victories in battles. It must have been a magnificent city.

As I strolled through its remains, I was disappointed at all that was left. Following the over-running of the city by successive waves of barbarians, it had been used effectively as a quarry to provide building material for what became the medieval town on the flat land down by the Tiber where a water supply could still be found. As an outdoor museum, I felt that more could have been done to bring it alive but the Italians appeared to be very blasé about their historical heritage. Mussolini hadn't helped by driving the wide Via dei Fori Imperiali smack bang through the middle of it. He deserved to be hung from a lamp post for that alone.

Trajan's Column, 40 metres (131 feet) of marble, celebrated his two campaigns in Dacia (now Romania), scenes from the action spiralling round the column. Originally a statue of Trajan had stood on top of the column: this had been replaced by one of St. Peter in 1587 – more Papal mischief. Nearby, there was quite a lot left of Trajan's Markets, a multi- storey complex of 150 shops and offices from which, among other functions, free corn had been doled out to the poor to keep them quiet. Little remained of the Forum built by Trajan in front of the Markets. The Arch of Septimus Severus was well preserved although badly weathered: relief panels, now barely discernible, celebrated his victories over the Parthians (now Iran and Iraq) and in Arabia. A section of the Temple of Vesta where the Vestal Virgins kept the Sacred Flame alight had been partially restored. In the adjacent remains of the House of the Vestal Virgins, some headless statues of them stood around the central courtyard. The Arch of Titus was in honour of him knocking shit out of the Jews in Judea, which culminated in the Jewish Diaspora. I felt like adding some graffiti to the effect that we had him to thank for the mess that Israel and Palestine was in now. The 25 metres (81 feet) high Arch of Constantine had been erected following his victory over his co-emperor Maxentius at the Battle of Milvian Bridge. Sculptures on it showed battle scenes. His victory temporarily re-united the two halves of the Empire split by Diocletian but Constantine later re-introduced the split, building his own capital of the Eastern Empire at Constantinople (Istanbul now). That half of the Empire survived in ever-decreasing size until 1453 when the Turks finally over-ran Constantinople.

The piece de resistance among the ruins of ancient Rome was the Colosseum, Rome's greatest amphitheatre, commissioned by Emperor Vespasian in 72 AD and completed by his son Titus in 80 AD. It had been built on the site of an artificial lake created by Nero in the grounds of his extravagant palace the Domus Aurea (Golden House). Vespasian had wanted to return to public use land expro-priated by Nero after the great fire of 64 AD to build his palace. Ironically, the Colosseum took its name from a colossal statue of Nero, 35 meters (114 feet) high, which stood nearby. While the remains were impressive, it had been seriously vandalised over the years. Most of the façade had been stripped away to build churches, bridges and palaces during the Renaissance: most of what was left was the inner wall. The original structure had been 50 meters (162 feet) high and 188 meters (611 feet) in diameter with 80 archway entrances. 100,000 tons of travertine (limestone) had been needed for the outer walls. The inner walls were of brick. The archways in the façade had used a variety of column styles – Doric at ground level; Ionic at the second level above; and Corinthian for the third level. A fourth storey had been added later to accommodate the riff-raff. Poles had been erected above the upper level to support the velarium, a huge awning to shade the spectators from the sun. It was raised by ropes fastened to bollards in a ring around the outside of the stadium which could still be seen. A labour force of 20,000, mostly slaves and prisoners of war, many of them Hebrews, had been used in the construction.

It could seat 55,000 spectators. The inaugural session lasted 100 days during which 9,000 animals perished. The arena had a wooden floor, covered in sand to soak up the blood, animal faeces and urine. A network of rooms and passages under the floor was used to accommodate the gladiators and wild animals pending their entrance into the arena and to store stage props for the shows so that they could be hoisted up into place. The shows usually opened with animals doing circus tricks or else fighting each other. They included lions, leopards, elephants, hippos, crocodiles, giraffes, hyenas, ostriches and zebras brought across from Africa, tigers, panthers and bears from elsewhere in the Empire. Men would be brought on to fight the animals or in the case of Christians, sacrificed to them. This was followed by the gladiators who fought each other to the death. Reports that the arena could be flooded for mock sea battles are now discounted: there was another venue over in Trastevere on the other side of the Tiber where this could take place.

The local satirist, Juvenal, had said that Roman emperors ruled with "bread and circuses". I had seen where free grain was handed out at Trajan's Market: now I had seen the circus in the Colosseum. The Roman underclass of slaves and poor could be kept quiet. But eventually the envious hordes of so-called barbarians outside the Empire's borders could not be kept in check and the downfall chronicled in Edward Gibbons' "Decline and Fall of the Roman Empire" came to pass. More recently, Emperor Berlusconi had managed to ensure that history repeated itself, doing a Nero and bunga-bungaing while Italy's economy burned.

5

THE GREAT WALL, CHINA
SEPTEMBER, 2002

In 1997, I took early retirement from Shetland Islands Council following a management re-organization and immigrated back to New Zealand. Since my mother was still alive, I took a trip back to Shetland every couple of years. On my way back to New Zealand in September 2002, I had booked a tour through China with Travel Indochina, an Australian firm based in Ho Chi Minh City (Saigon), which took in a visit to the Great Wall. The distances involved and the resulting transport logistics combined with the language barrier dictated group travel rather than my usual independent approach. I had taught myself some basic Putonghua (Mandarin Chinese), the numbers, greetings, how to ask the way and the price of things and haggle, directions, how to order a meal or a beer – just basic survival vocabulary. However, I couldn't read Chinese script so most things were likely to be inscrutable.

I had taken a brief tour into mainland China before in 1991, crossing from Hong Kong to Macau by jetfoil, then by road to Guangzhou (formerly known as Canton) via Foshan, returning to Hong Kong by rail via Shenzhen and the New Territories. On that occasion, I had used Kuoni Travel, a Swiss firm specialising in long-haul tours from Europe. On my way to New Zealand in 1971 I had

had a very brief stopover in Hong Kong and had made myself a promise that I would come back. It had taken me 20 years but I had finally made it. At that time Hong Kong was still a British colony. It had initially been occupied in 1841 at the end of the first Opium War between Britain and China. China had tried to stop the import of opium from India carried out by British traders and Britain had sent gunboats to ensure it could continue. Modern day Columbian drug barons have an interesting role model. The treaty at the end of the war left Britain with Hong Kong Island. At the end of the second Opium War in 1860, Britain took the Kowloon Peninsula. Finally, in 1898, they persuaded the decaying Chinese Empire to grant them a 99 year lease on the New Territories, stretching inland from Kowloon.

In 1991, Kai Tak Airport was still in operation. Coming in to land past the high rise flats brought back the same nervous thrill as twenty years ago. The tour group was based in a hotel in Kowloon. We took the Star Ferry across the harbour to Hong Kong Island and the Peak Tram (actually a funicular railway) up to the Peak, at 552 meters (1,794 feet), the highest point on the island. The view was magnificent over the central city below and across to Kowloon and the New Territories. To the south, lay Aberdeen Harbour and Repulse Bay and to the west Lantau and some other outlying islands. We took a bus around to Aberdeen Harbour, the original "Fragrant Harbour" from which Hong Kong took its name. We boarded a sampan for a cruise on the harbour, passing massive, multi-storey floating restaurants including the aptly named Jumbo. On the way back we stopped at the Man Mo Temple on Hollywood Road, dedicated to the gods of literature (Man) and war (Mo) in the ancient Chinese Taoist religion, the pungent smell of incense filling the air from the smoking spirals hanging from the ceiling. We walked down the aptly named Ladder Street and along to Cat Street Market, an Aladdin's cave of antiques.

A half hour ferry ride took us across to Cheung Chau Island, the hills of Lantau Island rising to the west. The tiny island had an old, traditional feel to it after the modern, bustling city, reflecting its history of piracy and fishing. The narrow streets were crowded with small shops, contrasting with the shopping malls and designer outlets we had just left. We saw junks being built and fishing nets mended.

The following day we caught a hovercraft across to Macau, a tiny Portuguese territory, measuring just 16 square kilometres, at the mouth of the Pearl River. It had been ceded to Portugal as a trading post in 1557 and consisted of a small peninsula and two adjoining islands, Taipa and Coloane, linked by a causeway and joined to the peninsula by bridges. Macau's prosperity depended on gambling which was illegal in both Hong Kong and China: the large pineapple shaped Lisboa Casino was a prominent landmark on the waterfront. We visited the ruins of the Jesuit Sao Paulo Cathedral, nothing remaining but an impressive façade above a flight of steep steps. It had been built in 1602 by Christian refugees from Nagasaki in Japan, fleeing from persecution there and destroyed in a fire in 1835. The streets in the old centre with their Portuguese names and architecture, the buildings painted in pastel colours, were reminiscent of Lisbon. In the Largo do Senado square, attractively paved with a wave pattern of black and white tiles, the colonnaded Leal Senado (Municipal Council Buildings) and the central Post Office were fine colonial style buildings. Portuguese restaurants abounded. We visited the Ah Ma Temple from which Macau took its name – Ah Ma Gau – Gau meaning harbour. Ah Ma was the goddess of seafarers. Just across the narrow strait dividing Macau from China rose the skyscrapers of Zuchai Special Economic Zone, one of four such capitalist enclaves established in 1980 when China started to open up to the West.

The following morning we headed into China through the Barrier Gate. We stopped in Cuiheng Village to visit the birthplace of Sun Yat Sen, the revolutionary who had led the Kuomintang (Nationalist Party) movement which had deposed the last of the Emperors, Pu Yi, in 1912. The house where he was born in 1866 had been pulled down but the Portuguese style building where he later lived with his parents had been converted to a museum with period furniture and memorabilia of the great man, still revered in China. In Guangzhou we stayed in the White Swan Hotel, a luxurious establishment on Shamian Dao Island. Shamian Dao had started life as a sandbank in the Pearl River but in the 18th century foreign merchants were permitted to build warehouses there and after the Opium Wars it became a joint British and French concession, much like the Bund in Shanghai. It still retained a sleepy colonial feel with its Victorian architecture and the French Catholic Our Lady of Lourdes Chapel on the leafy main boulevard. It was a different story when we crossed a bridge and entered the maelstrom of the city centre, people everywhere. We made our way to the Qingping Shichang (Bright Peace Market) a street market which was neither bright, the air laden with pollution on an overcast afternoon, nor peaceful, with the hordes of shoppers and the harsh, honking sounds of the Cantonese dialect. This private market had been set up at Deng Xiaoping's instigation in 1979 as an experiment with the capitalist system and it had taken off big time. It resembled a zoo as much as a market with as much fauna on sale as flora – cats, dogs, racoons, frogs, anteaters, monkeys, owls – all for the pot. We were due a banquet dinner at the hotel that night: I decided that I wouldn't be asking any questions about what the dishes consisted of. There were live fish swimming in tubs of water and tangles of snakes coiling around each other in baskets covered with netting. In the traditional medicine section a nauseating array of ingredients was on display – bears' paws, tigers' penises, dried snakes and lizards, deer antlers, hallucinogenic mushrooms – it was enough to make you sick. On the way back to the hotel towards dusk, we hit the rush hour – very few cars contributing to the flood of humanity but bicycles, serried ranks of them sweeping over the bridges from the offices on Shamian Dao, like a scene from the annual mass migration of wildebeest and zebra from the Serengeti Plains to the Masai Mara Game Reserve, which I had seen in my Africa days. In the evening, after our banquet, which finished early Chinese style, I decided to go and find the snake restaurant which Michael Palin had visited in his re-run of Around the World in 80 Days – the Kwangchow at 43 Chianglan Road. I had a map of sorts but the scale was dubious and I couldn't read signs or street names in Chinese characters. I tried asking directions in my basic Mandarin and English without success; no-one spoke English and it occurred to me that most people probably didn't speak Mandarin either which in the spoken form was double-Dutch to a Cantonese speaker. The people were very friendly in spite of the language barrier and seemed intrigued to see a gweilo (foreign devil) wandering around the streets at night – there were still very few foreign visitors to China in 1991. Eventually, I came across the restaurant and had a look in the window – it was near closing time and there were few customers left. I could see a variety of snakes wriggling around in glass tanks and a waiter was holding one up by the tail for the approval of a customer. I was glad that I had already eaten.

I awoke early to the muffled sound of engines. My room looked right out onto the Pearl River and the shipping was on the move in the grey light of dawn. Already you could feel the throb of China's awakening economic power. We caught a train to return to Hong Kong, past paddy fields and sleepy villages. Just at the border was the high-rise city of Shenzhen, another of the Special Economic Zones where capitalism ruled in an enclave still largely segregated from the rest of China, but a harbinger of things to come.

Back in Hong Kong in 2002 there was a new state of the art airport west of Lantau Island – Chek Lap Kok. I realized that I could memorise the name by making a check-list of the things needed for a lap dance in one of Kowloon's nightclubs. The transportation from the airport was also state of the art: the new rail system took me in to Hong Kong Island in twenty minutes. Since my last visit, Hong Kong had changed hands, reverting to China in 1997 when the 99 year lease on the New Territories ran out. In theory, Britain could have held onto Hong Kong Island and the Kowloon Peninsula, but even an old war horse like Margaret Thatcher had realized the futility of that and agreed to unload the whole territory. As it had turned out, little appeared to have changed. Hong Kong still had its own money and stamps and its capitalism was as rampant as ever. Le plus ca change, le plus ca ne change pas.

I was staying in the Empire Hotel in Wanchai, the World of Suzy Wong territory, pubs, sleazy nightclubs and restaurants lining Lockhart

Road. I took a bus out to Stanley Village on the south side of the island where there were some good restaurants and pubs and a lively market. On the way we passed Repulse Bay where a block of flats on the hillside had a large square hole in it where normally you would have expected just more flats. I discovered that this was a feng shui (pronounced fung shway and meaning wind and water) solution to the problem that a dragon lived on the mountain behind and required a right of way. Apparently nothing was built in Hong Kong without first consulting a feng shui specialist. This branch of geomancy was all about respecting the flow of qi, the cosmic life force, through the landscape, locating and orientating buildings so as not to interfere with it. I was glad that in my career as a town planner I had not had to deal with this complication although dealing with Maori cultural beliefs in New Zealand had at times come close – like being asked to re-route a major road to avoid disturbing a taniwha (water spirit) in a nearby river. In the evening I went to have a look at the new nightlife areas in Central District known as SoHo (standing for South of Hollywood Road and lying between Aberdeen Street and the Shelley Street escalator) and Lan Kwai Fong, off D'Aguilar Street. There were plenty of trendy pubs and up-market restaurants serving food from all over the world – Thai, Malaysian, Indian, French, Spanish, Italian – but it was all a bit too chyuppy (young upwardly-mobile Chinese person) for my liking; I preferred sleazy old Wanchai.

The following day I took an escorted tour into the New Territories, a strange mixture of high-rise new towns, agricultural land, reservoirs, mountains, marshes and beaches. We visited an old walled village, Kat Hing Wai, one of several around Kam Tin, dating from the 16th century. The walls were 6 metres (20 feet) thick with guard-houses on the four corners, slits to fire arrows at attackers and surrounded by a moat. About 400 people still lived there, all with the surname Tang, one of the original clans of Hakka people indigenous to the area. There was just one gateway into the village, carefully guarded by some old women dressed in traditional style with their trademark variation on the conical hat, eagerly watching that appropriate donations went into the box at the entrance. Inside, in the narrow lanes there were more ladies willing to pose for photographs for a fee and a street of souvenir vendors. It was all a bit like Disneyland but you could still get the feel of what life had been like before Britain became the landlord.

I had booked a couple of nights over in Macau before my flight up to Beijing, staying in the Hyatt Regency Hotel over on Taipa Island. Like Hong Kong, Macau had changed hands since my last visit, reverting to China in 1999. However, unlike Hong Kong, I soon got the impression that things had changed. They still had their own currency, the pataka, but it was as if some of the Portugueseness had drained away and it was noticeably busier. It was difficult to nail down what had changed; it was more just something in the ambience of the place. I caught a bus over to Coloane Island, the least developed part of the territory, although work had already started on an ambitious scheme to infill part of the area between the two islands to create new land for a range of commercial projects including new casinos. Coloane appeared to have been neglected by the Portuguese. It had remained a haven for pirates until 1910. The causeway linking it to Taipa Island hadn't been constructed until 1969. It was still rural with farmland and stands of pine trees and other woodland. Coloane Village had retained its traditional Chinese character with a narrow main street and even narrower lanes leading off it, lined with a range of shops and some inviting looking restaurants. On higher ground above the main road stood the Chapel of St. Francis Xavier, with a cream and white façade and a bell tower. It had been built in 1928 to house an arm bone of the famous missionary who had died on a nearby island. On the waterfront at the far end of the village, the Tom Kong Temple was dedicated to the God of the Sea; inside, a four feet long whalebone had been carved into a model dragon boat with red-coated, top-hatted oarsmen.

In the evening, I went for a meal in Fat Siu Lau Restaurant in Rua da Felicidade. A hybrid cuisine known as Macanese had evolved in Macau, a fusion of Portuguese cooking methods and Cantonese ingredients with influences from Portugal's other colonies in Africa, Brazil, India, Malaysia and Indonesia. I had peri-peri prawns, the fiery sauce made with coriander and chillies, followed by African chicken, marinated in garlic, chillies and coconut milk, then roasted in a hot oven until blackened, accompanied by a bottle of Portuguese Vinho Verde. Afterwards, I went for a drink in the bar of the Lisboa Casino. A group of Russian girls were sitting round a nearby table, casting glances in my direction, obviously on the game. To round off the evening, I paid a visit to a large, garishly neon-lit massage parlour on the Avenida da Praia Grande, to continue the research into Chinese female anatomy that I had started on my first visit to Hong Kong in 1971. A report on the fieldwork and findings will be published at a later date.

In Beijing, the Travel Indochina tour group had assembled in the Qianmen Hotel, not far from the Temple of Heaven. We set off for Tian'an Men Square, scene of the massacre of students and their supporters seeking greater democracy in 1989. The square was huge, allegedly able to hold a million people and a bit sterile in spite of the crowds of sightseers. It was flanked by the Great Hall of the People where Communist Party legislation was rubber stamped and opposite it, the National Museum, both built in the 1950s. In the middle of the square stood Mao Tse Tung's mausoleum, a long queue snaking towards the entrance.

Mao had come to power in 1949 after a long struggle from the time he co-founded the Chinese Communist Party in Shanghai in 1921. Initially the communists were allied with the nationalists under Sun Yat Sen and General Chiang Kai-shek trying to wrest control of the country from the war lords who effectively ran it. But in 1926 Chiang Kai-shek double crossed them and from then on the struggle was against the nationalists, apart from the 1937 to 1945 period when they both fought against the invading Japanese. In 1949 the communists came out on top and Chiang Kai-shek and his supporters withdrew to Taiwan. Industries and financial institutions were nationalised and agricultural cooperatives set up in the countryside, the landlord class mostly exterminated. However, economic development didn't happen fast enough for Mao's liking. In 1958 he launched his Great Leap Forward project. Steel production was to be started in rural areas on a cottage industry scale: this diverted farmers from agriculture which combined with consecutive bad harvests brought famine – it was estimated that between 30 and 40 million people died of starvation. Mao's reputation in the Party suffered and to retain power he launched the Cultural Revolution in 1965. Youth, in the form of brigades of Red Guards, were to be given their head to carry through a social revolution, root out in-grained privilege and make everyone equal. All forms of authority were to be challenged – parents, teachers, university professors along with intellectuals including writers and artists. Authority figures were challenged in public to subject themselves to self-criticism and "struggled" (a euphemism for abused) by Red Guards. Many were beaten and even killed, labelled "revisionists", "capitalist roaders" and "running dogs". Others were banished to the countryside for "re-education." Priceless cultural and historical artefacts and buildings were destroyed. Mao's leading supporter, Lin Biao, produced the Little Red Book ('The Thoughts of Chairman Mao') which became the Red Guards' bible. A personality cult grew up around Mao. In 1967 the PLA (Peoples Liberation Army) had to intervene to curb the worst excesses and some Red Guards were prosecuted but the cult continued until Mao's death in 1976. During his latter years, when he was incapacitated by motor-neuron disease, the Gang of Four led by his wife Jiang Qing, a former B-grade actress, took the lead. After his death, the Party tried to pass the blame for the excesses of the Cultural Revolution onto the Gang of Four and they were arrested and put on trial. In court, Jiang Qing argued that she had been Mao's dog and when he told her to bite someone, she bit them. Her death sentence was commuted to life imprisonment but she hanged herself in prison in 1991. After the trial, the official Party line was that Mao had been alright in his earlier days but in latter years he "had made some mistakes". He certainly had but his giant portrait still hung above the Tian'an Men Gate (Gate of Heavenly Peace) which led towards the entrance to the Forbidden City, our next destination.

The Forbidden City or Imperial Palace had been built between 1406 and 1420 by Emperor Yongle of the Ming Dynasty, using a workforce of 200,000, and had been the court of the emperors until the last one, Pu Yi, was deposed in 1912. The Meridian Gate took us across the surrounding moat and through the 10 metres (33 feet) high wall into the Palace complex, which covered an area of a square kilometre, then across the winding Golden Water River over a marble bridge to the Gate of Supreme Harmony which led into a courtyard where the main ceremonial buildings stood – the Hall of Supreme Harmony succeeded by the Halls of Middle Harmony and Preserving Harmony. The main buildings in the Palace were strung out along a south-north axis through the middle of the compound in a series of courtyards entered through ornate gateways. The architecture was repetitive, double roofs curling upwards at the eaves and gables, walls all painted the same shade of dark red. Gables were lined with carved dragon and phoenix figures to protect against lightning and fire. Most buildings were roped off at the door; you could see the interiors but not go inside. On the platform outside the Hall of Supreme Harmony stood large bronze sculptures of a tortoise and a crane, both symbols of longevity – emperors since the first one, Qin Shi Huang had been obsessed with the idea of eternal life. A large incense burner stood in front of the Hall. Inside we could see the Dragon Throne from which successive emperors had ruled. The stairs leading down from the Hall of Preserving Harmony were divided by a ramp of solid marble weighing 250 tons and decorated with dragon motifs. Scattered throughout the complex were huge metal urns which had held water to fight fires which were a constant danger among the wooden buildings.

The Gate of Heavenly Purity led into the former living quarters of the Palace, occupied by three large buildings, the Palaces of Heavenly Purity and Earthly Tranquillity and the Hall of Union. The former Palace had contained the emperor's bedroom; the latter had housed the empresses. The Hall of Union was where concubines had been selected. The interiors were lifeless; no attempt had been made to bring the history alive – the world of eunuchs, concubines and mandarins.

Immediately north of the Forbidden City lay Beihai Park around Beihai Lake, a peaceful enclave surrounded by tree-lined paths with restaurants and bars. On Jade Island in the lake, the White Dagoba, a Tibetan style shrine, towered above the trees. Further north, the Drum and Bell Towers originally dated back to the rule of Kublai Khan, when they stood in the centre of his new capital city, Dadu. They had been moved slightly and rebuilt during the Ming dynasty and renovated since. The bell in the 33 meters (108 feet) tall Bell Tower had been rung at 7.00 am to signal the start of the day; the drums had been beaten at 7.00 pm to mark the start of the night and then every two hours until 5.00 am.

We moved on to Liulichang Street for some lunch and shopping. The street had been tarted up as a tourist magnet and was a bit kitsch but there were several interesting antique shops, a shop selling Chinese lanterns and fans, a book shop specialising in old books and manuscripts, some calligraphy specialists and the Zhangyiyuan Teashop with a large ornamental ceramic teapot at first floor level. Two young hill-tribe girls from South China, in traditional costume, were selling packets of tea in the street, square boxes of their products suspended from poles held over their shoulders.

We had a walk through a hutong, the narrow residential lanes lined with single-storey houses typical of old Beijing but rapidly disappearing in the face of redevelopment. We visited a house where the owners provided home-stay accommodation for foreigners. The layout around a central courtyard created a very pleasant living environment, much preferable in my view to the high rise blocks of flats where the residents were being decanted to as the old houses got knocked down.

In the evening, I went to have dinner at the Quanjude Restaurant in Qianmen Dajie (Avenue) just south of Tian'an Men Square, which specialized in Peking Duck. Virtually every part of the duck was used in the meal. The appetiser allegedly contained liver, heart, intestines, tongue and skin from between the webbed feet. The main course was cut into bite sized pieces. It was served with wafer thin pancakes, spring onions and hoisin sauce – made from beans, garlic and spices. The etiquette was to roll the meat in a pancake with some spring onion and dipping sauce and eat with the hands. At the end, soup was served made from the remains of the duck, including the bones.

The following morning, we left early to visit the Great Wall at Mutianyu, 90 kilometres (55 miles) north-east of the city. The air pollution level was pretty high when we left Beijing but it had cleared a bit by the time we got to the wall, although it was still hazy. Nevertheless, the crenellated wall and square watchtowers on the ridges high above us made an impressive sight. There was a rash of souvenir stalls and hawkers near the cable car station where we stopped and a dromedary was standing waiting patiently to provide rides. This section of the wall had been sensitively restored and you could walk along the carriageway between the battlements and explore the watchtowers. I was accosted by a Ming warrior in full battle regalia carrying a lethal looking halberd, who demanded tribute in return for posing for a photograph. I didn't like to refuse. At this point the wall was about 8 meters (26 feet) high and the carriageway on top about 7 meters (22 feet) wide – wide enough for two chariots to pass or for 6 men to march abreast. The upper wall and towers were faced with brick although the lower courses of the wall were of granite.

The history of the wall went back to 500 BC when the various warring states built walls on their boundaries to protect themselves from troublesome neighbours. The first emperor, Qin Shi Huang, connected up parts of these walls and extended them to form a continuous barrier along the northern frontier during his reign from 221 to 210 BC and some additions were made by the subsequent Han dynasty. These early walls were made of rammed earth, compacted between scaffolding of boards, rather than brick and stone but remnants could still be seen. The existing wall dated from the Ming period with work starting around 1550 AD and continuing for the best part of 100 years. The Ming builders used much more robust materials as could be seen at Mutianyu. Once China had been unified, the need for a wall was to protect the empire from the marauding nomads who lived to the north. The Chinese were settled farmers cultivating the rich alluvial soils along the Yellow River (Huang He) and to the south. The Mongols and related tribes to the north were nomadic pastoralists who grazed their flocks of sheep, goats, cattle and horses wherever they could find pasture, moving with the seasons. Whenever there were droughts, they were tempted by the rich spoils in the farmland to the south. This conflict is known as the "steppe versus the sown" and became a feature of world history with the Mongols and then the Turks making incursions into Eastern Europe, reaching as far as Vienna at times. A similar conflict developed in the 'Wild West' of

America where the homesteaders or "sodbusters" came up against the cattle ranchers who had previously had free run of the prairies on the Great Plains.

Both the Qin and Ming walls were built using massive manpower and resources and with great loss of life. In the case of the Qin wall, it brought down the dynasty when the people rebelled against the forced labour and taxes it had involved during the ten years of its construction. Recently, an attempt has been made to measure the east-west length of the Great Wall accurately. Previously it had been estimated at around 6,000 kilometres (3,790 miles). The old Chinese name for the wall, Wan Li Chang Cheng, means the 10,000 Li Great Wall, a li measuring about half a kilometre, suggesting that they thought it was about 5,000 kilometres (3,125 miles) long. The problem is complicated by the existence of branch walls leading off the main line and the tortuous alignment of the wall to comply with feng shui principles and take advantage of the topography. The new research has come up with the figure of 8,850 kilometres (5,500 miles) for the Ming wall from where it reaches the Yellow Sea to its terminus in the Gobi Desert at Hu Mountain in northern Liaoning Province. This figure includes some stretches of lake, river and mountain where a wall was superfluous and some sections where trenches were used instead but regardless, it was a mind boggling set of fortifications. Along the line of the wall there were nearly 8,000 beacon and lookout towers. The wall was designated a UNESCO World Heritage Site in 1987.

The ironic thing is that in spite of all the effort, it didn't work. The Mongol warlord Ghengis Khan was able to breach it and sack much of China in 1215 AD and his grandson Kublai Khan invaded and set up the Yuan dynasty which lasted from 1279 to 1368. The Mongols breached the wall again in 1549 and sacked Beijing, prompting the Ming dynasty to undertake their massive upgrade. Finally, the Manchus from Manchuria got through it to set up the Qing dynasty in 1644, although in their case they were let through by a Chinese general who preferred to see them ruling China than the leader of a peasant revolt who had overthrown the last Ming emperor.

Re-entering Beijing on the way back from the Great Wall in the tour bus, I was struck by how the traffic had changed in China since my last visit to Guangzhou eleven years ago when I had witnessed an avalanche of bicycles crossing a bridge over an arm of the Pearl River at rush hour with few cars to interrupt the flow. Now the tables had been turned; there were still plenty of bicycles but they were far outnumbered by cars. Beijing was well designed to cope with vehicle traffic although with over 14 million people the congestion was already chronic, even with relatively low car ownership per head of population. It was frightening to think what congestion and air pollution levels would be like when ownership reached Western levels. Like all Chinese cities, Beijing was laid out on a rigid rectangular grid with the streets orientated north-south and east-west. It was very easy to navigate once you got the hang of the naming system: streets were called "jie" or "lu", jie generally being wider and "dajie" (big street) an avenue. The central stretch of a street would have the prefix "zhong" while further out the prefixes would be the compass points – "bei" (north), "nan" (south), "xi" (west) and "dong" (east). In the evening, I decided to have a look at the new entertainment area in Sanlitun Lu out in the Dongcheng area in the east of the city and try to master the metro system to get there. It proved remarkably easy, with signs and information in English and I arrived at my stop Dongsishitiao without any problems. Sanlitun was a street of Western type café-bars, pubs and restaurants favoured by Western expatriates and local yuppies. It was all a bit too artificial and contrived for my liking and I didn't stay late.

The following morning, we went to visit the Temple of Heaven (Tiantan), built in 1420 and once used for imperial ancestor worship. At the winter solstice, the emperor would come to honour his ancestors and pray for a good harvest in the coming season. The buildings in the complex were divided into two main groups: the northern group, centred on the Hall of Prayer for Good Harvests (Qiniandian), was semi-circular in layout, representing Heaven; the southern group had a square layout, representing earth. We entered the complex through the North Heavenly Gate and approached the Hall of Prayer for Good Harvests, its three tier, pointed roof made of

50,000 blue, glazed tiles with a golden top. It stood on a three level marble terrace, each level surrounded by a balustrade. The circular shape of the roof represented the sky, the blue colour of the tiles, Heaven. Inside, the roof had no beams, spars or nails to support it, just 28 wooden pillars, the central four, 20 meters (66 feet) tall, representing the four seasons. In the southern group of buildings, the Hall of Heaven was enclosed by the semi-circular Echo Wall. According to our guide, if someone faced the wall and spoke, the sound would carry around the wall to someone at the other end. With the number of tourists all trying this at the same time it was difficult to verify. The Altar of Heaven was enclosed by two walls, the outer one square, enclosing an area representing the earth, the inner one circular enclosing Heaven. The stone in the centre was considered to be the most holy place in the empire, the centre of the earth.

On the way out to the Summer Palace in the afternoon, we stopped at the zoo to see the Giant Panda. I'm not a great fan of zoos, having become used to seeing animals in the wild in East Africa, but I suppose it's the only practical way for people to see rare animals and it would be a pity to visit China without seeing their most iconic one. I was glad that I hadn't seen one on my previous visit to Guangzhou in the street market which had resembled a zoo.

We approached the East Palace Gate (Dongmen) to the Summer Palace through a brightly painted, ornate wooden structure called a pailou, a sort of triumphal arch. The Palace in its present form had been built from 1888 by the Empress Dowager Cixi (pronounced Tsuhshyi) following the destruction of the old Summer Palace a little to the east and the associated structures in this area, by British and French troops during the Opium Wars in 1860. This area had long been a royal park developed around the beautiful Kunming Lake and a 60 metres (200 feet) artificial hill called Longevity Hill. Cixi was believed to have misappropriated money intended to upgrade the navy to rebuild the Summer Palace in this location. She could argue that at least some of the money went for maritime purposes as part of it was used to refurbish a marble boat with stone wheels to resemble a paddle steamer where she used to take afternoon tea. The diversion of funds had unfortunate consequences as the navy suffered a humiliating defeat by the Japanese in 1895. Near the entrance was the Hall of Benevolence and Longevity where the young Emperor Guangxu dealt with state business when the court moved here from the Forbidden City during the heat of summer and where Cixi presided after she put him under virtual house arrest in 1898 in the neighbouring Hall of Jade Ripples after he had attempted to open up China to foreign ideas. Cixi had acted as regent since 1861 when her young son inherited the Dragon Throne and then subsequently for her nephew Guangxu, effectively ruling the country - not bad for someone who had started out as a concubine of the third rank. We passed her living quarters, the Hall of Happiness and Longevity and the Garden of Virtue and Harmony where she enjoyed performances of Chinese Opera. We walked through the Long Corridor, a covered walk-way which ran along the edge of the lake for 700 metres, the ceiling beams decorated with paintings, some of which had been vandalised by Red Guards during the Cultural Revolution. Half way along the Corridor, a series of temples ascended Longevity Hill, culminating in the 35 metres (125 feet) high Pagoda of Buddhist Virtue on the summit. At the end of the walk-way was Cixi's famous marble boat, the two-storey, wooden superstructure designed to look like marble to match the hull. From there we took a cruise on a dragon-prowed pleasure boat across the lake to South Lake Island, connected to the mainland by the photogenic Seventeen Arches Bridge, a big bronze ox lying at its landward end, intended to pacify the water spirit and protect the surrounding land from floods.

In the evening, we caught the overnight train to Xian, travelling 1st class, soft sleeper style in four person compartments with double-decker bunks. I slept like a log on the 15 hour trip. In Xian, we were staying in the Bell Tower Hotel, right in the centre of the city. After breakfast, we drove 30 kilometres (20 miles) east to see the Terracotta Warriors. They had been discovered in 1974 by some farmers digging a well. A mile to the west rose a huge mound, the tomb of China's first emperor, Qin Shi Huang, which they were guarding. The tomb had not yet been excavated but according to the 'Book of the Han Dynasty' written about a hundred years after Qin's death:

"Inside the tomb, the sarcophagus was afloat on a mercury sea, lit by lamps burning human fat and dotted with gold wild geese."

It was believed that the tomb was laid out like a map of China with the Yellow (Huang He) and Yangtse (Chang Jiang) Rivers filled with mercury and pearls set into the ceiling to represent stars. Soil tests had detected very high levels of mercury in the mound.

The pits containing the warriors were housed in a large building with a semi-circular roof, like a giant Nissen hut. From a surrounding walk-way you could look down on the serried ranks, over 6,000 infantrymen in the main pit along with cavalry and their horses and charioteers. The figures were life-size or possibly slightly larger than life compared to contemporary Chinese. A second pit, still under excavation, contained a mixed army of infantry, cavalry and chariots in battle formation with over 1300 armoured warriors and 90 wooden chariots. A third pit was believed to be the command centre with a group of 68 warriors, giving in all nearly 8,000 figures with the horses. All the faces were different; each man an individual. It was believed that they had been made individually from coiled clay, rather than from moulds. The detail of their uniforms, armour and helmets was exquisite. They had originally been painted, but the paint had quickly faded on exposure to the air. They had also carried a variety of arms - swords, halberds, spears, cross bows – mostly of bronze but some iron. Many of these had survived and had been discovered to have been chromium plated, an anti-erosion technique not re-activated until modern times. In a separate excavation, nearer Qin's tomb, two bronze chariots with their horses and riders had been found, half-size scale models and beautifully crafted. They were housed in a separate museum along with the weaponry.

The pits containing the warriors had originally been roofed over as shown by remains of pillars and beams and covered with earth. However, after the death of Emperor Qin in 210 BC the subjects of his successor rose up in rebellion against the heavy taxation and forced labour involved in building the Great Wall and the repressive regime generally, broke into the enclosure and systematically destroyed much of the dead emperor's defending army. Whether or not this was symbolic to give the old tyrant a hard time in the next world can only be speculative but it left modern day archaeologists a nightmare to piece together the broken pieces of all the king's horses and all the king's men. But they had done a magnificent job and thousands of Humptys were back on guard. How much longer they can stave off excavation of Qin's tomb remains to be seen.

In the souvenir shop, one of the peasants who had stumbled on the warriors' site was autographing copies of a new, glossy publication 'Valiant Imperial Warriors 2200 Years Ago' and looking distinctly uncomfortable about it. The expression on his face said "I'm a celebrity, get me out of here." He bore a striking resemblance to one of the warriors in a photograph in the book, perhaps modelled on an ancestor. The site had been declared a UNESCO World Heritage Site in 1987. If I was to draw up my own personal short-list for the New Seven Wonders of the World, the Terracotta Warriors would certainly be on it.

The following morning, we had a tour of Xian. The city had been the capital of China for over a thousand years, the starting point of the Silk Road, China's main link to the alleged barbarians in the rest of the world. At the height of the Tang dynasty in the 8th century it had housed over a million people, the largest city in the world at the time. The modern city held over six million and further development was being promoted by the government as part of its policy to promote growth in the west of the country: an area south of the centre was designated as a 'High Technical Development Zone'. The central part of the city was enclosed by a high wall dating from 1370 AD during the Ming period; the Tang dynasty wall had been much longer. The Ming wall was still impressive, rising 12 metres (39 feet), 18 metres (59 feet) wide at the base, the carriageway on top 12 to 14 metres (39 to 45 feet) wide and surrounded by a wide moat. It stretched for 14 kilometres (9 miles) in a rectangular shape but was not continuous now so it wouldn't have been possible to walk all the way around it. We mounted it near the south gate for a view over the city and a look at the impressive watch towers. Our hotel was right beside the massive Bell Tower (Zhong Lou) with its distinctive green, three tiered roof, which, with the Drum Tower (Gu Lou) a little to the west, had served the same purpose of marking day and night as their counterparts in Beijing. Nearby was the Great Mosque, serving Xian's substantial Moslem minority, the Hui (pronounced Hwey) people, who lived in the narrow streets around the mosque. The building looked more like a Chinese temple than a mosque from the outside but as infidels we weren't allowed inside. We drove down to the Big Goose Pagoda in the south of the city which had been built in 652 AD to house Buddhist scriptures brought back from India by the travelling monk Xuan Zang. Built from wood and brick, it stood 64 metres (208 feet) high, the seven storeys representing the stages of reaching nirvana. Outside was a large green statue of Buddha and near the entrance a monk in a brown robe was standing beside a smoking incense burner which dwarfed him. In the afternoon we had some free time before catching a flight down to Chongqing for a cruise down the Yangtse River through the Three Gorges. I took a wander through the maze of narrow, dusty streets in the Moslem quarter, lined with shops and pavement stalls selling inviting looking food – noodles, dumplings, broth, a variety of bread and skewered meat cooking on charcoal braziers. At one point I got lost and asked directions from a man with a wispy beard, wearing a white skullcap and selling pieces of mutton in sesame buns, who amazingly understood my basic Mandarin and even more amazingly I understood his directions to the hotel.

When we took off for the flight to Chongqing, the extent of the air pollution enveloping China's cities became apparent. We rose through a yellow, opaque bubble before bursting out into blue sky. In Chongqing, we were billeted in the Renmin Binguan (Hotel), modestly modelled on the Temple of Heaven in Beijing. Chongqing was even more polluted than Beijing or Xian, buried in a haze of smog into which the massed ranks of high rise buildings disappeared. The Yangtze, at 6,300 kilometres (3,900 miles) the third longest river in the world, was dirty brown; whether it was just mud carried down from upstream or something more toxic was anybody's guess. With a population of 3 million in the city and 14 million in the metropolitan area, Chongqing was a major industrial centre and it showed. In the morning, I got up early and went to watch the locals doing their early morning Tai Chi exercises in a square near the hotel. With the amount of pollution in the air, I wasn't tempted to do anything involving deep breathing.

Our cruise boat, the Yangtze Star, was tied up at a pontoon in the river. She was a substantial vessel with three storeys above deck level and an open sun deck on top, bar, restaurant, and lounges, all beautifully fitted out. We were accommodated in comfortable two person cabins with portholes for watching the passing scenery and there was plenty of open deck space for even better views. The cruise was scheduled to last three days down to where the giant Three Gorges Dam was already well under construction. We got underway after breakfast and made our way downstream towards the first stop at Fengdu. Here we saw vividly illustrated what the effect of the Three Gorges (Sanxia) Dam would be. We had already seen markers on the valley sides showing where the water level would rise to – 135 metres higher in 2003 when the first stage was finished; 175 metres in 2009 on completion of the project. At Fengdu this meant that the existing town would disappear underwater, a new town to replace it, shiny white, high up on the hillside on the opposite bank. Fengdu was known as Devil Town, as along with Mingshan mountain which rose above it, it was supposed to be the abode of Yinwang, the Emperor of Hell. We took a chairlift up to the temple dedicated to him, garishly decorated with sculptures of grotesque devils. We moored for the night and after dinner were subjected to a concert by the ship's staff. Fortunately, since Chairman Mao was now out of favour, we weren't treated to a rendition of 'Dong Fang Hong' (The East is Red), a catchy little number by a group called the Red Guards which had been top of the pops during the Cultural Revolution. However, I'll set it out below as an example of the musical lyrics typical of communist China and lower the curtain on the staff concert:-

Dong fang hong
Tai yang shang (The sun rises)
China produces Mao Zedong

He works for the happiness of the people
He is the saviour of the Chinese people
The east is red.

Early next morning we entered the first of the gorges, Qutang. It was only 8 kilometres (5 miles) long but spectacular; the river narrowed to 100 meters, the cliffs rising almost vertically on either side. An hour later we were into the Wu Gorge, stretching for 44 kilometres (27 miles). The river was wider here and the gorge walls not quite so precipitous, allowing views of some impressive mountains including Goddess Peak. Through the gorge, we passed another doomed town, Zigui, the old town along the river bank already looking derelict, the gleaming new town rising above it on the hillside. It was a surreal sight. We stopped and took a side tour in a large rowing boat up the Shenndong Stream, a shallow tributary. Three oarsmen forward and two aft propelled us along with another man in a conical hat on the steering oar. Upstream, the current grew stronger and three men who had been sitting behind me got out, fixed a rope to the boat and began towing us along, wading through the shallows at the edge of the stream. This was to illustrate the system that had been operated on the main river before navigation works and a dam further downstream had reduced the speed of the flow through the gorges. Gangs of men known as "trackers", working from narrow paths cut along the base of the gorge walls, had painfully hauled boats upstream using ropes, just like our team were now demonstrating. It must have been back-breaking work.

Around 4.00 pm we entered the third and last of the gorges, Xiling and shortly after we emerged from it, arrived at the site of the giant Three Gorges Dam where we stopped to view the construction site. This was to be the largest dam in the world, 2 kilometres wide and 185 metres high, the final reservoir stretching back 645 kilometres (400 miles) to Chongqing. It would have power stations at either end, a ship elevator for smaller craft and a five-lock ship canal for larger vessels. The dam was intended to control the seasonal flooding which had plagued residents along the Yangtse for millennia, generate power to reduce China's reliance on polluting fossil fuels, improve navigation, boost fisheries and recreational use of the river and provide irrigation water for drought stricken areas of north China. Set against this it would eventually displace 1.3 million people, result in the loss of agricultural land and historic sites, accumulate vast quantities of silt and concentrate pollutants. In addition, there was the risk of catastrophic failure in a country prone to severe earthquakes. There was also concern about the effect on environmental systems and rare wildlife such as the endangered Yangtse species of dolphin, sturgeon and alligator. That evening, we had the captain's farewell banquet, a delicious meal efficiently served by some of the stars from the previous evening's concert – an object lesson on why it is invariably wiser to stick to the day job.

The following morning we passed through the lock in the Gezhou Dam and in the afternoon disembarked in Yichang from where we continued by bus to Wuhan, further downstream, where we were to spend the night. Wuhan was another huge industrial city and river port (ocean going ships could reach this far) with over 7 million people. In the evening, a group of us set out in a taxi with Katrina, the Aussi tour leader, to look for a restaurant which she had been to on a previous trip. It soon became apparent that the taxi driver didn't know where we were going and neither did Katrina. She appeared to know about as much Chinese as I did, which was not a lot – she hadn't been in China long – and my earlier suspicions that she was allergic to maps (we never got handouts to show where we were going on excursions) were borne out. Back at the hotel, I had ripped the street map of Wuhan out of my Lonely Planet guide to take with me so that I could see where we were going and I passed it to Katrina in the hope that she might be able to locate the restaurant on it. I might as well have given her a copy of some of Einstein's calculations. We drove around for about an hour and then gave up. Back at the hotel, the restaurant was officially closed but we managed to persuade them to rustle us up some food. It had been an object lesson on how not to travel in a country where you don't know the language and the script. I always got a card from the hotel where I was staying with the address in the local script which I could show to taxi drivers to get me back there again. Likewise if I was going to a restaurant or a bar, I would get the hotel staff to write down the address in the local script to show to the taxi driver. I don't know what sort of training Travel Indochina provided for their operatives but I could have taught Katrina a thing or two – talk about the blind leading the blind.

The following morning, we flew down to Guilin. The scenery around the city was as spectacular as I had seen anywhere in the world, sheer limestone pinnacles rising from green paddy fields, the river Li winding its way through it all. This was the stuff of traditional Chinese paintings, misty peaks, bamboo forests. With a setting like that, Guilin was a tourist town although it had its share of industry too – there was more than water vapour in the haze shrouding the romantic landscape. We went to visit Reed Flute Cave, a massive cavern in the limestone with neon-lit stalactites and stalagmites and the huge Crystal Palace of the Dragon King said to be able to hold a thousand people. In the square in the city centre, a large mural depicted a futuristic impression of Guilin with beautifully designed tower blocks aping the limestone pinnacles, a placid Li River providing the foreground. Just beyond the square, two stately pagodas rose from islands in two lakes, the parkland around them planted with banyan and willow trees. It was all very idyllic. We were staying in the Universal Hotel down by the river, one of the best places in town. At night I went for a stroll along the river and became aware that there were quite a few girls touting for business in the street, the first place in China that I had seen this. On my return to the hotel, there was a group of girls outside the massage parlour which had a separate entrance and their gestures made it clear that there was more on offer than a foot massage.

Next morning, we boarded a cruise boat for a four hour trip down the Li River to the little tourist Mecca of Yangshuo, nestled among the limestone karst peaks. The mountain scenery along the river continued to astound; you could give your imagination free rein as to the shapes the contorted peaks conjured up, reflected in the names given them by the local people - Expectant Husband, Mighty Lion Riding a Carp, Dragon Head Hill, Penholder Peak. The rice harvest had begun and we saw farmers working in the fields, setting up bundles of rice to dry.

Water buffalo were grazing on a flat tongue of land jutting out into the river. Fishermen were working from canoes and bamboo rafts. Yangshuo had all the hallmarks of a hippy hang-out, a main street of Western style café-bars, restaurants, cheap accommodation and souvenir shops but it had not entirely lost its traditional character and the surrounding landscape was stunning. In the evening on a small lake at the Yangshuo Resort Hotel where we were staying we saw an exhibition of fishing using cormorants. The birds would dive in from the bamboo canoe, catch a fish, then obligingly swim back to the canoe where the fisherman would prise the fish from its beak and off it would go again. Now and then the fisherman would ease the collar around a bird's neck which prevented it from swallowing the fish and let it eat one as a reward. As the son of a fisherman I had always been interested to see how fishing was carried out in the places I'd visited and I'd seen many techniques in my time but this was unique.

We flew on to Shanghai, probably the fastest growing city in the world. The Bund, the waterfront along the Huangpu River, which flowed north into the Yangtse, was lined with impressive buildings from the time when this had been a European trading enclave under the Concession system, mostly dating from the early 20th century. Across the river, the Pudong area presented a futuristic vision of high rise towers dominated by the Oriental Pearl TV Tower. We took a cruise on the river, the banks lined with shipping, shipyards, docks and depots, a hive of industry. Back on land we had time to explore the Bund area and the main shopping street, Nanjing Road, running inland from it. I had a walk around the Peace Hotel which still had a 1920s feel to it as if you might meet Noel Coward at any moment. Further along was the Customs House with its distinctive clock-tower. Later we visited the Yu Gardens and Bazaar in what had been the Chinese quarter of the city in colonial times. It had a strangely artificial feel to it like the Chinatown area of Manchester, an impression probably created by its current domination by the tourist trade. But the Yu Gardens dating from the Ming period were genuine enough with their artistic rockery and Dragon Wall. We had a look at the Huxinting Teahouse, built in the 18th century and approached across a zig-zag bridge. I bought some dumplings from a street vendor, which were some of the best I've eaten.

We travelled by bus to Suzhou to visit a silk factory and see some of the famous formal gardens. On the way we stopped in Zhouzhuang, a water town, criss-crossed by canals like Venice and a UNESCO World Heritage Site. We had a cruise through the canals in a small rowing-boat under arched bridges and overhanging foliage and wandered through the narrow streets with vendors selling everything from prawns to grotesque masks. In Suzhou we saw the whole fascinating process of silk making which was developed in China and where the patent was jealously guarded until some cunning industrial espionage in the dark ages resulted in the industry establishing in Turkey and then later in Italy. But for centuries the Silk Road had been the only source of this fabulous material for the Western world. We went on to visit the Ming dynasty Garden for Lingering In where we lingered long enough to wander through the 3 hectares of buildings, ponds, sculptured rocks, trees, shrubs and potted plants. A covered walkway, inlaid with calligraphy, connected the major features. The Garden of the Master of Nets, laid out in the 12th century, was much smaller. It featured a beautiful lotus pond which could be viewed from walkways. A courtyard in an inner garden contained the Master's study with Ming furnishings.

From the tour end in Shanghai, I flew back to Hong Kong. I had booked a couple of nights in the Silvermine Beach Hotel over on Lantau Island. I took a bus across the island to visit the Po Lin Monastery with its Big Buddha. The east side of the island was remarkably quiet and rural bearing in mind the presence of the airport and its associated urbanization just on the other side of the island beyond the central range of mountains. Big Buddha lived up to his name, the seated bronze figure rising 26 metres (85 feet) from a plinth at the top of a flight of 260 steps, lined with statues of Buddhist saints. More large statues of goddesses knelt along the edge of the plinth looking out at the mountains. Back down the steps, a giant incense burner, several times the height of a man, stood between the Big Buddha and the main hall of the monastery, where saffron robed monks were chanting, the eerie, mellifluous sound seeming to echo back off Lantau Peak behind. I caught the next bus down to Tai O, a traditional fishing village, with stilt houses crammed around a muddy estuary, shops selling live seafood and dried fish.

I was having breakfast the following morning when the waitress asked me if I was leaving that day. When I confirmed that I was, she politely suggested that I should hurry as a typhoon warning had been issued and the ferries would probably stop running. I took her advice and none too soon, as the wind had risen substantially by the time I got on board the ferry. The crossing was very rough, spray flying, the little ferry 'Xin Xing' burying her bows, shuddering and tossing. A number of passengers were seasick and others looked frightened. Back at the Empire Hotel in Wanchai, the heavens opened and the rain came down in torrents. I decided to spend the afternoon in a pub. The Old China Hand pub in Lockhart Road was hooching. With the typhoon warning, all the offices had been closed and the expatriate money crunchers from the financial world had descended on the pub for the afternoon. A gaggle of Thai and Philippine girls in the corner were on the lookout for rich gweilos with the aim of relieving them of their stress and some of their bonuses. Hong Kong's capitalist economy was working just fine as the music throbbed, the wind howled and the rain pelted down. Above the din, I thought I heard Chairman Mao turning in his grave.

6

PETRA, JORDAN
MAY 2006

FROM TIME TO time over the years, I had considered a trip to Israel but had always been put off by the security situation. Not being religious, I didn't see a visit there as a pilgrimage but I had been so indoctrinated with Christian mythology in my youth that the places associated with it had an aura of fascination and I felt that I should see them as part of my further education in the University of the World. Friends who had been to the ancient city of Petra in Jordan had come back with enthusiastic reports about it and I discovered that trips there could be organised from Israel as Jordan had a marginally better political relationship with the Israelis than most other Arab countries. I also liked to vary my airlines and routes back to Britain from New Zealand and when planning my 2006 trip, I discovered that the Emirates airline were offering the best deal, coupled with remarkably cheap stopovers in Dubai. I hadn't seen much of the Arab world: just a stopover in Cairo on my way back from East Africa to Britain in 1970; a trip across to Morocco from Spain in the 1980s; and what I had seen of Arab culture in its Swahili hybrid on holidays to the Kenyan coast when I was living there. I had seen Arab dhows in the harbours at Mombasa and Lamu, a former Arab colony on a small island north of Mombasa, two of my favourite places in Kenya, and been fascinated by the romance of the trade between the East African coast and the Arabian peninsula. Many of the dhows had come from Oman and I found that I could arrange a day trip there from Dubai and see the other end of the trade route. I organized my itinerary for May 2006 to take in all those places.

Dubai appeared to be one huge building site: I later discovered that 18% of the world's cranes were located there at the time. It occurred to me that it could appropriately have been re-named Ucrane if a former Russian territory hadn't already patented something very similar. Dubai had mushroomed from a pearl-diving and fishing village to a metropolis of well over a million people during the course of the 20th century, most of its growth since the 1960s. It was a remarkable story. The ruling Maktoum family had moved there in 1833 from an inland oasis. The original settlement was Bur Dubai on the south side of the Creek, a saltwater inlet about 10 kilometres (6 miles) long by 300 metres wide, providing a sheltered harbour. During a smallpox epidemic in 1841 a separate village was developed on the other side of the Creek at Deira, which outgrew Bur Dubai. In 1892 Britain negotiated a Protectorate over the Trucial States, as the Emirates were then known, and adopted Dubai as a port of call for ships on their way to India. In 1894 Sheikh Maktoum made Dubai a tax free area and merchants from India and Persia (Iran) moved there. By the beginning of the 20th century, the population was still less than 10,000. In the early 1930s the pearl diving industry collapsed after the Japanese developed the technique of producing artificial cultured pearls and the Maktoums moved into the re-export business, taking advantage of the tax free status. After 1947 when India banned imports of gold to protect their currency, gold smuggling from Dubai became big business. Smuggling across the Persian Gulf to Iran was also lucrative. In 1959 the Maktoums borrowed money from Kuwait to dredge the Creek and develop the harbour to accommodate bigger ships: in 1960 an airport was built. The boom began to take off: money was spent on infrastructure; mains electricity; piped water; and roads – until then transport had been provided by donkeys and camels. In 1966 oil was discovered which provided a major boost to the economy. It wasn't on the scale of other fields in the Arabian Peninsula, only providing about 5% of GDP (Gross Domestic Product) but the profits were invested in infrastructure to support the trading, financial services, tourism, real estate and manufacturing sectors which really fuelled the boom, the wheels oiled by free trade zones for manufacturing, duty-free sales at the airport, tax holidays for businesses and personal tax free status for expatriates. In 1975 the population was 183,000: by 2006 it had grown to well over 1.5 million. Bizarrely, over 90% of the population were expatriates, mainly from India, Pakistan, Bangladesh and the South-East Asian countries including the Philippines and Indonesia, which provided cheap labour for the construction boom and menial jobs in general.

I was staying at the Oasis Beach Hotel, one of a strip of similar luxurious establishments strung out along Jumeirah Beach, including big names like Le Meridien, Ritz-Carlton and Sheraton. Just behind, the multi-storey, mega-bucks Dubai Marina development was under construction. My stopover deal included a tour of the city. Just to the north of the hotel, towards the city centre, an artificial island, the Palm-Jumeirah, shaped in plan like a palm tree encircled by a breakwater halo had been constructed to provide luxury waterfront villas, apartment blocks, 30 hotels, restaurants and retail outlets – the design maximised water frontage, doubling the length of the Dubai coastline. Local law had been amended to allow foreigners full freehold titles to property with automatically renewable residence permits. David Beckham was rumoured to have bought one of the villas: a total of 4,500 residential units were to be provided. With a diameter of 5 kilometres (3 Miles) it was the largest artificial island in the world and a workforce of 40,000 had been involved in constructing it. The tour guide said that two similar islands were under construction, one near the new harbour at Jebel Ali and another beyond the Creek at Deira. A larger, even more ambitious project, called the World, as the islands would be shaped like a map of the world, was underway further offshore just a bit to the north of the Palm-Jumeirah. Just beyond the island, the guide pointed out the Madinat Jumeirah, a complex containing hotels, shops, a mock-traditional Arabian Souk (market), Venetian style canals with "abras" (the local version of gondolas) and entertainment venues, including a theatre, the architecture inspired by the traditional multi-storey residential buildings in Saudi Arabia and the Yemen topped with wind towers to provide natural air-conditioning. Just beyond were two of the most iconic buildings in the city, the Burj al Arab and Jumeirah Beach hotels. The Burj al Arab, designed like a dazzling white sail, sat on an artificial island linked to the shore by a causeway, looking like a giant luxury yacht. At 321 metres (1,053 feet) it was the world's tallest hotel and allegedly the most luxurious, claiming to go off the Richter scale of hotel classification to warrant seven stars. Peasants weren't allowed in, so I never got to vet their claims. The nearby Jumeirah Beach Hotel was S-shaped, looking like a surf wave in profile, another architectural gem. We stopped to photograph the Jumeirah Mosque, another beautiful building. Only completed in 1998, it looked much more venerable with its majestic dome and twin minarets, the creamy-white stonework decorated with geometric patterns in relief, echoes of the Taj Majal. The museum was in the heart of old Bur Dubai, housed in the 1787 Al Fahidi Fort where the original rulers had lived, and which had later been converted to a prison, its yellow, crenellated walls surmounted by towers at three of its corners. In the courtyard a handsome traditional dhow was on display and a reconstruction of a traditional house called a barasti, made from woven palm fronds in a flimsy timber framework, with a wind tower on the roof. The wind tower was simple but ingenious: flat boards were fixed together to form a horizontal cross; a thatched, pitched roof above directed any wind from any direction down an open shaft into the house below, providing a primitive, but effective, air conditioning system. There was also a display of Bedouin costumes, weapons and jewellery. In the underground gallery, there was a multimedia presentation on the growth of the city: dioramas complete with life-like waxwork mannequins, holographs and old film footage illustrated aspects of traditional living – the Koranic school, the souk, the home; an explanation of pearl diving; a natural history section on the wildlife of the desert; and an archaeological section, including a recreated tomb grave. Adjacent to the Museum, at the waterfront, early 20th century Persian merchants' houses with decorative, screened windows and wind towers had been restored. Built of limestone, coral and gypsum, these two storey buildings with interior courtyards and ornate, carved wooden doors lined narrow lanes. There were cafes, restaurants and art galleries, the whole neighbourhood making a pleasant contrast to the high rise landscape of the new city. The historic Shindagha Waterfront area to the north, dating from the 1860s, had also been miraculously preserved and restored, including the Sheikh Saeed al-Maktoum House, which had belonged to the grandfather of the present ruler. A Heritage Village with barasti houses, a camel yard and a souk had been re-created and a Diving Village with a pearling display. There were several restaurants in the area.

We caught an "abra" (water taxi), open motor boats with an overhead awning to provide shade from the sun, across the Creek to Deira. The wharves fronting Baniyas Road were lined with working dhows, still trading to Iran and the Persian Gulf ports and even as far away as India and East Africa. It was a bustling waterfront scene, reminiscent of Sinbad the Sailor, rendered surrealistic by the backdrop skyline of skyscrapers. Deira was "souk land", the Spice Market smelling of cloves and cinnamon from open sacks, the Gold Souk with shop after shop packed with gold jewellery, watches and artwork and other markets, including a Perfume Souk, selling everything under the sun. This was Footballers' Wives' territory: Posh Spice Beckham would be in her element. On the way back to the hotel we passed the iconic National Bank of Dubai building and then crossing back over the Creek by bridge saw the snow-white roof of the Creek Golf and Yacht Club, designed to look like a dhow's sails, a spiky version of the Sydney Opera House. The tour guide told me that the city had world class facilities for golf, tennis, motor racing, horse racing, rugby sevens and even an artificial ski slope – my mind boggled at that last one. Driving along the main drag, Sheikh Zayed Road, we passed the Dubai World Trade Centre, then the Emirates Towers – like twin Stanley knives standing on end, one housing the Maktoum dynasty's offices, the other a luxury hotel. The guide pointed out the Burj Dubai skyscraper which was well on the way to completion, designed to be at least 700 metres (2,275 feet) tall, (it ended up at 828 metres [2,691 feet]) it would be the tallest building in the world by quite a margin, accommodating offices, residential apartments and a hotel.

I had booked a Dune Bashing/Bedouin Barbeque tour for the following afternoon. I'm not a petrol-head by nature but I found bombing up and down the sides of precipitous sand dunes in powerful 4WDs exhilarating in the extreme, requiring a very high order of buttock-clenching. The Bedouin driver was clearly enjoying himself and highly competent, competing to outdo the antics of his fellow drivers, as the vehicles swarmed over the dunes like black beetles. Afterwards, as dusk was falling, we headed to a Bedouin camp for a barbeque. Camel rides were on offer but I lacked the Lawrence of Arabia affection for these bad-tempered, smelly bastards and declined: I watched a demonstration of falconry instead although I didn't much like the look of the bird either – an evil, vicious looking beast – and so was its handler. The barbecue was excellent: mutton, goat, and chicken with rice and salad. Afterwards a Bedouin band struck up on a small stage and a bit later a belly-dancer appeared, looking exotic and full of eastern promise. The illusion was shattered when she emerged later to mingle with the punters and I heard her broad Birmingham accent.

The following morning I was picked up early by a driver to take me to the Musandam Peninsula in Oman for a dhow cruise in the fjord-like inlets there. The driver said that it would take over two hours to get to Khasab, the main town in Musandam. We drove through some of the other Emirates comprising the UAE with exotic, romantic Arabian Night names but playing copy-cat with Dubai in pushing up the skyscrapers – Sharjah, Ajman, Umm al-Quwain, Ras al-Khaiman. The border checks into Oman were friendly and perfunctory; this wasn't suicide bomber country. Musandam was a rugged massif of dolomite limestone and shale, rising to 2,087 metres (6,847 feet) in Jebel Harim (Woman's Mountain). It was cut off from the rest of Oman by the UAE Emirate of Fujairah. It protruded out into the narrow Strait of Hormuz at the mouth of the Persian Gulf, looking across to Iran. The population was only 27,000, 12,000 of which lived in Khasab, the rest scattered among isolated mountain villages and fishing villages along the coastline. We stopped at the Golden Tulip Khasab Hotel, just outside the town, for a coffee. The hotel was surrounded on three sides by water, the terrace where we sat, overlooking the sea. It was an attractive, comfortable looking property, obviously geared to the modern tourist economy – Musandam was becoming a popular diving venue. The driver said that there were two other smaller, traditional, cheaper, Omani-owned hotels in town. The whitewashed, flat-roofed houses of Khasab were set in a rocky, steep-sided wadi (canyon). The old souk, down near the harbour, seemed to specialise in cigarettes and electrical appliances, particularly TVs. The driver explained that there was a thriving trade in smuggling those items across the strait to Iran in exchange for goats. It seemed an odd trade but the fleet of fibre-glass speedboats with state of the art outboard motors moored in the harbour suggested that it was a lucrative one. There was an old Portuguese fort with watch towers down near the harbour. The new souk and town centre were about 3 kilometres (2 miles) inland, with the post office, bank, grocery stores and some restaurants. Back down at the harbour, I boarded the dhow which was to take me out cruising. The three man crew welcomed me aboard. It was comfortably fitted out with cushioned benches under an overhead canvas awning with adjustable sun blinds along the gunwales, colourful carpets covering the deck. The Musandam coast was deeply dissected by steep-sided, fjord like inlets called "khors". We set off out the largest of them, variously spelled Khor Shim or Khor ash-Sham. One of the crew, who spoke good English, said that there were half a dozen villages scattered around the khor only accessible by sea and living off fishing and goat herding. Fresh water had to be shipped out to them on barges and the children were transported to school in Khasab by speedboat. We saw a school of dolphins plunging through the sparkling water. The crew rustled up a delicious lunch of kebabs and barbecued chicken with rice, pitta bread and salad. They even had cold beer for sale from an ice box – I suspected that this was a bit of private enterprise on their part. We moored at Telegraph Island where the British had set up a telegraph station in 1864, a link in the communications chain with India. In this isolated, searing hot, spot, personnel had a tendency to go mad. When one was carted off, disappearing around the headland where the khor changed direction, his colleagues would say he had "gone round the bend". The expression had become enshrined in the English language. I had a swim and then we made our leisurely way back to Khasab, accompanied for part of the way by more dolphins. I had a few more beers. I wasn't going round the bend; quite the contrary, I was regaining sanity after the consumer madness of Dubai.

Flying on towards Cairo, I got to thinking about what the point was of a place like Dubai. Apart from some rapidly dwindling oil, it had no natural resources. Nothing would grow there naturally without irrigation – water was seriously deficient. The climate was lousy: from May to October the daytime temperature rarely fell below 40C (104F) with humidity around 90%, too hot to venture outside the door. Even in the relatively cooler so-called winter months it was often uncomfortably hot during the middle of the day, strong winds could bring sand storms and what little rain fell, tended to come in downpours which could cause flooding. Unless you were addicted to sand dunes, the landscape was boring. A good indication of the environmental carrying capacity of the place could be gleaned from the aptly named nearby Rub al-Khali desert, the Empty Quarter – fit for bugger all. The Arab culture and religion was repressive, male dominated and anally-retentive, even in the relatively relaxed form practised in Dubai. Everything about the city was artificial and contrived from the artificial ski slope to the bogus belly-dancer from Birmingham. It was Las Vegas, Disney Land, Tales from the Arabian Nights all rolled into one. The purpose of the cancer-like, debt-fuelled growth, an orgy of conspicuous consumption, oiled by tax-free incentives, was difficult to explain other than as an ego-trip for the ruling royal family. Why would you want to create a state where 90% of the population were foreigners? Wasn't that just building up problems for the future if they started to exercise their numerical muscle in order to get a say in how the place was run? Was it wise to put so many eggs in the tourist basket in a place with so little going for it in terms of natural attractions as opposed to man-made ones? Could the real estate market possibly absorb the sheer number of luxury apartments and villas being built?

Who in their right mind would buy a house there anyway? How long would it be until Arabs with the Bin Laden/Al Qaeda/ Taliban mentality started to take steps to punish the glaring breaches of Islam in a place that tolerated Western decadence in the form of alcohol and Russian prostitutes? I got the answer to some of these questions following the global financial melt-down of 2008. Property prices fell by 50%; many projects ground to a halt; debt repayments had to be drastically rescheduled. Filthy oil-rich big brother Abu Dhabi had to step in to bail out Dubai: the Burj Dubai had to be financially propped up and renamed the Burj Khalifa after the ruler of Abu Dhabi. At the same time cracks had begun to appear in the Palm-Jumeirah project. Inadequate environmental impact assessment at the design stage had necessitated radical amendments to the breakwater to avoid the water around the palm fronds becoming stagnant due to the disruption of tidal flows. It was discovered that the island was sinking at the rate of 5mm a year: coupled with the   projected sea level rise due to global warming, this was bad news for David Beckam and Posh Spice. Cost over-runs had meant that the number of villas had had to be increased, squeezing them closer together, to the annoyance of punters who had pre-bought properties. Some of the planned hotels were cancelled. The dream wasn't over for Dubai yet but it had turned into a bit of a nightmare.

I had booked to stay three nights in Cairo, to re-visit the Pyramids but also to collect my air ticket to Israel. My travel agent in New Zealand had been able to book a flight but not pay for it. Getting to Israel from the Arab world wasn't easy. Emirates, which flew practically everywhere, wouldn't touch them with a bargepole. Most Arab countries wouldn't let you in if you had an Israeli stamp in your passport. Israel was the pariah dog of the Middle East. But the Egyptians, keen to earn an unscrupulous buck whenever possible, did have connections. The office where I was to collect and pay for the ticket was conveniently located in an arcade of shops out behind the Nile Hilton Hotel where I was staying. It was tiny, not much bigger than a toilet, with four men crammed into it. When I produced my credit card to pay, one of them looked embarrassed and said it was cash only. I had to go and find an

ATM machine. When I got the ticket, I saw that it was for an airline called Arkia (ARK in its abbreviated form.) I pointed out that my itinerary showed the carrier as Air Sinai. Not a problem, I was assured. So I was to fly into Israel on the aerial equivalent of Noah's Ark, operated from a hole in the wall by an Egyptian cowboy outfit. As it turned out, the flight was on Egypt Air and there were no problems – all the two-legged animals on board arrived safely at Ben Gurion Airport near Tel Aviv, en route for the zoo called Israel.

I had booked a seven day tour starting in Tel Aviv and ending in Jerusalem after which I was to catch a bus down to Eilat on the Red Sea for a trip into Jordan to Petra. On the taxi ride into Tel Aviv from the airport along the Ayalon Highway it became apparent that this was a substantial city with some impressive high rise buildings – 2.5 million people lived in the Greater Tel Aviv metropolitan area. Unlike most of the settlements in Israel, many of which pre-dated Biblical times, Tel Aviv was a 20th century creation. In the second half of the 19th century, substantial numbers of Jews had begun to return to Palestine (as Israel was then known) which was part of the Turkish Ottoman Empire. I had always been under the impression that the re-population of Israel by Jews didn't happen until after Britain had captured it from the Turks in 1917 during World War I and subsequently taken over its administration under a Mandate from the League of Nations. I had thought the current political shambles in the Middle East could be put down squarely to yet another fine mess created by British Imperialism, stemming from the Balfour Declaration in 1917 by the then British Foreign Secretary which stated that: "His Majesty's government favourably views the creation of a national Jewish home in Palestine." But it wasn't that simple. For a start, the Jews had never completely abandoned Israel. After their first rebellion against Roman rule had resulted in the total destruction of Jerusalem, they were banned from living in the new city built by the Romans. After defeat in a second rebellion in 135 AD their communities in Judea were broken up, many were sold into slavery and sent to Rome and elsewhere in the Empire; and thousands fled to Egypt and North Africa and east into Mesopotamia where some had remained after a previous exile by Nebuchadnezzar

500 years earlier. This was known as the Jewish Diaspora. But the Jews had remained in Galilee to the north and by the time of the Crusades many had returned to Jerusalem. When the Jews who had migrated to Spain on the back of the Moorish conquest were expelled from there in 1492 along with the Moors, many of these Sephardim returned to Palestine, especially the Galilee area. The influx in the late 19th century was mainly of Ashkenazim from Eastern Europe, especially Poland and Russia following pogroms against them. Some of them settled in the ancient port of Jaffa, now merged into Tel Aviv. Jaffa became over-crowded and some Jewish families moved out and built houses in the sandy flats just to the north in Neve Tzedek. Others followed and in 1909 a plan for a new town centred on Herzl Street and to be called Tel Aviv was adopted. In 1925, a Masterplan for further expansion was drawn up by the Scottish urban planner, Sir Patrick Geddes.

I was staying in the Metropolitan Hotel in Trumpeldor Street. The tour didn't start until the following morning, so I set off on foot to explore the city. Trumpeldor Street ended at the beach, a wide expanse of golden sand with surf breaking off the shoreline, extending south to Jaffa and north to the old port which had been closed down in 1965 in favour of a new deeper-water harbour at Ashdod to the south and had now been redeveloped as a nightlife centre. Luxury multi-storey hotels lined the esplanade to the north. Just behind the beach to the south, the shocking pink, stepped pyramid of the Opera Tower caught the eye, looking like an ancient Mesopotamian ziggurat. It housed a shopping centre, cinema and apartments. I carried on down Allenby Street, called after the British General who had captured Palestine from the Turks. At the junction with King George and Sheinken Streets, the Carmel Market spilled down Ha-Carmel Street. There was cheap clothing and household goods, a colourful display of fruit, vegetables and flowers, areas for fish, meat, bread, olives and spices. The area around here was known as the Yemenite Quarter, settled by Jews from the Yemen around the turn of the 20th century. With its maze of narrow lanes and Moorish style houses, many in a poor state of repair, it had a distinct Arabic atmosphere. According to my guidebook the pedestrianized Nahalat Binyamin Street, which branched of Ha-Carmel, had a craft market on

Fridays and Tuesdays and its cafes, bars and restaurants were lively at night. Further south-west past the 34 storey Shalom Tower office block was the oldest part of the city, Neve Tzedek, which still had its pattern of narrow streets but was undergoing gentrification. There were some smart shops, restaurants, cafes and bars in Shabazi Street. I headed back to Allenby Street and then turned north into Rothschild Boulevard. This was Bauhaus country, the architectural style developed in Germany from 1919. Tel Aviv had the greatest number of these buildings found anywhere in the world, some 4,000 of them, built mostly in the 1930s and 40s. Because of them, UNESCO had designated Tel Aviv as a World Heritage Site. Many of them had been painted white, giving rise to the name "White City" but pollution had rendered most of them distinctly off-white. It was a simple, functional style with rectilinear shapes, strips of horizontal windows and overhanging balconies. Some had been designed to resemble the ships which had brought the immigrants, with round porthole style windows. Further north was Rabin Square, where Prime Minister Yitzhak Rabin had been assassinated by an ultra-religious Jew in 1995 because he had dared to sign the "Oslo Accords" with the Palestinians and shake hands with their President, Yasser Arafat. The Middle East "problem" was created as much by divisions within the Jewish community as it was by disputes with the Moslem Palestinian Arabs. A memorial beside City Hall marked the spot where Rabin had been shot. In the centre of the square, a big glass and iron monument was a memorial to the Holocaust. It wasn't the most cheerful of places.

In the evening, I took a taxi down to Jaffa to try out one of the harbour front fish restaurants. The driver stopped in a little square where the continuation of the road was blocked off by a barrier of big, square, concrete blocks. He said it was as close as he could get to the restaurants for security purposes and gave me directions of how to get there – about 100 metres away. The Arab-run restaurants had out-door tables with white tablecloths set out along the edge of the quay, the little harbour full of fishing boats and yachts inside a sheltering breakwater. It was a picturesque and romantic setting but there were very few customers: I didn't know if there had been a recent security incident but something was obviously keeping people away – the food wasn't the problem, the meal and service were excellent, although I was glad that I was a fisherman's son and had learned at a young age how to eat bony specimens like the St. Peter's fish I had at the aptly named Fishermen's Restaurant. On the way back to the hotel, I got the taxi to drop me in Sheinken Street to sample a couple of the bars there: it seemed to be a pretty lively area.

In the morning, the tour guide collected me from the hotel. It was a small group in a 12 seater mini-bus. There was an upper-class, ex-public school, ex-military Englishman around my age, who, I later discovered, had spent time on a kibbutz in his youth; a tall, dark, good-looking American woman in her mid-fifties who was married to an Italian Jew but wasn't Jewish herself; and a group of four Jewish Indians from Kochi in Kerala – a husband and wife in their thirties and her parents in their sixties. I hadn't realized that there were Jewish communities in India but on a later visit to Kochi, I visited the synagogue there which had once served a sizeable congregation but most of them had by then emigrated to Israel. The group on the tour were visiting relatives who were now living in Jerusalem. The tour guide Noam was originally from Russia and had spent time in the Israeli military. Just before we turned onto the Ayalon Motorway, we passed the triple towers of the Azrieli Centre, looking like giant cheese graters. Noam said that there was an observatory on the 49th floor of the round tower with a magnificent view of the city. To the north, we saw the towers of the Diamond Exchange. According to Noam, Israel was the world's largest exporter of polished diamonds, importing raw stones and processing them. He said that Israel's economy was now heavily weighted towards new technology including bio-tech industries and with a speciality in weapons technology. As we drove north up the coast, I was surprised at how green and fertile looking the landscape was with citrus orchards and wheat fields and wooded areas. I remarked on this to Noam and he said that it hadn't always been like that. Before the arrival of Jewish settlers in the late 19th century the coastal strip had been very sparsely populated with sand flats and dunes backed by malarial swamps. The settlers had been able to buy the land because the Arab owners and the Ottoman Sultan, who had to ratify sales, saw it as useless. Jewish philanthropists in Europe, particularly Baron Edmund Rothschild and his family started buying up land for colonists. The first Jewish farm colony had been established by a consortium of East European Jews at Petah Tikvah just east of Tel Aviv in 1878, followed by Rishon LeZion nearby in 1882. Baron Rothschild had later put money into these settlements to set up Israel's first winery at Rishon LeZion and to drain the malarial swamps at Petah Tikvah. David Ben Gurion, who later became Israel's first President, had been head of the Worker's Union at the winery. Settlement was given a boost when the World Zionist Organization was founded in 1897 with the aim of creating a home for the Jewish people in Palestine and the Jewish National Fund set up to purchase land for settlement. Many of the early settlers from Russia like Ben Gurion had strong socialist tendencies and the first kibbutz, essentially a collective farm, had been established at the south end of Lake Galilee in 1909 and the movement had taken off from then. In the coastal strip, it was found that citrus fruit – oranges, lemons, grapefruit – did particularly well and Australian eucalyptus trees were found to be particularly effective in draining the soil.

We stopped at the ruins of Caesarea, which had been built by King Herod just before the time of Christ, on the site of an ancient Phoenician settlement, and dedicated to the Roman Emperor – the Romans had annexed Israel in 63 BC but had allowed the local rulers to remain as puppets. It had become the Roman capital of the Province and the main seaport, protected by a massive breakwater. There wasn't a great deal left to be seen of the Roman city: the hippodrome, used for chariot racing, on the way into the site; the impressive 4,000 seater theatre at the south end with the remains of Herod's palace on a promontory nearby; and an aqueduct leading north which had extended for 17 kilometres (11 miles) bringing water from the foothills of Mount Carmel. The city had declined after the departure of the Romans and conquest of the area by the Moslem Arabs in the 7th century but had had a new lease of life under the Crusaders who had built a fortress down at the Roman harbour, substantial remains of their citadel and walls still standing. In 1261 the Mameluk Sultan overran the fortress, destroying what was left of the city and it was buried in blowing sand until workers on a kibbutz established there started finding artefacts and the site was excavated.

We had a brief stop on the heights of Mount Carmel above Haifa to view the Baha'i Temple and gardens extending down the hillside below us. As if there weren't enough religions in Israel already, this was the world headquarters of the Baha'i faith which had been founded in Iran in the mid 19th century. Its founder (the Bab) had been shot by a firing squad (religions other than Islam weren't popular with the Ottoman Turks) and his successor (the Baha'Ullah) spent 25 years in jail in Akko (Acre) just up the coast from Haifa. On his release, he had visited Mt Carmel and decided that this was the place where the remains of the founder should be buried and the golden domed Shrine of the Bab became his tomb. The Baha'i believed that no religion had a monopoly on the truth and their aim was to integrate the teachings of all holy men. Perhaps wisely, they had decided not to put this theory to the test in Israel as the Baha'Ullah had decreed that it would be sacrilegious for members of the faith to reside in Israel and banned Israeli citizens from becoming members – the centre was run by volunteers from overseas. The Baha'i were no fools: Israel was no place for a reasonable, compromising, religion. The gardens were a beautiful sight, descending the slope in nineteen terraces, with grassy lawns, trees, flowerbeds, fountains, ornate balustrades and sculptures. Haifa was Israel's main port and an important industrial centre but there was no sign of all that up here in this peaceful spot.

We drove north to Akko (Acre), an ancient port already mentioned in a 19th century BC Egyptian text and one of the Phoenicians' harbours. Shortly after the Crusaders took Jerusalem in 1099 AD, they also seized Acre and made it their main port of entry to the Holy Land. It was recaptured by Saladin shortly after he had defeated the Crusaders in a battle at the Horns of Hittim in 1187 but Richard the Lionheart soon won it back in the 3rd Crusade and it remained the last bastion of the Crusaders until it was finally over-run and virtually destroyed by the Mamelukes in 1291. It had remained semi-derelict until the 18th century when the Ottoman Turks had rebuilt

the Crusader walls, built mosques, baths, khans (inns for camel caravans) and repopulated the city. What was to be seen within the walls
of the old town now was that Ottoman city, little changed since its
resurrection. UNESCO had designated it as a World Heritage Site.
We drove through the walls on Weizmann Street and parked on open
ground near the El-Jazzar Mosque, its green dome and pencil slim
minaret dominating the area. Down past the mosque, the Citadel
and Museum of Heroism overlooked an archaeological site where
part of the old Crusader city had been excavated lying 8 metres (26
feet) below current street level. Some of the knights' halls had been
preserved with Gothic arches (I was later to be reminded how similar
it was to the quarters of the Knights of St. John on a visit to Rhodes).
The Citadel had been used as a jail during the British Mandate and
Jewish underground fighters, aiming to set up an independent Jewish
state, had been imprisoned and executed there. Their story was told
in the Museum. We continued down through narrow, winding streets
and arrived at the souk where fruit, vegetables, fish and household
items were on display. The old town was predominantly Arab with
street names and signs in Arabic script and the minarets of mosques
rising above the rooftops: the new town outside the walls was Jewish.
Adding to the ethnic complexity of Israel was the fact that there were
1.7 million Arabs living within its borders, out of a total population
of 7.5 million, excluding the Palestinian territories of the West Bank
and Gaza. Of the Arabs living in Israel, 10% were Christian. Among
the Moslems were around 150,000 Bedouin and some Druze communities, a mystical sect which had split off from mainstream Islam
a thousand years ago and believed that Mohammed had been super-
seded by yet another Prophet. Down by the harbour, enclosed by a
breakwater and crammed with fishing boats and yachts, a clock-less
clock tower marked the Khan el-Umdan, a former inn for camel caravans, built around an inner courtyard. Some fishermen were mending nets on the quayside. I had grilled fish for lunch in the Doniana
Restaurant up on the ramparts above the harbour. There was a lighthouse on the headland beyond and some boys were diving off the
sea wall.

Right on the Lebanese border, at Rosh ha-Nikra, we visited sea caves eroded in the cliff face from the white chalk rocks. The caves were accessed by a cable car and tunnel, with vistas across the sparkling blue sea, where a grey Israeli navy ship lurked just offshore. The border post above the grottoes was heavily guarded by soldiers. Some Japanese girls tried to pose beside one for photographs but he waved them away and said something in Hebrew which I assumed was along the lines of "Fuck off." This wasn't ceremonial duty: things could get ugly on the Lebanese border. A former railway tunnel linking the two countries had been blocked in, symbolic of the political relationship between them. We headed east, inland, following the Lebanese border, at one point driving right along the high, razor-wire topped fence which marked it. The Englishman, who I had privately named "Hooray Henry", remarked that we were close enough to see the flies on the bride at a Lebanese wedding. Noam laughed uproariously but the Indians didn't look amused. I was beginning to worry about some of my fellow tourists. The American woman, Linda, didn't seem very interested in proceedings. She had spent most of the time reading a paperback rather than watching the scenery, even when Noam switched on his microphone to point out something along the way. In both Haifa and Akko she had asked me: "Where are we now?" She obviously hadn't majored in map reading. I had noticed the younger Indian trying unsuccessfully to engage Henry in conversation in Akko and been answered in monosyllables. This wasn't Henry's normal style: he was apparently fond of his own voice and turned up the volume to hear it better. We turned north, driving along the edge of the Hula Valley, where a swamp in the valley of the River Jordan had been drained to provide fertile agricultural land, and arrived at the Kfar Gil'adi Kibbutz where we were to spend the night in the hotel attached to it. This was almost on the north border and looking from the wooded hotel garden, Lebanon lay just on the other side of the valley to the west. This area had come under rocket fire from across the border in periods of unrest in the past.

In the morning we set off for the Golan Heights. We stopped to see one of the sources of the River Jordan at the Banias waterfall, 33 metres

(107 feet) high with an emerald pool beneath it. Nearby, the towers and battlements of the ruined Nimrod Castle, built by the Crusaders, towered above the road. The snow-capped limestone peak of Mount Hermon rose to the north, straddling the border with Syria, at 2,814 metres (9,230 feet), Israel's highest point, where ski-fields operated in winter. We passed through the Druze village of Mas'ada and further south stopped at the Quneitra Viewpoint. From here we could see the camp of the United Nations' peacekeeper force of a thousand troops guarding the Disengagement Zone, a strip of neutral, unoccupied territory between the Israeli and Syrian borders. Beyond the camp, the white walls of the Syrian ghost town of Quneitra were visible: it had been   destroyed by Israeli forces in 1967. When Britain gave up its Mandate over Palestine in 1947, the United Nations proposed carving up the area between a Jewish and an Arab state. The Jews had accepted this but the Arabs didn't agree. In early 1948 when the British left, Israel declared independence for the area they had been provisionally allocated. War broke out immediately with all their Arab neighbours and at the armistice in 1949 the Golan Heights were part of Syria; the Left Bank, including eastern Jerusalem went to Jordan; Egypt occupied the Gaza Strip; and Israel was left with the rest. In 1967, following threats from Egypt, Israel launched the pre-emptive Six Day War, at the end of which they had captured the Golan Heights, the Left Bank, the Gaza Strip and the Sinai Peninsula. In 1973 in the Yom Kippur War, the Arab countries made a surprise attack on Israel and initially made some inroads into their territory but Israel recovered and drove them back, the 1967 borders remaining at the end of hostilities. Israel later handed the Sinai back to Egypt and the understanding with the United Nations was that the Palestinian territories in the Left Bank and Gaza would not remain permanently part of Israel. Israel, however, had made it clear that they intended to hold onto the Golan Heights for strategic reasons: it was a high plateau of hard, black, basalt rock overlooking the Sea of Galilee and the upper Jordan Valley and therefore a perfect base for Syrian artillery. It was now sparsely populated: 90% of the population had fled to Syria in 1967, only the Druzes remaining in their villages. Some Israeli settlers had since moved in and there were

vineyards, apple and pear orchards and cattle ranches, complete with cowboys.

Down on the shore of the Sea of Galilee, we visited the archaeological site at Capernaum which was believed to have been Jesus' base for his preaching mission in the area. A synagogue site had been excavated and a church built over what was believed to have been the site of St. Peter's house. Further along the shore at Tabgha was where the loaves and fishes miracle was supposed to have been performed. A church built over the site in 1982 had preserved a floor mosaic from a ruined 5th century church which included a design with loaves and fishes. Down by the shore, another church marked the spot where the resurrected Christ had supposedly passed on the leadership of the movement to Peter. High on a hill above, there was a magnificent view out across the lake from the octagonal Church of the Beatitudes where Christ allegedly preached the Sermon on the Mount – "Blessed be the meek, for they shall inherit the earth." (He forgot to add: "after the arrogant, hard-nosed bastards have made it unfit for human habitation.") We passed through Tiberias, originally founded in Roman times, its lakefront esplanade lined with restaurants, cafes and bars and turned inland to visit Nazareth. Just past the junction we saw the hill known as the Horns of Hittim, where the Crusaders had been heavily defeated in battle by Saladin: shortly afterwards they were driven out of Jerusalem by him. Not far from Nazareth, Noam pointed out the little Arab village of Kafr Kana where Jesus was believed to have turned water into wine at a wedding. If he'd been around during Prohibition in America he could have made a fortune. I had been to some weddings where, judging by the queues outside the toilets, the opposite effect had been achieved without divine intervention. Our destination in Nazareth was the Basilica of the Annunciation marking the spot where the Angel Gabriel had appeared to tell Mary that she was up the duff to God. (He may have put it more politely but, hey, how do you sugar that sort of pill?) The remains of her house are allegedly preserved in the crypt. The Basilica was completed in 1969 on the site of earlier Byzantine and Crusader era churches and its 60 metres (195 feet) high dome dominated central Nazareth – it was said to be the largest church in the Middle East. Like Akko, Nazareth was an Arab town; the red roofs of a new Jewish extension could be seen on a hilltop above. Noam took us for lunch to an Arab take-away which he said made the best shwarmas in Israel and he was right. We moved on to Tzipori, the Roman capital of Galilee Province. It had obviously been a substantial city with colonnaded roadways, and a 4,500 seat amphitheatre. A reconstructed Roman Villa had some magnificent mosaics which had been excavated on the site including some relating to the cult surrounding the Greek god of wine, ritual madness, ecstasy and debauchery generally – Dionysus, or as the Romans called him, Bacchus, and there were some explanatory boards in English about the cult. Worshipping him seemed to have mainly involved drunken orgies. Having had a gutsful of Jesus and his do-gooding all morning, I decided that Dionysus was more my kind of God. We made our way back to the shore of the Sea of Galilee where we were staying the night in the hotel attached to the Nof Ginosar Kibbutz. In the bar in the evening after dinner, I was having a drink with Noam and Henry and the subject had got round to the Palestinian "problem". I happened to mention the "illegal" Jewish settlements in the West Bank. "What's illegal about them?" Noam bridled. "Well, the United Nations seem to think so for a start," I replied: "and wasn't their eventual removal part of the agreement in the Oslo Accords?" "Oh! That! Yitzakh Rabin should never have signed that and he paid for it. Jewish immigrants keep pouring in," Noam ranted, "and they have to live somewhere. Anyway a lot of that land is just wasted by the Arabs." "But won't it make it very difficult to return the West Bank to the Palestinians eventually?" I asked. "That'll be the day," Henry snorted. He had obviously picked up some Zionist attitudes in his time on the Kibbutz in his youth.

In the morning, I walked down to the reedy lakeshore. It was a beautiful, still morning with a haze over the water. The Indians were there and I got chatting to them. The younger man was a chief librarian, his father in law an ex senior civil servant with the Indian government and they both seemed highly intelligent and well informed. The women didn't have much to say until I mentioned Henry and the old lady said "Oh! That man!" Her daughter went on to pass a few humorous comments about him which suggested that she didn't miss much. We went together to the Yigal Allon Centre attached to the kibbutz to see the "Jesus Boat". This 8.2 metres (27 feet) long wooden fishing boat had been found when the lake level fell in 1986 and it had been excavated from the anaerobic mud which had preserved it. It had been carbon dated to the time of Christ and so was the type of craft the fishermen among his Disciples would have earned their living on. He, of course, wouldn't have needed it: he could walk on water. I decided to go and see if I could emulate him. The hotel had a swimming beach with a raft moored offshore from which some boys were diving. I waded in and for a long way out never got past my knees: I thought: "Just have faith and you can carry on like this right out past the raft." I could imagine the astonishment on the boys' faces, reaching for their waterproof cell phones: "Mom, Mom! I've just seen a man walking on water." "Don't be silly, Dear. You know that's impossible. He was probably wearing stilts." Nice one, Jesus. I would never have thought of that. The reverie ended abruptly. I stepped over an underwater ledge and was up to my neck, swimming. I realized that if another Messiah was on the way, it certainly wasn't me. We drove down the lake shore, past the earliest kibbuzim at its south end and arrived at the Yardenit baptismal site on the River Jordan where John the Baptist was supposed to have baptised Jesus. I was amazed at how insignificant the Jordan was: a reasonably competent pole-vaulter could have cleared it in one mighty bound. Compared to some of the rivers I'd seen – the Nile, the Volga, the Mekong – this was just a dribble from a leaky tap. Some white clad pilgrims were busy being baptised: I hoped they would remember to keep their mouths closed while submerged. The water looked none too clean and hepatitis can afflict even the saved. We continued south along the Jordan Valley to the border crossing point into Jordan at the King Hussein Bridge and then turned west heading for Armageddon.

There wasn't much left of Armageddon even before Armageddon had arrived. It was just a "tel", a pile of rubble representing the remains of around twenty cities which had been destroyed and rebuilt on the same site over the centuries, the latest dating to 400 BC. The Hebrew name for it was Har (Mount) Meggido. Its fame came from the Book of Revelation in the Bible where it is identified as the place where the last great battle on earth between good and evil will take place following the second coming of the Messiah. At least that's how it's interpreted: I've read the relevant passages and they make no sense to me, just the demented ravings of a deranged mind or someone who's been on something a lot stronger than communion wine. The city had occupied a strategic location in the foothills of the Samarian Hills, the flat, fertile, Jezreel Valley lying to the north with the Heights of Galilee rising beyond. The main road south passed close by, following low ground between the Sumerian Hills and Mount Carmel to the west. Over the centuries marauding armies heading to and from Egypt, Mesopotamia and Assyria had passed this way and flattened Megiddo as they passed if it got in their way. Egyptian records showed that in 1486 BC a Canaanite city there was destroyed by the Pharaoh Thutmose III. Even long after the city had gone, General Allenby defeated the Turks nearby in a major battle in World War II. It occurred to me that if Armageddon was coming, this was as likely a spot as any for it to start. Israel had atomic weapons and one of their arch enemies, the champions of militant Islam, Iran, were believed to be clandestinely working in the same direction. Iran supported the fanatically anti-Israeli Palestinian groups Hezbollah in Lebanon and Hamas in the Gaza strip. From what I had seen of the Israelis, they were hard-nosed, bloody-minded and self-destructive enough to use any weapons at their disposal if any one threatened to take the "Promised Land" away from them again. Army recruits were taken up to the hilltop fortress of Masada, where 1,000 fanatical "Zealots" had committed suicide rather than surrender to the Romans in 73 AD, and made to swear an oath: "Masada shall not fall again."

We returned to the Metropolitan Hotel in Tel Aviv for the night. I went along to the Gaucho Restaurant near the hotel for an Argentinean steak. At the entrance, I was gone over with a metal detector by a security guard. Here the "War on Terror" had been going on for years, long before the US launched their modern version of the Crusades against Moslem extremists following the 9/11 attack. At the end of the meal, the waiter brought the bill. It was in Hebrew except for a hand-written message at the bottom, signed with a smiley face (the only one I'd seen all night) saying "Service not included": Shylock was alive and well and still after his pound of flesh. In the morning we set off towards Jerusalem via Be'er-Sheva and the Dead Sea. This was a separate tour, no longer our intimate mini-bus but a 48 seater, almost full, the sort of tour I dreaded where we would be herded round behind a flag. But Noam was still there and if he was his usual, casual, disorganised, self, with a bit of luck we would probably lose most of them before we got to Jerusalem. We headed south parallel to the coast, past Ashdod and Ashkelon, strongholds of the Philistines in Biblical times and then swung east, passing alongside the high, razor-wired fence which formed the boundary of the Gaza Strip. Gaza had had a limited amount of autonomy since 1994 when the Palestinian Authority had been set up following the Oslo Accords the previous year and Israel had forcibly removed the last of the "illegal" Jewish settlements there in 2005. But the Hamas group, which didn't recognise Israel's existence, had recently won political control and occasional rockets were being lobbed across the border from the Strip. The nearby town of Sderot had registered a few hits but the rockets were neither very accurate nor powerful and traffic seemed to be flowing normally along the road. (The situation escalated the following month with the kidnap of the Israeli soldier Gilad Shalit by Hamas following which Israel launched "Operation Summer Rains", staging armed incursions into the territory, killing a couple of hundred militants and over a hundred civilians in collateral damage.) Be'er Sheva, on the fringe of the Negev Desert and known as its capital, was Israel's fourth largest city with a population of nearly 200,000. It had grown very quickly and it showed: it looked as if it had been thrown together without much thought. We had passed some Bedouin camps on the road into Be'er Sheva and saw some more as we headed for Masada. The government was trying without much success to herd them into planned villages but they preferred to do their own thing, although their nomadic lifestyle had been reigned in. Just north of here, in the West Bank, was the town of Hebron, perhaps the most dangerous potential flashpoint in the whole troubled area. It housed the Tomb of the Patriarchs, where Abraham and his family were supposed to be buried. Ironically, Jews and Arabs accepted that they had this common ancestor, the Arabs descending from one son Isaac, the Jews from the other, Ishmael and his son Jacob. They were both Semitic people originating in Mesopotamia, their languages, Hebrew and Arabic, closely related, the script reading from right to left in both cases. The word for "peace" in Hebrew, "shalom" was cognate with the Arabic "salaam" but there hadn't been much of it in Hebron recently. In 1929, during the British Mandate, militant Arab nationalists had staged a revolt against what they saw as encroaching Zionism and massacred members of the ancient Jewish community which had lived there for centuries. The aftermath of the 6 Day War was pay-back time and a group of ultra-religious Jews moved in and built settlements in the town centre. In 1994, one of them, Baruch Goldstein, a doctor, originally from Brooklyn, New York, had opened up with a sub-machine gun at worshippers in the mosque in the Tomb of the Patriarchs during Ramadan, killing 29 and wounding 200. Now it was stalemate, the autonomous Palestinian Authority controlling the Arab section of the city, an Israeli Defence Force garrison protecting the Jewish enclave. The Tomb was segregated with one end containing a mosque and the Cenotaph to Isaac; the other a synagogue and the Cenotaph to Jacob. Abraham and his wife Sarah supposedly lay in the middle, like two stone dead members of a United Nations peacekeeper force. Of course it was all Jehovah's fault as usual: he had told Ishmael's mother that her son's descendents would be a great nation in perpetual conflict with the offspring of Isaac. So far he'd been dead right.

Masada was perched on a mountain top, over 400 metres (1,300 feet) above the Dead Sea and accessed by cable car. In 43 BC, King Herod had upgraded an earlier fortress and built a couple of palaces for himself in case he needed a bolt hole either from his masters the Romans or his subjects who were none too happy with his role as a Roman front man. After his death, the Romans had kept a small garrison there and in 66 AD a group of fanatical Jewish "Zealots" had captured it in a revolt. The Romans crushed the revolt, destroying Jerusalem in 70 AD and then patiently setting about recapturing

Masada. The siege lasted two years. They built a wall around it to prevent escape; then using prisoners of war as slave labour set about building a huge ramp, still to be seen - and brought up siege engines. When the defenders saw that the game was up, the men killed their own wives and children and then drew lots for who was to kill and be killed in a suicide pact. Nearly 1,000 died in all. The remains of Herod's palaces, a synagogue, bathhouses and water cisterns hewn out of the rock could still be seen.

From the fortress' ramparts, there was a spectacular view out across the Dead Sea, shimmering in a heat-haze. Like the Sea of Galilee, it was just a lake, although a big one, extending 76 kilometres (47 miles) from north to south and 16 kilometres (10 miles) wide. The mountains of Jordan stretched along the far side including at the north end Mount Nebo from which Jehovah had allegedly showed Moses the Promised Land, and then topped him before he had a chance to get there - the old sadist. Those Biblical dens of iniquity, Sodom and Gomorrah, may in fact have existed near the southern end, as ancient city ruins had been found there with evidence of destruction by fire. There were plenty of pillars of salt around there as well, but none had so far been identified as Lot's wife. She had taken a last nostalgic look back at where the good times had rolled and been turned into one by God. It didn't pay to mess with Jehovah. This was the guy who had told Abraham to sacrifice his son Isaac to him and when the silly old bugger was about to do so said: "Nah, Abraham. Let him go; I was only joking. Just kill a sheep or a goat or something instead." That was just about as sadistic as it gets. With a God like that, no wonder the Jews and the Arabs were at each other's throats.

We wound our way down to the shore of the Dead Sea to the little tourist resort of Ein Gedi. Noam told us that there were toilets and changing rooms in the shop. I couldn't see any signs for the toilet so I went over to ask an assistant. She gave me a dirty look and waved an arm vaguely towards a corner. I found the changing room but no sign of a toilet. I went back to the woman. She was talking to another assistant and ignored me. I butted in and told her I still couldn't find the toilet. She looked furious. "Round the corner, at the back" she shrilled, pointing in the same direction and turned her back on me. I found it this time, behind a curtain at the end of a dead-end corridor. It was obviously designed to be as difficult to find as possible. I'm not normally tempted to punch females in the face but that Jewess came close. I had found Israelis generally to be unfriendly and off-hand if not down right rude like this one. I remembered a conversation I'd had with a friend back in the Shetland Islands who'd come to the Dead Sea to get some relief from the skin disease, psoriasis. He'd said that by the time he'd left Israel, he was beginning to think that perhaps Hitler hadn't got it so wrong after all. At the time I'd thought that was taking it a bit far. Now I wasn't so sure. It's amazing how you can get things out of proportion when travelling; minor grievances can build up into irrational hatreds. I'd noticed that Paul Theroux seemed to suffer from this syndrome from time to time as well. I changed and made my way down to the shore. Floating in the Dead Sea was a weird experience. I can't say that I enjoyed it. You couldn't swim in the dense water with a 30% salt content and had to be careful not to get the chemical stew in your mouth or eyes; and when I tried to stand up to wade out, it took a major effort to get my legs forced to the bottom. The Dead Sea was the lowest point on the earth's surface, over 400 metres (1,300 feet) below sea level and sinking fast, at a rate of nearly a metre (3 feet) a year. The Dead Sea was dying. It had no outlet; the previous outflow to the Gulf of Aqaba was now just a dried up wadi. With reduced inflow, evaporation in the searing heat was having a dramatic effect. Evaporation over the centuries had already concentrated minerals in the water which were the basis of a lucrative chemical industry at the south end of the Sea, including the production of potash for fertilizers, and of course the therapeutic muds used in the health spas like Ein Gedi. The mineral extraction industry was also contributing to the lowering of the water level. The main problem, however, was that the major top-up source, the River Jordan, had been reduced to a dribble through extraction of water to irrigate crops and for drinking water supplies to the burgeoning population. Schemes had been mooted to top the Dead Sea up from the Red Sea and even the Mediterranean but all the options were expensive and involved serious environmental risks. Night was falling by the time we got into Jerusalem and booked into the Grand Court Hotel in the new part of the city.

In the morning we started our tour of the city on Mount Scopus for a panoramic overview from the north. Below us we could see the old city with its massive encircling wall, the new city spreading out over the hills to the west. Above the old city to the east, the Mount of Olives dropped down to the Garden of Gethsemane and the Valley of Jehoshaphat. Just inside the walls, the sun glinted on the golden roof of the Dome on the Rock, the Moslem holy of holies. We made our way round to the Mount of Olives with its extensive Jewish cemeteries. When the Jewish Messiah finally arrived, the plan was that he would assemble the resurrected in the Valley of Jehoshaphat below and lead them into Jerusalem through the Golden Gate. There was a big demand among Jews for places in the cemeteries, to be first in the queue for resurrection. Unfortunately, the Moslems had got wind of this plan in the 7th century after they'd built the Dome on the Rock and bricked up the Golden Gate. Moslems 1 Jews 0. But if the Christian Messiah could walk on water, a few stone blocks shouldn't be a major problem to the Jewish one – just another brick in the wall, as the song goes. There were also some attractive churches and chapels on the slopes of the Mount, the Russian orthodox Church of Mary Magdalene, with its onion domes and the little Basilica of Dominus Flevit (Jesus Wept) among them. At the foot of the Mount, we stopped at the Basilica of the Agony with its striking Byzantine style murals on the façade. Adjoining it was the Garden of Gethsemane where Judas had betrayed Jesus to the Romans and then later hanged himself from an olive tree. The tree may well still have been around as the grove was believed to be 2,000 years old. The alleged tomb of the Virgin Mary was nearby down a long flight of steps. We drove around to Mount Zion, a hill just outside the old city wall on the south side, beside the Zion Gate. A building there was claimed to cover the tomb of King David who had captured Jerusalem around 1,000 BC for the Israelites and made it their capital. There was considerable doubt in academic circles about the authenticity of this site but his cenotaph was there draped in velvet until somebody came up with a better idea.

We climbed a staircase from the courtyard outside to the first floor of the building and entered a bare room where the Last Supper was supposed to have been held. This was clearly stretching credibility a bit as the building had been constructed by the Crusaders so presumably it was just the location that was claimed to be kosher. However, it was a pleasant enough room for a nosh up with Gothic arches and some stained glass windows. The latter had apparently been installed by the Moslems when they had temporarily used the building as a mosque after they'd turfed the Crusaders out. Jesus would have turned in his grave about that if he hadn't already vacated it. To stretch credibility even further, just next door, the Church of the Dormition was supposed to mark the spot where the Virgin Mary had died. It seemed to me that it was extremely lucky from the point of view of the staff at the Jerusalem Tourist Authority, trying to package Jesus Tours to fit the time frame of Americans who never liked to spend any longer in one place than they could help, that King David had decided to be buried, Mary to die and Jesus to have his Last Supper, all within shot-put range of each other. But there you are; miracles can happen if the Bible is to be believed. When we were in the alleged Last Supper room, Noam had started to tell us the story of Jesus' last days when I saw Henry appear at the door bellowing into his cell phone: "I'm at the Last Supper." I suppose it was a bit less banal than the usual cell phone performances in public – "I'm at the bus stop, Dear. I'll be home in five minutes." Henry ranted on a bit longer, oblivious to all around him, until he caught Noam's eye and ended the call smartly. Those two were bosom buddies but if looks could crucify, Henry would have been hanging up there with Jesus.

We moved on to visit the new city. Jerusalem had fallen on hard times in the last few centuries of Ottoman rule. In their early days, Suleiman the Magnificent had built the current walls between 1537 and 1541 and generally tidied things up after centuries of fighting over the city by Crusaders and then various Moslem dynasties vying for power. However by the mid 19th century it had become a backwater and judging by contemporary reports, a rundown slum. In 1856 the Ottoman Sultan had issued the Edict of Tolerance, allowing religious freedom in his Empire, and Jews had started moving back in the 1860s. Rather than live in a slum, they started building new settlements outside the walls. Jerusalem was now a city of approaching 800,000 people. We passed the impressive King David Hotel. This had been the administrative headquarters of the British during their Mandate over Palestine. In 1946 the Zionist paramilitary terrorist group Irgun, led by a future Prime Minister, Menachem Begin, had carried out a bomb attack on it, killing 80 people and injuring hundreds more. This had been one of the catalysts leading to Britain handing over their Mandate to the United Nations in 1948. We drove past the ultra-modern Supreme Court building and the low-key parliament, the Knesset and stopped at the Israel Museum to visit the Shrine of the Book where the Dead Sea Scrolls were kept - parchments found in caves at Qumran which included the oldest versions of the Old Testament scriptures ever located. We didn't stay long: Noam had forgotten that it was closed. However, that had a silver lining: it gave us longer at Yad Vashem, the Holocaust museum, on the outskirts of the city. Walking through that dismal story, brought alive by a variety of audio-visual techniques was a harrowing experience. I had not generally been favourably impressed with the Israelis I had met so far, but being forcibly reminded so graphically of what their forebears had gone through in Hitler's concentration and death camps, it was no wonder that they weren't a barrel of laughs. We moved on to look at the stained glass windows by the Russian-Jewish artist, Marc Chagall, in the synagogue at the Hadassah Medical Centre. Each of the 12 windows represented one of the 12 tribes of Israel and their colour and design were stunning. On the way back to the hotel, we passed through John the Baptist's birthplace and old stomping ground in the pleasant, wooded village of Ein Karem.

I walked up to the Mea Shearim district, an enclave of ultra-orthodox Hassidic Jews (Haredi). It was like emerging from a time capsule into an 18th century East European Jewish shtetl (ghetto), untidy, narrow streets lined with two storey, terraced houses, some with the first floor overhanging, balconies strung with washing. The men were dressed entirely in black from their wide-brimmed fedora style hats to their doc Martins with long, heavy, black coats. Most had beards and long side curls of hair hanging down from beneath their hats. They reminded me of scarecrows, sinister ones at that. The women wore long dresses with long sleeves, shawls and head scarves, not an inch of flesh in sight. The Haredi rejected the modern lifestyle; TVs, cars and modern technology were anathema to them. They spoke Yiddish as they considered that Hebrew should only be used in religious contexts. They didn't even believe in Israel: for them, there could be no truly Jewish state until the coming of the Messiah. They were looking forward to Armageddon. They took Jehovah's award of the Promised Land to the Jews literally and wouldn't give an inch of land back to the Palestinians if they had their way – and they were disproportionately powerful politically because of the proportional representation system of voting in Israel. Although they were a minority (albeit in Jerusalem a large one, constituting perhaps a third of the population I was told) ultra-religious and other right wing political parties could hold governments to ransom in the coalitions normally needed to govern under this voting system. It had come as a surprise to me to learn that the majority of Israelis were "secular", just paying lip service to Judaism for weddings and funerals like most so-called Christians. The Haredi had no time for them, spitting and throwing stones at "immodestly" dressed women and girls.

Ben Yehuda Street, extending west from Zion Square and the Nakhalat Shiva area to the south was the liveliest nightlife area of Jerusalem, with bars, restaurants and nightclubs. Nakhalat Shiva was one of the oldest residential settlements established outside the Old City walls in the 19th century and the original buildings in its narrow lanes had been restored in the 1980s. I had dinner in La Guta, a French restaurant and got another written reminder that service wasn't included. The food hadn't been very good and the service slow and unfriendly so I wrote "Tips not given" on the bill and kept my shekels in my pocket.

The following morning, the tour bus parked outside the Damascus Gate in the north wall and we walked into the Old City to the Via Doloroso, the route that Christ was believed to have followed to the Hill of Golgotha where he was crucified. Like all the tourist sites on the Jesus trail in Jerusalem there was no real evidence that we were on the right track here. There was a theory that Jesus would have been tried at the Citadel, down at the Jaffa Gate on the west side of the Old City and would therefore have followed a completely different route. But every Friday, the Franciscans dutifully paraded past the Stations of the Cross marked out along the route we now followed and once more myth and theory had become fact. There were similar doubts about the location of the Church of the Holy Sepulchre where we ended up. It was believed to mark the site where Christ had been crucified and buried: the final five Stations off the Cross were identified inside, including Christ's tomb. The church was looked after jointly by the Catholic, Orthodox, Armenian and Coptic branches of the Christian faith, occasionally falling out and fighting with broomsticks over who had the right to sweep where. The Protestants of course thought they'd all got it wrong and believed Jesus had been buried in the Garden Tomb outside the Damascus Gate. Archaeological investigations had dated the tombs there to around 700 BC but when has scientific fact ever been allowed to get in the way of religious beliefs? The site of the Holy Sepulchre and some of the other Christian sites in Israel had been identified by the mother of the Eastern Roman Emperor Constantine early in the 4th century AD, after he had been converted to Christianity and legalised it throughout the Empire. This was 300 years after Christ's death and folk memories must have faded by that time. However, there is evidence that the site would have been outside the city walls in the time of Christ (the current walls dated to the 16th century and had left out Mount Zion which was previously inside) so she may well have got it right.

We walked down towards the Wailing Wall in the Jewish Quarter. In Ottoman times, the city had been divided into four Quarters: Moslem; Jewish; Christian; and Armenian. There were few Armenians left, but these divisions were still recognised. Between the 1948 war and the Six Day War in 1967, Jerusalem had been partitioned between Jordan and Israel, the Old City falling wholly in Jordan, the new city divided along the Green Line into Jordanian Eastern Jerusalem and Israeli Western Jerusalem. The Old City still retained the character of an

Arab bazaar, the narrow, bustling, streets packed with shops with tri-lingual signs in Arabic, Hebrew and English. We walked through the Cardo, the excavated main street in the Roman city built out of the ruins of the one they destroyed after the Jewish revolt in 70 AD. It lay well below modern street level, partly restored to resemble the origi-nal colonnaded avenue, partly reconstructed with arcades of shops. We entered the wide plaza in front of the Western Wall, which was all that remained of the Temple on the Mount which had been destroyed by the Romans, actually just its retaining wall. A gaggle of black clad Hassidic scarecrows were facing it, praying fervently and bobbing their heads as if they were head-butting it. Noam delivered a spiel about it, among other things mentioning that there was a segregated section for female head-bangers. He also pointed out where there were toilets up a stone staircase on a building at the side of the square. When he had finished, Linda, who as usual had given Noam less than her full attention, asked me: "Where did he say the Ladies was?" I pointed up the steps. When we reassembled to get back on the bus, she came up and accused me of sending her to the wrong place. "Don't tell me you went into the Gentiles?" I said. "I wanted the ladies section of the pray-ing wall," she complained. I had come across this failure to communi-cate with Americans before, even intelligent ones: two nations divided by a common language summed up Britain and America pretty well.

High above us, the area known as the Temple Mount to the Jews and the Haram ash-Sharif to the Moslems contained the golden domed Dome of the Rock and the Al Aqsa Mosque. It was here that King Solomon had built the first temple to house the Ark of the Covenant containing the tablet with the Ten Commandments given by God to Moses accord-ing to Jewish belief. It had been destroyed by King Nebuchadnezzar of Babylon in 586 BC and subsequently rebuilt only for the Romans to do it over again. Following Mohammed's death, his followers had set out to spread the faith at the point of the sword and captured Jerusalem in 638 AD. They had built the Dome of the Rock as a shrine covering the lump of rock which Abraham had supposedly been going to use as a butcher's slab to sacrifice his son Isaac and from where Mohammed allegedly ascended on his horse to heaven to join Allah and the 40 Virgins. It was therefore a sacred spot to both Moslems and Jews and consequently another potential flashpoint for trouble.

In the afternoon we went into Bethlehem to see the Church of the Nativity which was claimed to be built on the place where Jesus had been born in a manger. Bethlehem, although now just a suburb of Jerusalem, was one of the West Bank cities handed over to the Palestinian Authority for self government following the Oslo Accords. It had now become a virtual prison surrounded by a perimeter wall consisting of a combination of 5 metres (16 feet) high wire and mesh fences on a concrete base and 8 metres (26 feet) high solid concrete walls with watch towers, bordered by deep, moat-like ditches. It brought back disturbing memories of a former Concentration Camp I had seen in Germany. We had to go through immigration controls to get in. This had all come about through the "intifadas" (shaking off) when Palestinian impatience at continued Israeli occupation of their territory and the lack of progress towards statehood had boiled over into violence, initially between 1987 and 1990, when it had mainly just consisted of throwing rocks and Molotov cocktails and strikes but again between 2001 and 2005 when suicide bombers had come into the picture. In 2002, Ariel Sharon had initiated the wall building strategy, ostensibly to keep out the suicide bombers. The system was to extend to 670 kilometres (420 miles) throughout the West Bank. Sharon was now lying in a coma following a massive stroke and negotiations with the Palestinians was at stalemate. Noam had abandoned us at the border check. "Not coming with us?" I had asked innocently. "You must be joking," he said. The authenticity of the church as marking the birthplace of Christ was even more dubious than the scene of his death. Historians doubted whether Mary and Joseph would have been required to report to Bethlehem, so far away from Nazareth, for bureaucratic reasons – it was like someone from Birmingham having to go to London to pay their poll tax. However, in the church, down some stairs, in the Grotto of the Nativity, a fourteen pointed silver star marked the spot where the saviour may or may not have been born. If he'd left it until now, he would have had a hell of a time making it back to Nazareth through all the security barriers.

I caught a bus for the 300 kilometres (187 miles) six hour drive down through the Negev Desert to Eilat on the Gulf of Aqaba. There had been an ancient port city there which was mentioned in the Bible's Book of Exodus but the Ottomans had developed Aqaba next door in Jordan as their outlet to the Red Sea and there was nothing much on the site of Eilat when the modern city was founded in 1951. Now it was a vibrant tourist resort of 50,000 people specialising in diving on the coral reefs and desert safaris into the Negev. The layout was odd with the airport runway splitting the town centre off from the main hotel zone, developed around a lagoon, where I was staying in the Caesar Hotel. Israel only had 12 kilometres (7 miles) of coastline here. Beaches, hotels and diving facilities stretched all the way down the western shore to the Egyptian border at Taba. Looking east, you could see a giant Jordanian flag flying at the far end of Aqaba. The hotel zone around the lagoon was very attractive with some beautifully designed hotels. The stepped pyramid cum ziggurat style that I had seen in Tel Aviv was popular; my hotel looked out across the lagoon to the modestly named King Solomon's Palace Hotel which had had a serious attack of zigguratitis and even the humble Holiday Inn on the other side had a slight touch of it. It was all a bit Las Vegas but it suited the mood of the place. I liked it. A little bridge crossed the mouth of the lagoon and breakwaters enclosed a marina with some impressive yachts in it. A promenade lead-ing east towards the Jordan border passed the palatial Royal Beach and Dan Hotels. On the west side of the bridge, North Beach, the closest one to town, was a pleasant stretch of golden sand packed with swimmers and sunbathers. Along the strip of coast down to the Egyptian border was the Coral World Underwater Observatory, where you could watch marine life through large windows some 5 metres (16 feet) below water level and there were tanks with other specimens unlikely to participate in the live show. You could take trips in glass-bottomed boats; there was a "Yellow Submarine" submersible; and you could swim with the dolphins. Inland to the north, the International Birdwatching Centre was on a kibbutz near a salt marsh, where species migrating between Africa and Eurasia could be seen in Spring and Autumn. For such a desolate loca-tion, there was a lot to do.

A representative from the tour company arrived at the hotel early to take me to the Jordanian border at Wadi Araba. I had to wait a while until some other tour group members arrived and then there was slow progress through Israeli Immigration; things were even slower on the Jordanian side. The tour guide who was to take us to Petra met us and there was more delay while we waited for a second mini bus to turn up; the group was too big for one. I had read somewhere that Petra had been chosen by the BBC as one of the 40 places you had to see before you die. I was beginning to wonder if any of us on this tour would make it. We eventually set off north up the Desert Road, the guide pointing out where Wadi Rum of Lawrence of Arabia fame lay, just to the east. A two hour drive took us to Wadi Musa (Valley of Moses), a small town at the entrance to the Petra site, with hotels, restaurants and shops. Just outside the town, the guide had shown us the spring where Moses was supposed to have struck a rock with his staff and brought forth water. There was a further long delay while we waited for ponies which were to take us down the track to the famous Siq, which led into the site. Some people grumbled that we would be faster walking but the guide was adamant: my suspicious mind suspected that he didn't want to lose his commission from the pony trek operator. While we waited, I recalled a poem which described Petra as "a rose-red city, half as old as time." It was getting older by the minute and our time to see it reducing proportionately. When the nags arrived, it was apparent that none of them would have got a job with the pony express: my one stumbled a couple of times and almost collapsed but we made it to the finishing line. The Siq (Shaft) made a dramatic entrance to the ancient city. A gorge, over a kilometre long, its walls around 200 metres (650 feet) high and narrowing at one point to just 2 metres (6.5 feet) it followed a line of weakness caused by a fault line in the soft, rose-red Nubian sandstone. Stone channels which had carried water could be seen along both sides of the Siq. The Nabataeans, who had built the city, had become expert hydraulic engineers, developing a system of dams, cisterns, channels and ceramic pipes to collect, store and distribute water throughout the valley. They were able to supply their own needs and those of the camel caravans that passed through along the trade routes and created the city's wealth.

The Nabataeans were a semi-nomadic people from northern Arabia who migrated north to the Petra area around 600 BC. They had been involved in the frankincense and myrrh trade from the Arabian Peninsula along the "Incense Route" and "Kings' Road" leading north to Damascus in Syria. Petra was a more strategic location for them as it could also control east-west routes to Gaza, Egypt and Mesopotamia. Spices from India and gold, ivory and slaves from East Africa also came in via Arabian ports and the Gulf of Aqaba. It became an entrepot on the Silk Road from China. There were copper mines and smelters nearby and bitumen from the Dead Sea was valuable for waterproofing ships and embalming corpses. At the height of its power between 100 BC and its annexation by Rome in 106 AD Petra had a population of around 30,000. As we neared the end of the Siq, the magnificent Hellenistic façade of the the Khazneh (Treasury) appeared before us, framed between the narrow walls of the chasm. Forty-three metres (140 feet) high by 30 metres (97 feet) wide with a façade of six columns surmounted by a triangular pediment, all carved out of the rose-red rock, it was a stunning sight, not least for the way it just suddenly appeared. Nabataean architecture was a mixture of styles borrowed from other civilizations which they encountered through their trade links – Egyptian, Assyrian, Hellenistic (Greek) and Roman. They had traditionally lived in tents and it was believed that many continued to do so in Petra even after it became a substantial town. (Shades of the late lamented Colonel Ghadafi. I had also seen people living in Yurts [felt tents] in Ulan Bator, the capital of Mongolia.) The Kazneh was the tomb of a Nabataean king (the "Treasury" label had come from a legend that the urn carved near the top of the building had held the Pharaoh's treasure) but there was nothing to see inside. The façade was carved with figures, believed to be gods, and animals, with a gorgon's head in the pediment. Further along on the left, we walked through the Street of Facades, 44 tombs cut into the rock wall, and came to the Theatre, again carved out of solid rock. After a Roman refurbishment, which had desecrated some tombs, it had been able to seat 7,000 spectators. High on the cliff face on the other side of the valley we could see the Royal Tombs carved into the red rock. The track led us downhill to the city centre with a 6 metres (20 feet) wide colonnaded street, which had probably been lined with shops. The remains of a public water fountain, the Nymphaeum, could be seen beneath a pistachio tree. Little remained of the markets and Royal Palace. An arched gate had led into the temple precinct where the remains of the Qasr al Bint Temple stood. Some ruins marked the site of the public Baths. All the earlier delays meant that there was no time to climb up to any of the higher level sites such as Al-Deir (the Monastery) or even the Royal Tombs. In retrospect, I realized that an overnight stay in Wadi Musa would have made more sense to do the site justice. Petra had continued to prosper for a while after the Romans occupied it. But a massive earthquake in 363 AD did a lot of damage including to the vital water management system and the main trade routes shifted – Palmyra in Syria became the focus for the Silk Road and more direct routes across the Indian Ocean to the Red Sea using the monsoon winds rather than creeping along the coast diverted the spice trade away. Another earthquake in 551 AD delivered the coup de grace and it became a backwater, virtually abandoned by the late 8th century and almost forgotten until interest was awakened by the Swiss explorer J.L. Burckhardt who came across it on his travels in 1812.

On the way back to Eilat, we stopped briefly in Aqaba, Jordan's port city at the head of the Gulf of Aqaba, looking down the Saudi Arabian coast – the border was only 20 kilometres (12 miles) to the south. Since 2000, the Jordanian government had been putting a lot of money and effort into diversifying the city away from the heavy industry and port activities, which had boosted it in the 1960s and 70s. The aim now was to create a tourist centre, specialising in diving on the coral reefs, to rival Eilat just across the Israeli border. It had been made a Special Economic Zone with tax breaks and duty free status. A major city centre clean-up had been carried out and new hotels were sprouting up. The result was a very attractive city. The port still dominated the waterfront near the city centre but the main central boulevard, King Hussein Street, palm trees lining the central reservation and with restaurants and up-market looking shops, led down to a very pleasant area around the 14th century fort built by the Mameluke Sultans, the Museum and a tall flagpole flying the Jordanian flag. We had a sund-owner on the terrace of the Movenpick Resort Hotel overlooking the marina and time didn't seem to matter as much as it had earlier in the day. By the time we got back to Eilat, "Shabbat" (the Jewish Sabbath) had started – it ran from sunset on Friday night to sunset Saturday. I had been told in Jerusalem that everything ground to a halt there, even the buses. Here in secular Eilat, nobody seemed to be paying it much heed, the bars and restaurants were as lively as ever and there wasn't a black-clad Hassidic scarecrow to be seen anywhere, shaking his fist at anyone enjoying their self and spitting at little girls with bare arms.

At Eilat Airport the following morning, on my way back to Tel Aviv, they were having a training session for security personnel. A 12 year-old (O.K. she was probably 18) collared me when I entered the Departures Hall to check my baggage. She had a look at my passport and I heard her alarm bells ringing. "You've been to four Arab coun-tries in the last two weeks," she announced. "What were you doing there?" "Just visiting as a tourist" I replied. "Have you got any tourist material, guide books or anything like that?" Fortunately I had and dug one out from my hand luggage. "What about souvenirs? Have you bought any?" Again, fortunately, I had succumbed under pressure to buying my mother an ornamental vase in the Cairo souk. This time I had to dig it out from the bowels of my suitcase and unwrap it for her. She proceeded to go through everything in my suitcase and hand lug-gage with a very fine tooth comb. Time was ticking on and I hadn't got to the check-in desk yet. She was looking at my passport again. "You have a British passport but you live in New Zealand" she said. "How is that?" I explained that there were no real advantages in taking out New Zealand citizenship unless I wanted to move to Australia, which I didn't. "When did you arrive in Israel?" she asked. "Oh! God, I can't remember," I said, "You'll see the stamp in my passport." This was obvi-ously a mistake. "No, I need you to tell me," she said. I did some mental arithmetic. "A week past last Thursday, maybe?" I tried. By this time a supervisor had appeared. They had a long discussion and my passport was pored over. The check-in was closing. I was beginning to panic. Eventually the supervisor seemed to reach a conclusion, handed back my passport and the two of them took my luggage across to the check-in desk. "Sorry for the delay, Sir" the Trainee said. "But we can't be too careful here. Have a nice day." I'm sure she was still suspicious. She would make a good Mossad (the Israeli Secret Service) agent one day.

The following morning I was watching TV in the Departures area at Ben Gurion Airport when a news report appeared which seemed to be about a rocket attack somewhere in the north. I went to look for an English language version of the "Jerusalem Post". Sure enough, the Hezbollah in Lebanon had been firing katyusha rockets at an Israeli Airforce air traffic control base near Safed, 10 kilometres (6 miles) from the border. A soldier at Manara Kibutz, just south of the one I had stayed at, had been wounded by a sniper from across the border and mortar fire had also been coming across. A week ago, I would have been right in the line of fire. (Shortly afterwards, Israel sent troops into the Lebanon and there was widespread fighting with the Hezbollah.) The little girl at Eilat airport had been right: you couldn't be too careful in Israel. Armageddon could come any day.

7

TAJ MAHAL, AGRA, INDIA
MARCH 2008

IN NOVEMBER 2007, I came across the web site of the New 7 Wonders foundation on the internet and decided to visit the two "Wonders" which I had not yet seen, starting with the Taj Mahal in Agra, India. Before I took a trip up there in March 2008, I had only been in India once, purely by accident. On my way back from a holiday in Thailand in 1991, the flight was due a stop in Delhi but the airport was fogged in. We flew on to Karachi in Pakistan and sat on the tarmac for hours waiting for Delhi to clear. By the time we got back there, the crew were due a rest break, so we were booked into a hotel near the airport for a sleepover. I was so tired that I made no attempt to see anything of the city. Before we left, a buffet lunch was laid on and I had a generous helping of chicken vindaloo curry with chapattis. Not long into the flight disaster struck – Delhi Belly with a vengeance. Fortunately, an American lady sitting next to me had a supply of Imodium which eventually got it under control. I have rarely been bothered with stomach problems on my travels since a bout of dysentery at Makerere University in Uganda on my first venture abroad. It wasn't a very good introduction to India.

Apart from the opportunity to see another of the New Seven Wonders of the World, I had long been fascinated by India. I was familiar with much of the culture from my time in East Africa, where the "Asians" had dominated the commercial world. One of my best friends at Makerere University had been Jasu Patel, a Hindu whose forebears had come from Gujarat. While still at primary school, I had devoured a seven volume history of the British Empire and been enthralled by the stories of Clive of India, the Indian Mutiny and the Black Hole of Calcutta. Before my trip, I had read a fascinating book 'Shantaram' by an Australian prison escaper, Gregory David Roberts, who had fled to Bombay and become involved in the underworld there. I had also read V.S. Naipaul's 'India, A Million Mutinies Now' and Christopher Kremmer's 'Inhaling the Mahatma'. I had not bothered to learn any Hindi as I assumed, correctly as it turned out, that English, as the former colonial language and the language of commerce, would be widely spoken.

I flew to Mumbai (formerly Bombay) from New Zealand in March to avoid the heat build-up before the June monsoon and the colder conditions in North India in winter. Mumbai was hot and steamy even at that time of year. On the drive in from the airport I got a foretaste of the sheer size of the place, over 17 million people and the consequent congestion. The roads had not been constructed to deal with that and the traffic was horrendous. It was slow progress in the taxi into the Colaba area of the city centre where I had, appropriately enough, booked into the Taj Mahal Palace Hotel. Apart from its association with the main object of my trip, the central character in Paul Theroux's novel 'The Elephanta Suite' had stayed there and since our paths had crossed at Makerere University I had been a fan of his writing. The venerable old hotel dating from 1903 was later to become famous as one of the targets in the November, 2008 Moslem terrorist attack on Bombay.

Just in front of the hotel, leading to the Arabian Sea, stood the Gateway of India, built in 1928 to commemorate the visit of King George V and Queen Mary. The last British troops to leave India at independence in 1947 ceremonially marched through here on their way to the transport ships. I walked up to the 19th century Raj era town centre with its Victorian style buildings, Mumbai University, the High Court and across the street the grassy Oval Maidan where a cricket match was in progress. I took a taxi up to see the Victoria Terminus Railway Station, an elaborate gothic structure completed in 1887, looking more like a temple or a mosque than a place to catch the 8.15 to Delhi. The taxi took me on through the chaotic Crawford Market to the sordid red light district in Falkland Road with whores hanging out of the windows but I wasn't tempted to do any window shopping in spite of the driver's encouragement. In the evening I had a drink in the touristy Leopold's Café just behind the hotel, which featured in the book 'Shantaram' and the 2008 terrorist attack.

The following day I had booked a tour of the city. My guide, Mrs. Rama S. Khandwala from her business card, was elderly and looked far too frail to take on Mumbai's traffic and crowds, the heat and the humidity but then Ghandhi hadn't been the strongest physical specimen either and he had eventually defeated the British Empire. We visited the Mahalaxmi Dhobi Ghat, a huge expanse of water tanks where 5,000 dhobi wallahs (clothes washers) were scouring, beating and drying the city's dirty laundry. We came back south to the Mani Bhavan, a house where Mahatma Ghandi stayed frequently between 1917 and 1934 and from where he planned many of his campaigns against the British colonial regime such as the 1930 Salt March against the hated salt tax. It was now a museum with the room where he lived and worked preserved in its original state and elsewhere exhibits and pictures illustrating his life and works. Down the road towards Malabar Point was a Jain Temple, a sect of extreme vegetarians so focused on non-violence to all living things that they wouldn't eat root vegetables in case they were harbouring living organisms. Their monks and nuns would sweep the path in front of them in case they trod on ants or other insects contrary to their beliefs. On the slopes of Malabar Hill were the Hanging Gardens and on top the off-limits Towers of Silence where the Parsi dead were laid out for the vultures to pick clean. My guide Rama explained that the Parsis had come to India from Persia around the 10th century AD to escape persecution by the

Moslem rulers and worshipped the prophet Zoroaster. I was becoming bemused by the variety of religions in India. On the way back to the hotel we visited Chowpatty Beach, a popular evening rendezvous for the locals with food stalls and music but there was no way that I would have considered dipping a toe in the filthy looking water never mind risking a swim. All the Hepatitis A and B and cholera injections in the world wouldn't help.

I flew down to Kerala on the Malabar Coast, and transferred to my hotel the Trident Hilton Cochin on Willingdon Island via a bridge from the mainland. The island had been artificially created by the British in colonial times in 1931 from dredgings to create a deep water port to replace the old harbour at Fort Kochi (formerly Cochin). I had booked a tour with Swastik Tours and Travels. My guide, Vinayan, bore no resemblance whatsoever to a Nazi, polite and deferential to a fault. He took me across to Mattancherry on the peninsula to the west of Willingdon Island and just south of Fort Kochi. The ferry ticket cost 200 paise (2 rupees), just over 2 pence sterling. We visited the two-storey Dutch Palace, something of a mis-nomer as it was originally built by the Portuguese for the Maharaja of Cochin in 1555AD although it was extended and repaired by the Dutch in 1663. Inside, the Coronation Hall was where the Cochin Maharajas were crowned, their portraits decorating the walls. Other rooms had 17th century murals with scenes from the Indian epics the Ramayana and Mahabharata including a striking depiction in reds and yellows of Brahma emerging from Vishnu's navel. Nearby was the Paradesi Synagogue, India's oldest. Jews had first arrived in India in the 1st century AD at the time of the Diaspora when the Romans expelled them from Judea following their revolt against the Empire. The original synagogue on the site was built in 1568 but destroyed by the Portuguese. The existing building with its red tiled roof and clock tower dated from 1664 when it was re-built with Dutch help. In 1940 there were 2500 Jews living in the area which was still known as Jew Town but now there were only a dozen families left, the rest hav-ing emigrated to Israel. I had met one of those remaining families on a tour of Israel in 2006. Inside there were hanging oil lamps, crystal chandeliers and a beautifully crafted brass pulpit. The floor was covered in blue hand-painted Chinese tiles.

The narrow streets of Jew Town were lined with two-storey Dutch style houses, now mostly shops selling handicrafts, antiques, carpets, textiles, clothes, food and spices. We had a look in the Kochi International Pepper Exchange, a miniature stock-market, the upstairs floor a warren of cubicles with spice traders wielding telephones like weapons of war. Vinayan enticed me into the Euphoria Arts Emporium in Synagogue Lane where the carpet salesman was lying in ambush. I hadn't even been thinking about buying a carpet but I came out with a fine silk hand-made Kashmiri specimen regardless. Indians are even better salesmen than the Chinese and they take some beating.

We drove up to Fort Kochi and went to see the Chinese Fishing Nets on the shoreline looking out towards Vypeen Island. The nets were believed to have been introduced by Chinese traders some time between 1350 and 1450 AD. There is historical evidence that a huge Chinese fleet led by the eunuch Huang He at the behest of Emperor Zhu Di called here in 1421 and went on to visit the coast of East Africa. Gavin Menzies in his book '1421: The Year China Discovered America' claims that they went a lot further than that but few historians accept his evidence. However, there is no doubt that at the time the Chinese had bigger ships and better navigational technology than the Europeans and it is interesting to speculate what might have happened in world history if Emperor Zhu Di had not been killed in battle three years later and his successors turned inwards again rather than pursuing his dream of world exploration. The nets were extended from a framework of five wooden poles operating on a cantilever system and were lowered at high water. The catch seemed to be pretty meagre and one of the fishermen admitted that they were now more of a tourist attraction than a commercial fishing operation. Just behind the nets, there wasn't much left of the old fort which gave the area its name. Built by the Portuguese in the 16th century it was later taken over by the Dutch then the British. A block back from the beach stood St. Francis Church, erected by the Portuguese in 1510 and thought to be the oldest church in India. Vasco da Gama, the great Portuguese explorer, was buried here in 1524 but his body was taken back to Portugal fourteen years later. Further along the road, the Santa Cruz Cathedral, built in 1887, had some interesting murals on its ceiling. There was a legend in the area that Jesus' disciple Thomas (Doubting Thomas) had come to India and brought Christianity in the 1st century AD but this seems to belong in the same category as Gavin Menzies' speculations about how far Huang He's fleet got. Fort Kochi was a treasure trove of historical buildings – the 16th century Bishop's house was once the Portuguese Governor's residence, the Malabar House Residency was now a hotel, the Kashi Art Café was housed in an old Dutch building, the hotels and shops along Peter Celli Street were all housed in historic buildings. Just past a little sandy beach with a refreshment stall, was the poignant Dutch cemetery.

In the evening, Vinayan took me over to Ernakulam on the mainland, the modern part of Kochi, to see a performance of the traditional Kathakali dancing show in the Cochin Cultural Centre. This consisted of a series of vignettes from the Hindu epics, the characters in colourful costumes and headdresses, with hideous make up representing gods, demons and humans – the good guys with green faces. The singing, drumming and at times violent action sequences were a fascinating spectacle but not being familiar with the story lines or the language I soon lost the plot. Afterwards, Vinayan tried to interest me in an Ayurveda oil massage and steam bath at a nearby establishment but I had had my fill of Indian culture for one night and politely declined. I reckoned that he had already had a good commission day on me at the carpet emporium.

On my last night in Kochi, I went for dinner at the Taj Malabar Hotel at the north end of Willingdon Island facing Fort Kochi. This was a beautiful building set in spectacular landscaping and the seafood in their restaurant was some of the best I have eaten anywhere. There was hardly anybody in the restaurant and I had the almost undivided attention and recommendations of the staff while I was selecting my shellfish and fish from the array on display. The main course was served in a green banana leaf with herbs and spices and a coconut cream sauce and was absolutely delicious. And not a twinge of Delhi Belly the morning after.

The following day at 14.15 I boarded the Netravathi Express train at Ernakulam Junction bound for Goa, 850 kilometres (131 miles) to the north. Since we weren't due in Goa until 6.00 a.m., I had booked a berth in a sleeper coach. When I boarded, the cubicle where my berth was located was all occupied except my berth. An elderly man in a traditional white dhoti-kurta outfit greeted me in English and asked where I was from and where I was heading for. He introduced his fellow passengers, his wife, daughter and grandson. He then looked a bit embarrassed and pointed to his wife who was sitting on the bunk across the passageway leading through the carriage and asked if I would mind exchanging berths with her as she wasn't very well and they would be better able to look after her if she was closer to them. I readily agreed and as my new position was right by a window whereas I would have seen nothing of the countryside from my allocated top bunk I had the better of the deal. The family were very friendly and we chatted as the train chugged its way northwards. The old gentleman had been a senior civil servant with the government and was extremely well read and intelligent. He was fascinated by my nomadic lifestyle between New Zealand and the Shetland Islands and said that his one regret in life was that he hadn't been able to see the world. I had brought some cold chicken and chapattis to eat in the evening but the family insisted on sharing their meal with me and even produced hot, sweet, milky tea from a thermos flask. I slept well in spite of the frequent stops, 26 in all before we eventually arrived in Madgaon, my destination.

I was staying at the Fort Aguada Beach Resort at the south end of the seaside resort of Sinquerim. The hotel was on the site of an old Portuguese fort and overlooked the surf fringed beach. North along the beach on a sand bank lay the wreck of an ore carrier which had apparently been there for 8 years without any attempt to salvage it. The village was set well back from the beach, screened by a dense belt of coconut palms. I took a walk up the beach towards the wreck. The surf was pretty heavy and extended a long way out so it didn't look like a practical swimming beach. A few tourists were sunbathing and being massaged and some latter-day hippies were selling trinkets from palm frond shaded stalls but it was fairly quiet. I was told that the tourist trade had suffered from the recent murder of an English girl there on holiday. It didn't strike me as the sort of place where you were likely to get your throat cut. In the evening I walked through the village of Sinquerim and the neighbouring Candolim, both very quiet and had a meal of king prawns with chilli and garlic followed by suckling pig in the Bom Sucesso Bar and Restaurant. Goa, with a large Christian population, was one of the few parts of India with pork on the menu.

The following day I had booked a tour of the area. Goa had been colonised by the Portuguese in 1508 and they didn't leave until they were finally expelled by the Indian army in 1961, long after the rest of India had become independent. There was therefore still a strong Portuguese flavour in the buildings and the culture. We drove out to Old Goa, the original capital of the province, but now derelict apart from the impressive churches preserved as a UNESCO World Heritage Site. In the Basilica de Bom Jesus we saw the tomb of St. Francis Xavier, his body suspended in a glass case. He had been the pioneer in introducing the Catholic faith to the Far East, travelling as far as Japan. Nearby, were the imposing Se Cathedral, Asia's largest church and the attractive Church of St. Francis of Assisi. At its peak, Old Goa had had a population of 30,000 and was reputed to be richer than London or Paris at the time. However, after recurrent outbreaks of bubonic plague, it was abandoned in the mid 18th century.

We moved on to the new capital, Panaji (formerly Panjim) with the ornate Church of Our Lady of the Immaculate Conception dominating the centre. We walked through the historic Fontainhas area with its Portuguese style houses painted in pastel shades of yellow, ochre, green and indigo, reminiscent of old Lisbon. The former fishing village of Dona Paula down on the Arabian Sea front had been absorbed into greater Panaji and touristified.

I flew on to Delhi, from where I had booked a 'Golden Triangle Tour' taking in Agra and Jaipur in Rajasthan. On the drive in from the airport to my guest house in the Karol Bagh district, I began to get some idea of Delhi's size, over 14 million people in the conurbation and the traffic problems created by this. Next morning, my tour guide took me down to the Chandni Chowk (Silvery, Moonlit Square), the teeming commercial centre of Old Delhi. Here, among shops spilling out onto the pavements, we visited the Digambar Jain Temple, the Jami Masjid (Friday Mosque), India's largest with its soaring minarets and vast marble domes and saw the Sisganj Gurdwara, a Sikh temple. Here the various religions lived cheek by jowl in apparent harmony. The shopping streets were organized on a trade basis, one street specialising in gold and silver ornaments and jewellery, another in textiles and turbans, another in perfumes and cosmetics, electric goods here, bicycles there, spices somewhere else. Nearby, the imposing red sandstone Lahore Gate was the entranceway to the Lal Qila (Red Fort) built by the Mogul ruler Shah Jahan when he moved his capital here from Agra. There were seven old capitals within the boundaries of Delhi, this one the seventh constructed between 1638 and 1649 and called Shahjahanabad after the Emperor. The earliest Moslem rulers in India came from Persia and conquered the previous Hindu states in the late 12th century. We later visited the remains of their capital Qila Rai Pithora to see the soaring Qutb Minar (Minaret) built for the first Moslem Emperor and a strange cast iron pilar standing nearby which didn't rust. The later Mogul rulers were originally from what is now Afghanistan. The tomb of the Emperor Humayun was in another old capital and was the model for the Taj Mahal. Down towards the Jamuna River, a tributary of the Ganges, was the Rajghat, a memorial and shrine to Mahatma Ghandi, with an eternal flame burning in an ornamental lantern. The centre of New Delhi, the building of which started in 1911 when the capital of the British Raj was moved here from Calcutta (now Kolkata), stretched along the wide ceremonial Rajpath from the presidential palace with its fancy wrought iron gates to the India Gate, government buildings lining part of the frontage. In the evening, I had a meal at Karim's Restaurant, an unpretentious place tucked away in a narrow lane near the Jami Masjid serving authentic Mogul style cuisine like the delicious lamb curry which I sampled.

The following morning I was picked up by my driver Chintu to continue my 'Golden Triangle' tour. I hadn't expected this to be a one man tour as it wasn't particularly expensive but so it transpired. Chintu was from the state of Bihar, known for its crime and lawlessness and a hotbed for Maoist rebels. Chintu showed none of these tendencies even under severe provocation from the traffic on the Grand Trunk Road down to Agra. On this motorway there were, pedestrians, cyclists, holy cows, dogs, camel carts; traffic weaved in and out of lanes without signalling or the drivers even looking; in the motorway median strip near a spectacular white Hindu Temple was a vegetable stall, doing a roaring trade. Chintu was imperturbable. "It's just India", he explained. Further on I asked him what the garden shed sized brown piles beside the road were. "Dried cowshit" he replied. "The people use it for cooking." The built-up area seemed to go on forever.

We stopped at Sikandra to visit the tomb of the Mogul Emperor Akbar completed in 1612. He had ruled for 49 years and built our next stop, Agra Fort, between 1565 and 1573. The imposing red sandstone walls concealed some beautiful delicate buildings inside and a landscaped garden in the courtyard split in four to resemble the gardens in paradise. The guide showed me the room where Emperor Shahjahan, the builder of the Taj Mahal, was imprisoned by his son after he had been deposed. From the window you could see his masterpiece gleaming in the sunlight.

Chintu collected me before dawn to go and see the Taj Mahal, built for Emperor Shahjahan between 1632 and 1653 as a mausoleum for his third wife Mumtaz Mahal, who died having their fourteenth child. The building is often described as a symbol of eternal love but it crossed my mind that there might have been an element of guilt involved as well – fourteen children is too many for any woman. We arrived just as the sun was coming up, bathing the complex in a soft ethereal light. The white domed marble mausoleum with its four minarets, one at each corner of the plinth on which the building stood, was indescribably beautiful. I had seen photographs of it and live footage on videos and film but the real thing was in another dimension, the impact heightened by the early morning light and the serene atmosphere created by the elongated pond reflecting it and leading the eye towards it. The symmetry created by the mosque and matching guesthouse flanking the mausoleum and the entrance building facing it, beautiful buildings in their own right, added to the overall effect.

The buildings enclosed an ornate charbagh garden divided into four quarters, like the one I had seen at Agra Fort, with avenues of trees and bushes again leading the eye towards the mausoleum. Fountains played, glistening in the rising sun. Close up, you could see the semi-precious stones including jasper, jade, lapis lazuli and turquoise inlaid into the white marble. The exterior walls were decorated with Arabic calligraphy, painted and carved designs of vines, flowers and fruit and geometric and herringbone patterns. The 35m (115 feet) high dome was topped by a gilded bronze finial, ending with a moon with its horns pointing heavenwards. Inside, in an octagonal chamber, the cenotaphs of Mumtaz Mahal and Shahjahan stood side by side, although the bodies were actually buried at a lower level. The walls and caskets were again beautifully decorated in precious and semi-precious gemstones including sapphires, calligraphy and designs. The guide told me that a labour force of twenty thousand workers had been recruited and over a thousand elephants were used to transport building materials. Some of the materials used came from as far away as China and Arabia. The Taj Mahal was designated a UNESCO World Heritage Site in 1983.

When I emerged from the Taj Mahal gateway, still mesmerised by the experience, I was forcibly reminded that this was the day of the Hindu religious spring festival, Holi. A boisterous group of youths came running towards me and within seconds I was drenched with water and covered from head to toe with red and yellow powder. One of them applied a dot of red grease paint to the middle of my forehead just to complete the effect. Chintu came running across from his car to rescue me and got the same treatment. Later he explained that the festival was supposed to celebrate the end of winter and the onset of spring, the throwing of water probably symbolising rain for the crops, but now he said it was just an excuse for some legal hooliganism and at night it would degenerate into a drunken orgy. I told him that we had a few festivals like that in the West as well, like St. Patrick's Day.

We headed off for Jaipur in Rajasthan and stopped at the abandoned walled city of Fatehpur Sikri which had been built by Emperor Akbar between 1571 and 1585 and had been his capital for fourteen years. The reason for its abandonment was believed to be an unreliable water supply. There were some interesting buildings in the complex. The Diwan-i-Khas had been used for private audiences with the Emperor and its construction was unusual with a central pilar supported by carved brackets, inspired by Gujarati buildings according to the guide. The Panch Mahal, an open sided, five storey sandstone pavilion was where Akbar's wives could enjoy the cool evening breezes. In the Khwabgah, the Emperor's private sleeping quarters, the guide showed us the ingenious ventilating shaft near his bed.

Not far into Rajasthan I spotted a road block up ahead manned by a group of men and youths. "Not another Holi ambush, surely" I said. "No," Chintu replied, "a different sort of ambush." He got out of the car and chatted with the men for a while and I saw him giving them some money. When he got in and they let us through I said, "What was all that about?" "They're collecting a sort of unofficial road tax" he explained. "It's completely illegal, of course, but nobody worries much about that in Rajasthan." A bit further on the road works started and went on for miles and miles. Nobody was working as it was a public holiday for Holi but there were diversions onto dirt roads, coned off areas, unsigned ramps, every obstacle that an Indian bureaucrat could dream up. I had never seen road works extending for such a distance and I couldn't see how it was efficient or practical to have so much reconstruction going on at once. We were sitting at a single lane section controlled by a couple of policemen on a walky-talky waiting for our turn to go through when a car appeared speeding down the closed lane. One of the policemen rushed across and stopped it. The driver lowered his window and the next I knew the policeman was punching the man in the head, left, right, blow after blow. Chintu just shrugged and rolled his eyes.

In Jaipur, my hotel, the Trident Hilton, was just north of the city, looking out over the artificial Mansagar Lake to the salmon pink Jal Mahal (Water Palace) which appeared to be floating in it, the Aravalli Mountains rising behind it. The palace had been built as a summer retreat for the Maharajas and was due to be restored as a tourist attraction. The lake had originally been created as a water supply but its turquoise hue suggested the presence of an algal bloom.

In the morning, a guide arrived to take me on a city tour. Our first destination was the pale red sandstone Amber Fort, high on a hillside above the northern approaches to the city, protected by Jaigarh Fort on the hilltop. This had been the headquarters of the local Rajput rulers, who took over the area in the 11th century AD, before the present day city of Jaipur was built. We stopped below the fort, where a group of painted and caparisoned elephants were waiting patiently to take tourists up to it. I had ridden elephants before in Thailand and had found it a very pleasant experience, perched on those huge, placid, intelligent looking beasts. Swaying up to a Maharaja's fort in Rajasthan on the back of one made it easy to allow my thoughts to wander back to the high days of the Rajputs. We entered through the Suraj Pol (Sun Gate) leading into the Chaleb Chowk (Main Courtyard). Down some steps an ornately carved silver door led into the Shila Devi Temple where an image of the goddess Kali was flanked by two silver elephants. The lavishly decorated, three-storeyed Ganesh Pol (Elephant God Gate) led into an inner courtyard with the Aram Bagh pleasure garden in the centre. In the Jai Mandir (Victory Hall) mirrors in the ceiling would have glittered like stars in candlelight. The Zenana (Women's Quarters) was at the far end of the complex.

Jaipur (City of Victory) was a planned city laid out for Maharaja Jai Singh, work starting in 1727 and taking six years to complete. Known as the 'Pink City' since 1876 when the Maharaja decreed that the buildings should be painted pink, the colour of welcome, for a visit by the British Prince of Wales (later to become Edward VII), old Jaipur was surrounded by a crenellated wall punctuated by seven gates. The streets were laid out in a rectangular pattern, each block specialising in a different craft or trade. Yet another fort, Nahargarh, built in 1734, overlooked the city from a sheer ridge to the north-west. The new part of the city, now, as Rajasthan's capital, home to over 3 million people, sprawled out to the south and west.

Inside the city walls, we walked through the chaotic Tripolia Bazaar and into some of the streets leading off it. Cycle-rickshaws, auto-rickshaws and motorbikes weaved in and out of the cars, lorries and buses, the occasional camel cart adding to the congestion. The noise of engines and horns was deafening and the pungent traffic fumes caught in the nose. Jaipur was renowned as a shopping centre and everything imaginable was on display here in the bazaar. In the Johari Bazaar, jewellers, goldsmiths and silversmiths plied their trades. Their wares were on display in the streets, in the noses and ears and on the hands and wrists of the local Rajasthani women, dazzling in their brightly coloured traditional robes. A Jaipur speciality, enamelware, was on display, highly glazed and intricately decorated in shades of ruby, bottle green and royal blue. Women selling vegetables sat on the pavement displaying their produce and flower sellers offered garlands of marigolds.

We passed through the imposing Tripolia Gate towards the Royal Palace, now a museum, although the current Maharaja still lived in part of the complex, the seven-storey Chandra Mahal. Facing the entrance was the Mubarak Mahal (Welcome Palace) with a display of royal costumes on the first floor including beautiful Kashmiri pashmina shawls. Through the Rajendra Pol gateway, flanked by two elephants carved from single blocks of marble, was the Diwan-i-Khas (The Hall of Private Audience) which housed two huge silver urns, 1.6 metres tall and capable of holding 4,000 litres each. These had been used by the Maharaja to hold holy Ganges water for bathing when he went to London for King Edward VII's coronation in 1902. They feature in the Guinness Book of Records as the largest sterling silver objects in the world. The Diwan-i-Aam (Hall of Public Audience), the former ceremonial hall, with an enormous crystal chandelier hanging from the ceiling, was now an art gallery with exquisite Rajput and Mogul miniature paintings (mostly with religious themes), carpets, rare manuscripts, a silver throne and an ivory elephant howdah. In the Armoury there were shields, swords, daggers, guns and chain armour, harking back to the often bloodthirsty past. There was also a carriage museum and in a courtyard called the Pitam Niwas Chowk, in front of the Chandra Mahal, four ornately decorated gates represented the four seasons.

We emerged out into the Jantar Mantar, the observatory, con-structed by Maharaja Jai Singh, a keen astronomer, between 1728 and

1734. At first glance it resembled a children's playground. But there was serious stuff here, a bewildering array of large astronomical instruments for measuring time, the altitude and azimuth of all celestial bodies, the position of the stars including the Pole Star and the twelve signs of the zodiac and for all I knew possibly even the Maharaja's inside leg. The instruments were still used by astrologers and to predict the timing of the monsoon. The largest instrument, a massive sundial 23 metres (75 feet) tall, could measure time to within 2 seconds. Some restoration work was underway and a female brick-layer in a sari was busy re-paving the surrounds of one of the instruments.

We moved on to the Hawa Mahal (The House of Winds), five storeys of pink sandstone riddled with windows from which the women of the palace used to peek out at the street scene, hidden from prying eyes behind perforated mesh-like "jali" screens. It was hardly a building at all, really just a façade, one room deep with narrow walkways and designed to catch any evening breezes.

We drove back to Delhi and I caught a flight to Varanasi (formerly Benares) on the west bank of the Ganges, India's holiest Hindu city, with a history going back nearly 3,000 years, making it contemporary with Ninevah and Babylon. Hindu legend held that it was founded by Lord Shiva, one of the trinity of 'super gods' with Vishnu and Brahma. My tour guide Abuzar from Varuna Tours appeared at my hotel, the Taj Ganges, shortly after we arrived in the late afternoon. He suggested going down to the Ganges at dusk to see the Hindu Aarti prayers held every evening to pay homage to the goddess Ganga – the river itself was considered to be a goddess in the Hindu religion, he explained. On the drive down towards the river, Abuzar expanded on the role of the Ganges in the city's life. "Many people from all over India are making yatra – pilgrimage - here to bathe in the river. To visit once in a lifetime is every Hindu's dream – it is our Mecca. Bathing cleanses oneself of the bad karma from past lives and this life and prepares one for death and rebirth into a better life – we Hindus believe in reincarnation, you know. To die in Varanasi gives the best chance of achieving moksha – liberation from the cycle of life and death – so many old people come here to die. There are boarding houses full of them."

We parked some way back from the river as the traffic was horrendous, backed up at one point behind a bull ambling down the middle of the road. As we walked down towards Dasaswamedh Ghat, Abuzar pointed out another bull lying on the floor of a shop selling saris. Its picture appeared on their signboard. Abuzar said that it had started appearing at the shop every morning since it opened and spending the day there. Then, at closing time, it would get up and wander away. "You see, the bull Nandi was Lord Shiva's vehicle – means of transport – so since this is his city they get a lot of leeway here. Bulls are not much economic use, you can't milk them, so farmers often just let them loose to wander around. People feed them since they are holy." We arrived at the Ghat, a flight of steps leading down to the river – Abuzar said that there were about 100 Ghats along a 6km (4 mile) stretch of the river. We made our way to a flat roof area where chairs were set out to view the ceremony. A crowd was building up down below, Sadhu holy men in saffron robes, chai (tea) sellers, beggars, goats, a buffalo. Brahmin priests appeared and sat down cross legged on mats in front of little shrines, half a dozen of them. As darkness fell, lights came on, fairy lights picking out parasols fastened to wires above each altar. Oil lamps were lit, the flames flaring up; bells were rung; mantras were chanted. I'm not a religious person but the performance was very moving, the holy Ganges lying black and silent in the background.

I got up before dawn to go down to the Ganges again. Abuzar had booked us a row boat to view the early morning scene. As the sun came up bathers appeared, crowding every ghat. Some were performing their puja (worship) others washing clothes; some brave souls were setting out to swim across to the flat sandbank on the other side – the river was low at this stage of the dry season but it was still a long way in polluted water. In the soft, pink light of dawn, lighted candles floated downstream, borne on leaves; garlands of flowers, bright yellow marigolds, drifted past the boat. We rowed south - upstream - as far as the Harishchanrda Ghat where bodies were being cremated and then turned round. The banks were lined with temples and havelis (mansions) some belonging to Maharajas from all over India, including the Jaipur family and Jai Singh had built another of his observatories outside their one. Colourful murals of the various gods decorated some walls – I saw Ganga, Shiva, Hanuman the monkey god, Ganesh the elephant god. We saw the palace of the Raja of the Doms, the Untouchable (Dalit) caste who had the lucrative concession on cremations on the Ghats. Soon afterwards we came to Manikarnika Ghat, the main cremation ghat. Several pyres were burning and a body lay waiting, wrapped in a shroud – it was a 24 hour, seven day operation. Piles of firewood and dried cow dung were stacked up. Abuzar told me that the Doms picked through the ashes for any gold teeth, which they were allowed to keep and then shovelled the ashes into the river. We came ashore there and walked up past a large stone lingam (penis), a symbol of Shiva and fertility.

A labyrinth of narrow lanes led up towards our next destination, the Gyanavapi Mosque. The lanes were lined with barber shops, cobblers, spice shops, betel nut sellers; a calf was waddling slowly down the centre of the lane in front of us, pedestrians detouring around it. It's dangerous to try to interpret the expression on animal's faces as we tend to anthropomorphise them but this one had spoilt brat written all over its face. As we approached the mosque, I became aware of a large group of heavily armed soldiers up ahead. They stopped and frisked us and just as we were turning away an officer in heavy gold braid, wearing a turban   and with a fierce curly moustache appeared with a metal detector and went over us again. Whether it was a new toy he enjoyed playing with or he was just relieving the boredom and brightening his day by pissing off a tourist, I don't know. Abuzar explained the situation. "They are protecting the mosque against attack by Hindu militants following threats. In the 17th century, Emperor Aurungzeb demolished the Hindu Kashi Vishwanath Temple which stood on the site to build the mosque. The Vishwanath (Golden) Temple was rebuilt later just next door but it has remained a bone of contention between Hindus and Moslems and the government are worried. In 2006 a bomb was exploded by Islamic militants in the Sankat Mocham Temple to the monkey god Hanuman in the south of the city. Before that, in 1992, the Babri Mosque in the city of Ayodhya was demolished in a riot following a political rally organised by the Hindu nationalist Bharattya Janata Party. The mosque had been built by the first Mogul Emperor, Babur, on a site believed by the Hindus to be the birthplace of the god Lord Rama. The Hindus claimed that a temple had been destroyed to build the mosque but the Moslems disputed that. Anyway, after the Babri Mosque had been destroyed, riots broke out in the big cities, especially Mumbai and over 2,000 Moslems were killed. Before that, Hindu chauvinism was not a big factor in Indian politics. Now it is a big problem." Non-believers weren't allowed into either the mosque or the temple but Abuzar took me up onto the roof of a nearby shop to view the gold plated dome and spire of the temple. I felt it was a pity that things had turned out this way. Hindus do not proselytise, try to push their religion down other people's throats. The only way to become a Hindu is to be born one. It's a gentle religion and non-violence is the central plank of its offshoots Jainism and Buddhism. But old enmities were clearly bubbling up again. I read later that 20% of the population of Varanasi was Moslem.

In the afternoon, we drove about 8 kilometres (5 miles) north of Varanasi to Saranath, one of the most important Buddhist pilgrimage sites in India. This is where Buddha was supposed to have preached his first sermon in 528 BC after his enlightenment. The Damekh Stupa marked the spot where he had preached. Abuzar explained that a stupa was a burial mound or dome containing relics of the Buddha. This one was a solid, circular brick structure about 25m (80 feet) high and the same in diameter, the lower half in lighter coloured bricks, the upper half dark brown and narrower, with a conical top. The ruins of a Buddhist temple and an estimated 30 monasteries stretched north to a Deer Park. To the west, beyond a Jain temple, stood the remains of Ashoka's Dharmarajika Stupa and the base of the pillar on which the famous Lion Capital had stood. Ashoka was the greatest of the Mauryan Emperors, the first dynasty to unite India and adjacent lands stretching from Bangladesh to Afghanistan in the 3rd century BC, slightly earlier than the first Chinese Empire under Qin Shi Huang Di. Ashoka erected pillars all over his empire setting out his ethical code, including non-violence and religious tolerance. The Lion Capital was in the adjacent museum. It consisted of a 24-spoked Buddhist Wheel of Law surmounted by four lions sitting back to back. The base was a lotus. It had become the national emblem of India.

I took a short flight to Kathmandu, capital of neighbouring Nepal, birth place of the Buddha, where I was staying at the Everest Hotel. I had booked an early morning flight with Buddha Air. These 19 seaters flew close along the face of the Himalayas and then turned and came back so that everyone on board could get a clear view of the mountains. Yeti Air provided similar flights, but the thought of big hairy feet and hands on the controls so close to the world's highest mountain range put me off them. We flew past the peak of Gauri Shankar, sacred to Hindus and the Stetson-shaped Melungtse. Further west, Everest appeared with its close neighbour, Lhotse. We had picked a lucky break in the weather; sunlight bathed the snow clad peaks making them sparkle. It was perhaps the most awe-inspiring spectacle I had ever seen. Living in New Zealand, I was aware of the God-like respect accorded to Sir Edmund Hillary, the first man to reach the 8,848m (29,028 feet) summit of Mount Everest with Sherpa Tensing in 1953. My own respect for their feat soared as I saw for myself what a mountain they had had to climb. Everest was named in 1875 after Sir George Everest, the man who pioneered the mapping of India. In Tibet it was already called Chomolangma, Goddess Mother of the Earth. The rejection of such an evocative name in favour of a British bureaucrat says a lot about the colonial mentality. In 1956, the Nepalese had confused matters further by naming it Sagarmatha, Head of the Sky.

Back at Kathmandu Airport, I was met by my guide Amil and driver Deepak from Krishna Tours who were to take me round the city. We started in the old medieval core, the Durbar Square, a UNESCO World Heritage Site. The oldest building, the wooden Kasthamandap, after which the city was named, was originally built as a lodging for pilgrims and dated from the 12th century. However, most of the other structures, mostly Hindu and Buddhist temples, were built in the 16th and 17th centuries by the Malla dynasty. A gold-plated door led into the Hanuman Dhoka (Royal Palace) guarded by a red statue of the monkey god Hanuman and two fierce looking lions. The soaring 36m (120 feet) pagoda of the Taleju Temple dominated the square. Amil said it had been built by King Mahendra Malla in 1564. A ferocious looking black-faced statue of the Kala (Black) Bhairav, the most destructive manifestation of the god Shiva, stood nearby. He was wearing a garland of skulls and trampling a corpse, which Amil said was supposed to symbolise human ignorance. The faces of Shiva and his consort Parvati peeked from a third-storey window of the temple named after them. We went to see the three-storey brick house where the living goddess, the Kumari Devi, lived – a pre-pubescent girl considered to be an incarnation of the goddess Taleju. Amil explained that she was selected from a caste of gold and silversmiths on the basis of physical characteristics, her horoscope and her reaction to a terrifying sounding selection process involving a darkened room, deafening noises, men dancing in horrific masks and an array of over 100 buffalo heads. Candidates could be as young as four and were retired at puberty. She had to perform various ceremonial duties during the year.

We drove over to the Boudhanath Temple on the eastern outskirts of the city, a Buddhist temple which served as a centre for the 20,000 Tibetan refugees exiled in the city. From the gilded tower above the white-washed dome of the stupa, Buddha's blue eyes looked impassively out over the complex. Prayer flags streamed from the tower. An array of prayer wheels were being spun by the procession of pilgrims on their ritual clockwise circumambulation of the dome. Two figures sitting on elephants on the plinth were the ex-king and queen, according to Amil, who had been assassinated along with eight other members of the royal household by their drunken son in 2001. Amil said that the original temple had been built around 600 AD after the Tibetan king, Songsten Gampo, converted to Buddhism. It had had to be re-built in the 14th century after being destroyed by Mogul invaders from India. Shops and monasteries surrounded the shrine, with all the paraphernalia of Buddhist worship on display – butter lamps, horns, drums, plumed lama hats. A large prayer bell hung outside a monastery.

Nearby was the Hindu temple of Pashupatinath, on the bank of the sacred Bagmati River, a tributary of the Ganges. Amil told me that the temple was dedicated to Shiva, who took on many different forms, depending on which of his roles as creator, preserver or destroyer he was fulfilling. Here he was Pashupati, Lord of the Beasts. A number of Sadhus (holy men) in heavy make-up for the tourist cameras were sitting around, the scent of hashish hanging in the air around them. Amil said that a lot of them were bogus, just there to take money off tourists for posing for photographs. A cremation was taking place on the ghat across the river, smoke rising and hanging in the still air. Now in the dry season, the river was just a series of polluted puddles and I wondered how the ashes got away. Amil pointed out the royal cremation site outside the main temple building where the ten victims of the 2001 palace massacre had been cremated. He said that the motive of Crown Prince Dipendra for gunning down his parents and eight other family members and then turning the weapon on himself had never been established but that he had been a bit of a playboy, a heavy drinker and used drugs and he had quarrelled with his parents over the woman he wanted to marry. There had also been rumours that his uncle, Gyanendra, who succeeded to the throne, had been complicit in a conspiracy and Gyanendra was not popular with the people. The path back up to the car was lined with shops serving the pilgrim and tourist markets. A beautiful girl dressed in a pale blue salwar-kameez outfit (a loose tunic over pyjama-like pantaloons, tapered at the ankle) approached me and tried to sell me a circular mandala disk on a red ribbon for hanging around the neck. She was as bold as brass, not at all demure like Indian women. Amil explained that the geometric diagrams on the disc symbolised the universe and that they were used by Buddhists to aid meditation. I meditated for a moment and the girl was persuasive but the price she was asking was exorbitant and I eventually settled for giving her 50 rupees to pose for a picture which I could meditate over later.

We drove around the city on the ring road, heading for another Bhuddhist temple, Swayambhunath, on the western outskirts. We ground to a halt in a traffic jam. Up ahead there was a commotion and a wall of noise gradually came towards us, manifesting itself as a Maoist election campaign rally – a procession of flag bedecked vehicles, pedestrians, a sea of banners and placards. A Maoist insurgency had been underway in the rural areas for years and many lives had been lost but a ceasefire had now been negotiated and they had agreed to take part in an election which was due shortly. I had read in The Kathmandu Post that there had been violence at a number of their rallies resulting in deaths and they were accused of intimidating other parties but this crowd seemed to be good natured enough. Back in New Zealand, I read that they had won the election and formed the new government. One of their first actions had been to depose the unpopular King Gyanendra and declare a republic.

Swayambhunath Temple was on top of a hill, approached by a long flight of steps, the handrails lined with stone statues of animals and birds and very much alive rhesus macaque monkeys, sliding down the banisters. The architectural style of the temple was similar to Bhoudhanath. Amil explained that the whitewashed hemispherical dome symbolised creation and the earth, the Buddha statues set into it representing the four elements – earth, fire, air and water. The thirteen gilded rings on the tower demonstrated the stages of knowledge required to achieve enlightenment and nirvana. Nirvana was represented by the umbrella crowning the tower. The all-seeing eyes of the Buddha looked out from all four sides of the tower. A forest of small stupas crowded the surrounding terrace. On the way back to the hotel, we passed through the Thamel district of the city, backpackers' paradise, with cheap guesthouses, cafes and restaurants catering to the tourist trade.

The following morning, Deepak, my driver from the tour company, arrived at the hotel to transfer me the 200 km (125 miles) to Pokhara. Getting out of the city was painful, traffic jam after traffic jam. Matters seemed to be even worse for traffic coming into the city which was completely gridlocked, a line of mainly lorries stretching nose to tail for miles. Deepak explained that this was the main road in from India and that it was always congested. The scenery was rugged hill country, a series of river valleys with gushing rapids. Stone-built villages were surrounded by emerald green rice terraces. We passed the junction to Gorhka, the birthplace of the Shah dynasty, the current royal family. Approaching Pokhara, we followed the valley of the Seti (White) River, the light coloured soil showing in its heavily eroded banks suggesting where the name came from. In Pokhara, I had booked into the Fulbari Resort Hotel, in a spectacular location above the gorge of the Seti River, at the end of a long bone-jarring dirt road. A plaque outside identified it as one of "The Great Hotels of the World". The plaque looked as if it hadn't seen polish in months. I wandered around the extensive grounds. The swimming pool was dirty, only one of the six restaurants and bars was open, the casino was closed. In the Colonel Robert's Aviary, two colourful birds lay dead in one of the cages, a hole in the netting wire showing where a predator had gained entry. The rest of the aviary was decrepit, the remaining birds looking half-starved. No doubt at some time in the past the Fulbari had deserved its plaque. Now it was a disgrace.

I got up early hoping for a view of the mountains. The day before had been hazy and overcast and they had been hidden. I wasn't disappointed. The gleaming white peaks of the Annapurna Range with the distinctive shape of the "fish tail", Machhapuchhare, hung in the sky above me, looking close enough to walk to before breakfast, even though they were about 30km (20 miles) away. It was an awesome sight. A guide turned up with Deepak to take me around Pokhara. The Lakeside district, down beside the placid waters of the Phewa Tal (Lake), was touristy, the equivalent of the Thamel area of Kathmandu. The lake was bathed in hazy sunshine, presenting an idyllic picture with cattle and buffaloes grazing and lying along the shore in little stone-walled paddocks, fishing boats out on the water. Up in the old part of town we saw some traditional three-storey, red brick houses, typical of the Newari people who were native to this area and the Kathmandu Valley.

I flew back to Kathmandu where I had arranged a tour of the two other former royal cities, Patan and Bhaktapur. These, with Kathmandu, had been independent kingdoms under different branches of the Malla dynasty until the conquest of the Kathmandu Valley by Prithvi Narayan Shah, the ancestor of the current royal family, in 1768. The centres of all three were now UNESCO World Heritage Sites.

Pathan was now only separated from Kathmandu by the Bagmati River. The old centre, another Durbar Square, closely resembled

Kathmandu's equivalent, with a palace and an array of temples. The square was dominated by a brass statue of former King Yoganarendra Malla seated on top of a tall column, his head shielded by a cobra. The Krishna Mandir was built from carved stone rather than the more typical brick and timber and was surmounted by a shikhara, a corn cob like spire. Its three tiers fronted by columns had friezes depicting scenes from the Ramayana and Mahabarhata. Pornographic carvings decorated the roof struts. The two-storey Jagannarayan Temple was fronted by two stone lions, yet more porno on the roof struts. Two large stone elephants stood outside the Hari Shankar Temple where for a change the roof struts were carved with scenes of the tortures of the damned. The huge Taleju Bell hung between two sturdy pillars.

Bakhtapur was 16 kilometres (10 miles) east of Kathmandu along a congested road, some open country separating the two with fields of rice, wheat and vegetables. Bakhtapur, like the other two cities, had been badly damaged in an earthquake in 1934 which had destroyed many of the buildings in its Durbar Square. What was left had since been beautifully restored but the greater spacing of the buildings coupled with a traffic ban gave it more of a museum feel than the other two cities. The Sun Dhoka (Golden Gate) led into the royal palace, which had been badly damaged in the earthquake. The gate was made from gilded copper, elaborately decorated with representations of Hindu deities. On the roof struts of a small Shiva temple, camels, elephants and cows were fornicating.

The historic part of Bakhtapur was more spread out than in either of the other two cities, extending along a curved road from the Lion Gate through Taumadhi Tole to Tachupal Tole. This was part of the old trade route from Tibet to India. The oldest part, the Tachupal Tole, dated from the 12th century. Here the brick and terracotta base of the Dattatreya Temple was carved with yet more erotic scenes. The Bhimsen Temple was dedicated to the god of commerce. In the centre of the square was a statue of the strange man-bird hybrid of Hindu mythology, the Garuda, the god Vishnu's vehicle of transport. Taumadhi Tole was dominated by the five-storey, 30m (98 feet) high Nyatapola Temple, the highest in the valley, the roofs of the pagoda resembling a giant fir tree. The stairway up to it was flanked by stone guardians, two Rajput wrestlers at the bottom, then pairs of elephants, lions, griffons, and finally goddesses at the top. It was dedicated to Lakshmi, a bloodthirsty incarnation of the goddess Durga. A large chariot with wooden wheels stood outside the adjacent Bhairabnath Temple. It was used to cart around an effigy of the frightful god Bhairab during the Bisket festival due next month. Down a side street, in Potter's Square, clay pots were drying in the sun and craftsmen were operating treadle power wheels and mud covered kilns. It was a scene that had probably hardly altered since the middle ages.

I flew on to Kuala Lumpur in Malaysia, via Delhi. I was staying near the Petronas twin towers, the highest buildings in the world until recently over-topped by rivals in Shanghai and Dubai. Kuala Lumpur was an ultra modern city and squeaky clean – far too pristine for my taste after squalid, fascinating, India. It was a shopper's paradise but since for me shopping is a cross between purgatory and hell it didn't appeal to me. The city centre had an interesting mixture of old and new buildings. The cream-coloured, Moorish style Sultan Abdul Samad building, with its domes, minarets and clock tower sat in front of a forest of modern banks and office blocks. It was the former British colonial administration's headquarters, now the Supreme Court. The mock-Tudor style Royal Selangor Club looked out on a manicured expanse of grass with a backdrop of skyscrapers. In the middle of Dataran Merdeka (Independence Square), where the British flag was finally lowered in 1957, an ornate fountain was surrounded by flower beds and surmounted by a large, abstract sculpture. Alongside the venerable St. Mary's Cathedral was the confluence of two streams where the city had been founded by a group of Chinese tin prospectors in 1857. Kuala Lumpur meant "muddy confluence" in Malay, an inauspicious name for a city of over 7 million inhabitants and the capital of Malaysia. Nearby was the Masjid Jamek (Friday Mosque) the oldest in the city. Malaysia was a strongly Islamic state.

The following day I had booked a day trip to the old city of Melaka (formerly Malacca), a four hours drive down the motorway, through rather featureless scenery dominated by oil palm plantations.

Melaka's history paralleled that of Kochi in India; early Chinese trade contacts, then occupation by the Portuguese, followed by the Dutch and finally the British. Originally a sea gypsy camp at the mouth of the Malacca River, the site had been taken over by Sumatrans under Prince Parameswara in the 14th century. He was credited with introducing Islam to Malaysia. With its strategic location on the Straits of Malacca it became an important port in the trade between China, India, Arabia and Java handling tea, silk, spices, perfumes and opium. This attracted the Portuguese who captured it in 1511. Traces of their occupation could still be seen on Bukit St. Paul (ST. Paul's Hill) where the remains of their fortress, A Famosa, stood next the ruins of St. Paul's Church. At the bottom of the hill was another remnant, the Porta (Gate) de Santiago. Down on the waterfront was the Church of St. Francis Xavier, whose body I had seen in the Basilica de Bom Jesus in Old Goa. There were still some Portuguese speaking Eurasians left in the town, the result of mixed marriages with the Portuguese occupiers. We visited the "Portuguese Village" where some of them lived but it was a bit Disneylandish as it was a modern creation - there were no historic buildings in the complex – but there were some inviting looking restaurants with traditional Portuguese cuisine on the menus.

The Dutch legacy was most evident in Red Square, the old town centre, where the Stadthuys, the former town hall, built around 1650, was now an art gallery. Beside it stood Christ Church, dating from 1753. Both buildings were painted red, hence the name of the square, which was beautifully landscaped with shade trees, colourful flower beds and fountains. On the drive into the city, we had stopped at the attractive little Dutch style St. Peter's Church, dating from 1710. The Dutch had expelled the Portuguese in1641 and were in turn ousted by the British in 1824. The ornate Proclamation of Independence (Merdeka) Building commemorated Britain getting its marching orders in 1957. A reconstruction of the former Sultan's palace in traditional Malay style stood nearby.

Across the river was Chinatown, home to the earliest invaders of all. The early Chinese traders had taken local Malay wives, the resulting mixed-race group coming to be known as the Straits Chinese or the Peranakan culture, the men called Babas and the females Nonyas. Malaysian cuisine has become world famous and you can find chicken satay and laksa soup worldwide. But the Peranakan or Nonya cuisine is extra-special. I had lunch in a little Peranakan restaurant in China Town and the fish head curry I ordered was one of the tastiest dishes I have ever eaten. Along Jalan Hang Jebat, the main street of Chinatown, lined with antique and gift shops, we visited a Chinese temple, a mosque and a Christian church, almost next door to each other. Melaka was truly a melting pot. In the parallel Jalan Tun Tan Cheng Lock alias "Millionaires Row", elegant houses built by wealthy Dutch merchants had been renovated and decorated by equally wealthy Pernambukans to produce a stunning streetscape.

In November 2008 I switched on the television in my flat in New Zealand and saw smoke coming from the window of my room in the Taj Mahal Palace Hotel in Mumbai. Moslem terrorists, based in Pakistan, had attacked a number of Mumbai landmarks including the hotel, Leopold's Café, where I had had a drink and the railway station. I cast my mind back to the army cordon around the Gyanavapi Mosque in Varanasi and the officer who had gone over me with a metal detector. I now appreciated why he was being so careful.

8

CHICHEN ITZA, MEXICO
MAY 2008

THE LAST OF the New 7 Wonders which I had not yet seen was Chichen
Itza, the ruined Mayan city near Cancun in Mexico. I planned my annual migration route north with the sun to visit family and friends in
Shetland for May 2008 to take it in. I had been to Mexico briefly once
before on a day trip into Tijuana in 1996 as part of a tour of the western states of the USA but apart from a two hour stop in the airport
at Panama City in 1970 on a flight from Columbia to Jamaica, I had
never been to any of the countries of Central America. I planned my
itinerary to take in some of them as well as Mexico and visit some of
the other ancient Mayan sites.

Mexico City was huge: with a population of over 20 million it was
one of the largest cities in the world. Its location in an amphitheatre surrounded by mountains created a natural trap for the pollution belching out from its swarms of vehicles and poorly regulated
industries and power stations. Lurking nearby, were the towering
volcanic cones of Popocatepetl (Smoking Mountain) and its neighbour Iztaccihuatl (Sleeping Woman) still posing a threat of eruption.
The centre of the city had been built on an old lake bed. Lying in an
earthquake-prone area, this posed a serious threat of the phenomena

known as "liquefaction", where the soil turns like porridge following
tremors. Buildings were sinking on their foundations as was, even in
the absence of major earthquakes since 1985, when a tremor measuring 8.1 on the Richter scale struck and did major damage. To cap all
those natural perils, Mexico had a dreadful reputation for violence
arising from its strategic location on the drug trade route into the
United States from South America. It was the home of powerful drug
cartels which the government struggled to combat.

In spite of all these drawbacks, I found Mexico City a surprisingly pleasant place to visit with some impressive historic buildings
dating back to the Conquistadors, elaborate monuments, some very
good museums and pleasant parks providing greenery. Lying at 2,100
metres (7,000 feet) above sea level, the altitude of the Valley of Mexico
tempered the heat to be expected in its location just inside the tropic
of Capricorn, resulting in a benign climate. I was staying in the Royal
Hotel in the Zona Rosa, an up-market residential area west of the city
centre where many of the hotels, bars, clubs and restaurants catering to tourists were located. The centre of the city was the Plaza de la
Constitution, better known as the Zocalo. I had picked Mayday for my
first foray up there and the huge square (at 220 metres by 240 metres
[715 feet by 780 feet] one of the largest in the world) was thronged
with workers celebrating it as Labour Day. A temporary stage had been
erected outside the National Palace and trade unionists were harangu-
ing the crowds at full volume. The Miners' Union was prominent,
"Mineros" emblazoned on their red T-shirts. Baseball caps were the
order of the day rather than sombreros. The square had been used for
autos-da-fe (burning at the stake) by the Spanish Inquisition in early
colonial times: with the platform speakers whipping up a mood of rampant disaffection with the injustices being meted out to the working
class, any capitalist mad enough to show his face in the square could
well have suffered a similar fate.

The Square was dominated by the Metropolitan Cathedral, the
largest church in Latin America, its two monumental bell towers rising
67 metres (220 feet) above the Zocalo and with a central dome. The
smaller clock tower, between the bell towers on the main façade, was

surmounted by statues of Faith, Hope and Charity. Adjoining the front of the Cathedral, the main façade of the Sagrario Metropolitano (the Parish Church) was elaborately sculpted with figures of saints. It had taken from 1525 to 1813 to complete the Cathedral and now the problem was to keep it standing in the face of earthquakes and the unstable foundations. A lot of work had already been done underground to combat subsidence and maintenance was clearly a work in progress, judging by the amount of scaffolding and tarpaulin in evidence. Inside, the Altar de los Reyes was a baroque masterpiece of ornate, gilded carving surrounding two fine oil paintings. In the choir, there were two organs and the stalls were intricately carved in red wood. There were statues, oil paintings, sculptures everywhere, in an orgy of devotion to a god who had seen over 90% of the native population wiped out on his watch within decades of his arrival with the Conquistadors, through brutality and European diseases. The natives had been better off with the Aztec God of War, Huitzilopotchli: at least he just needed a regular supply of human sacrifices; and they were usually prisoners of war and therefore expendable. The east side of the Zocalo was taken up by the National Palace, which now housed the offices of the President and the Federal Treasury. It occupied the former site of the Aztec Emperors' palace. The walls around the internal staircase were decorated with magnificent murals by Diego Rivera, Mexico's most revered artist (although his wife, Frida Kahlo, might dispute that, her being a bit stroppy and a feminist to boot). The murals depicted Mexico's history from the founding around 1325 AD of Tenochtitlan (the Aztec name for Mexico City) by the Aztecs where, as prophesied, the wandering tribe saw an eagle seated on a prickly pear cactus, eating a snake; the conquest of Mexico in 1521 by the Conquistadores under Hernando Cortez; the colonial era; the independence struggle with Spain ending in success in 1821; the 1846-48 war with the USA which resulted in the loss of all the territory north of the Rio Grande; the 1864-67 occupation by France and the execution of their puppet Emperor, Maximillian; the revolution lasting ten years from 1910 with a cast including Pancho Villa and Emiliano Zapata; and finally, modern Mexico, seen as a struggle of the classes, reflecting Rivera's Marxist views. (He and his wife were friends of the exiled Russian revolutionary Leon Trotsky who was assassinated by a local Stalinist with an ice-pick in Mexico City in 1940. The assassin may well have been hired by the Man of Steel [Stalin] himself, in an act of international terrorism worthy even of the CIA.)

The remaining two sides of the Square were occupied by impressive buildings: the Supreme Court; the former City Hall; and the opulent Gran and Majestic Hotels, with jewellery shops at ground level. Just off the Square to the north, beyond the former Archbishop's Palace, was an archaeological site where the remains of the Aztec Templo Mayor were being excavated. This had been the heart of the Aztec capital city of Tenochtitlan which Hernan Cortez had razed to the ground when he finally conquered it in 1521. I subsequently saw a beautiful model of the city at the National Museum of Anthropology in Chapultepec Park. It had stood on an island in shallow, brackish, Lake Texcoco, connected to the shore by causeways and with an aqueduct bringing fresh water. Canals criss-crossed the island for moving people and goods, giving it a strong resemblance to Venice. When the Spaniards arrived in 1519, the city was estimated to have a population of around 300,000, larger than any city in Spain at the time and much bigger than contemporary London. The wider area of the Valley of Mexico held around 1.5 million people and the Aztecs had subjugated most of present day Mexico. The Conquistadors had been awe-struck by the city they saw, but not awe-struck enough to deter them from destroying it. There wasn't much left to see on the site of the Templo Mayor but on a subsequent visit, following my trip to the Museum where the excavated artefacts were on display, I was able to piece together a picture in my mind of the original structure and what went on there. A huge, stepped pyramid had been surmounted by twin temples, one dedicated to Huitzilopochtli, the God of War, the other to Tlaloc, the God of Rain and Water, twin obsessions of the Aztecs and other Mesoamerican cultures like the Maya. A block of volcanic stone on the platform in front of the temples had served as an altar where sacrificial victims were bent over backwards and had their hearts cut out with obsidian knives to placate the gods, their bodies being thrown down the staircase for disposal. In one ceremony alone, there was evidence that around 20,000 victims, mostly prisoners of war, had been sacrificed. The god of war doubled up as the sun god and it was him that needed large amounts of blood to persuade him to keep rising in the morning. The reclining figure of Chac Mool, believed to have been an intermediary between man and the gods, had also been found on the temple platform. He lay resting on his backside with his torso upright and knees bent, his head turned to look across his shoulder at us with a surprised look on his face, as if he'd been disturbed in the middle of a wank. He was cradling a bowl on his stomach which was thought to have been a repository for sacrifices including still beating human hearts. Two stone snake heads guarded the foot of the main staircase. It was thought that the pyramid may have represented the Hill of the Serpent, a sacred place in Aztec mythology. The Tzompantli shrine was a wall of human skulls covered with stucco. The Eagle Knights were two identical, life-size clay statues of Aztec warriors in eagle feather costumes. A gruesome, round, carved stone, which had been found on the site by chance in 1978 and led to the excavation, showed the dismembered body parts of a goddess who had fallen foul of the God of War. It had been a bloodthirsty spot.

From the Zocalo, I walked down Calle (Street) Madero towards the landmark Torre Latinoamericana, Latin America's tallest building when built in 1956 and at 182 metres (600 feet), still among the city's highest structures. Just across the street was the Casa de los Azuljeos, a mansion dating from 1596 but refurbished in 1737 with the blue and white Chinese tiles which gave it its name. Just ahead, bordering the Alameda Central Park, the Palacio de Bellas Artes, the city's opera house and main concert venue, was a beautiful building in white Italian marble designed in Neo-Classical style with an Art-Nouveau flavour. Its dome was crowned with an eagle with spread wings. Construction had started in 1905 but it hadn't been completed until 1934 due to the interruption of the Revolution. I walked through to the Paseo de la Reforma, a wide tree-lined boulevard laid out in the 1960s, and took a taxi back to the Zona Rosa. The traffic circles along the way held impressive monuments – a statue of Columbus; a monument to the last Aztec emperor, Cuauhtemoc; the Angel of Independence; and the naked bronze figure of Diana Cazadora (the Huntress). Just past the Torre Mayor, the tallest building in Latin America, the Boulevard entered Chapultepec Park which, as well as providing the site of the Museum of Anthropology, also had boating lakes, a botanic garden, a zoo and pleasant walking tracks through tree-shaded, landscaped parkland and gardens. It also housed the National History Museum in the Castillo de Chapultepec, built in the 18th century as a fortress but later serving as the palace of Emperor Maximilian and later presidents. It covered the history of Mexico from the Conquest to the Revolution.

The story of the conquest of the Aztecs by Hernan Cortez and his band of treasure-hungry Conquistadors was fascinating. Cortez was the son of a minor nobleman in Spain who had moved to the Caribbean to seek his fortune. The Spanish were already well established in Cuba and Hispaniola (present day Dominican Republic and Haiti) and Cortez became an important landowner and government official in Cuba. In 1519 the Governor of Cuba put him in command of an expedition to explore the interior of Mexico for colonization. He landed first on the island of Cozumel, off present day Cancun in the Yucatan peninsula, where the Spaniards already had a foothold on the mainland and then sailed up the coast to Veracruz, collecting more men on the way: by the time he set off inland from there towards Tenochtitlan he had 600 men, 15 horsemen and 15 cannon, not a large force to conquer an empire. To encourage his men not to give up, he burned his fleet of a dozen or so ships. On the trek inland, he formed alliances with some local tribes who were disaffected with Aztec rule and joined his expedition. He also massacred thousands of unarmed noblemen in the central plaza of the Aztecs' second largest city, either fearing treachery or as an example to others. In spite of this he was peacefully received in Tenochtitlan by the Emperor, Moctezuma II. Cortez later claimed that the Aztecs thought he was an old god Quetzalcoatl (the feathered serpent) returning but academics now dispute this. After his rearguard at the coast was attacked, Cortez took Moctezuma hostage as an insurance policy. Meanwhile, Cortez had fallen out with the Governor of Cuba who had rescinded his command of the expedition and sent an armed force to arrest him. Cortez marched back to the coast, defeated the Governor's men and signed on the survivors. While he was away from Tenochtitlan, the rearguard he had left behind had carried out a massacre in the temple and triggered a rebellion. Cortez attempted to calm things down and enlisted Moctezuma's help but the latter was stoned to death by his people when he appealed to them. The Spaniards had to retreat from the city and suffered heavy losses during the "Noche Triste" (Night of Sorrow) when they left, having to fight their way across a causeway. They regrouped, got reinforcements from Cuba, recruited more local allies, built pre-fabricated ships for assembly at Lake Texcoco and attacked Tenochtitlan in 1521, eventually defeating the new Emperor, virtually having to destroy the city block by block in the process. Cortez built a new city on the ruins of the old, draining Lake Texcoco to provide more building land as the city expanded.

In the evening I went for a meal in a restaurant not far from my hotel. This being Mexico, I had a Margarita as an aperitif – tequila mixed with lime juice and triple sec, served with salt around the rim of the glass. Mexican appetizers were called "antojitos" (a little of what you fancy), similar to Spanish "tapas". I had a taco al carbon – a small tortilla (maize pancake) folded over barbecued pork – served with side dishes of guacamole (pureed avocado, red pepper, onions and tomatoes) and salsa (fiery hot red sauce with tomatoes, chillies, onions and garlic.) For the main course, I chose the Turkey Mole, the "mole" being the sauce, a thick, pureed mixture of chillies, fruit, nuts, seeds, spices and chocolate. While I was eating, I thought about how much European cuisine owed to crops developed in the Americas: apart from the maize, beans and squash which had been the staples of Central American agriculture, where would Italian cooking be without tomatoes?; Xmas without turkey?; North Europe without potatoes?; and the whole world without chocolate? Add to the list the chillies, peanuts and avocados from my menu and a range of dishes worldwide owed a debt to Native American farmers. After dinner I caught a taxi up to Plaza Garibaldi to see the Mariachi bands which congregated there in the evenings to show off their talents to prospective customers. Dressed in tight maroon or black suits with shiny boots and belt buckles, some with the trade mark sombreros, these groups of 7 to 15 men armed with violins, guitars and trumpets were just about as Mexican as you could get.

The following day I took a bus tour to see the remains of Teotihuacan, reputedly one of the most impressive archaeological sites in the Americas. The ruined city lay about an hour's drive (50 kilometres [30 miles]) north-east of the city centre. It was a mysterious city as little was known about its inhabitants but it had bequeathed its gods to both the Mayans and the Aztecs. The early development of the city had been dated back to around 200 BC and it had suddenly been destroyed around 650 AD: internal revolt or barbarian invaders from the north were the prime suspects. At its peak, the city had held an estimated 125,000 people and covered 20 square kilometres (8 square miles). Archaeological evidence of the influence of the city had been traced all over Mexico and beyond into Guatemala and it was believed that the empire it controlled was more extensive than that of the Aztecs. We entered the site at the south end, opposite the Temple of Quetzalcoatl, the feathered serpent god who was still alive in Aztec mythology when Cortez arrived. Huge stone carvings of his head and that of the rain god, Tlaloc, also later worshipped by the Aztecs, decorated the walls of the temple. From the temple, the Avenue of the Dead stretched north for over 1500 metres (a mile) to the Pyramid of the Moon at the far end of the site. It was a big site but the excavated area still just covered about a tenth of the area of the city. The piece de resistance was the Pyramid of the Sun, the third largest in the world, as wide as the Great Pyramid at Giza in Egypt at 225 metres (738 feet) and although not as high at 65 metres (213 feet) and consisting of 2.5 million tons of stone and earth as compared with the Great Pyramid's 6.5 million tons, it was still a massive engineering feat. A steep flight of steps led up to the platform on top. It was believed to have been used to worship the sun god. At the end of the avenue, the Pyramid of the Moon was smaller, but as the land rose up towards it, it tended to dominate the site and from the top presented a panorama right across it. Just off the plaza in front of the Pyramid of the Moon was the Palace of Quetzalpapalotl (Bird-Butterfly) and an adjoining maze of residential structures and temples. An enormous stone serpent's head jutted out from the top of the steep staircase at the entrance to the complex. Inside there were brightly coloured murals of plumed jaguars playing musical instruments made from feathered conch shells, green parrots spewing water, hybrid bird-butterflies – the artist must have been on the tequila or something stronger from Colombia. The pyramids would originally have been coated in smooth stucco and painted in bright colours and must have been a magnificent sight. Just beside the Pyramid of the Sun, the museum held artefacts excavated on site and there was an impressive scale model of the city beneath the glass floor of the main hall. Hawkers were very much alive in the Avenue of the Dead, selling postcards, drinks and souvenirs and the occasional "genuine antique" furtively produced from the folds of a poncho.

On the way back, we stopped at a small rural artisan's workshop in the San Juan district called Mi Mexico Lindo Artesanias. Here we were given a demonstration of how mezcal, the rougher little brother of tequila, was made from the agave cactus plant followed by a tasting session. It must have gone to my head (no doubt that was the intention) as I ended up buying a beautiful but expensive sculpture of the head of the Aztec god of gods, Tonatiuh, made from obsidian with semi-precious stones inlaid – turquoise, lapis lazuli, agate, jade, serpentine. Our final stop was at Our Lady of Gaudeloupe Church, where we staggered out still stinking of mescal. In 1531, a local Indian Christian convert called Juan Diego had had a vision of a beautiful dark skinned woman on Cerro (Hill) de Tepeyac just above where the original church now stood. (He had probably been on the mezcal too.) She told him she was the Virgin Mary and that he was to go and tell the bishop to build a shrine there in her honour. Now, most of us just would have gone home and slept it off, but not Diego: he went to the bishop as instructed, who, to his credit, didn't believe him. But Diego kept going back to the hill and each time the same vision re-appeared until the fourth time her image miraculously imprinted itself on his cloak and the Bishop fell for it. A shrine was built to her, she became the Patron Saint of Mexico and in 2002 Diego had been canonized. It's amazing what a glass or two of mezcal can do for you. The baroque basilica we now stood in front of had been built around 1700 AD. It had twin bell towers, a yellow dome and relief figures of the Virgin carved on the façade. The cult of the Virgin of Guadeloupe caught on big time, probably because she was associated in the minds of the local Indians with the Aztec goddess, Tonantzin, who had previously been worshipped on the hill. (It was common practice for the Indians to merge Christian Saints with their old gods when they were forcibly converted to Christianity. Cynics like me may be tempted to think that the vision was a deliberate ploy engineered by the Church to popularise Catholicism with the Indians.) In the 1970s a huge new circular basilica, capable of accommodating 10,000 worshippers, had been built down below. We walked down to it through a beautiful park with trees, flowers, waterfalls and a sculptured recreation of the apparition scene. Down below, around the huge plaza in front of the new basilica, it became obvious what a big business the cult had become – it was virtually a self-contained little town with shops and accommodation for pilgrims. The Church was obviously raking it in: visions pay. I hoped the bishop had made it worth Diego's while and paid for the print job on his cloak. While we were there, a large group of young female pilgrims arrived at a canter, on foot, all dressed in the same colours like a sports team and obviously highly excited. The tour guide told us that some days thousands arrived, coming from all over Mexico and even further afield. Some of them completed the last part of the journey on their knees.

The following day, I flew down to Cancun on the east coast of the Yucatan Peninsula. Cancun had been built from scratch since the early 1970s as a tourist centre to act as a counter-weight to Acapulco on the Pacific Coast which was suffering from its own success. Cancun now had a population of nearly half a million. It was really two cities: Ciudad (City) Cancun, the commercial centre, on the mainland; and Isla (Island) Cancun, the Zona Hotelera (Hotel Zone) where the tourist business was concentrated on a former boomerang shaped sandy island, now connected to the mainland at either end by bridges and causeways and enclosing a sheltered scenic lagoon, the Laguna de

Nichupte. The narrow, 23 kilometres (14 miles) long island was perfect for its purpose, fringed with dazzling sugar-white sandy beaches on its seaward side, catering for surfers on the exposed eastern side, sheltered and ideal for swimming on the northern arm in the Bahia de Mujeres (Bay of Women): the lagoon was tailor-made for water sports. The beaches were lapped by turquoise water which shaded into deep blue as the ocean deepened. I'm no great fan of purpose-built "new towns" but Cancun came as a pleasant surprise. There was a touch of Las Vegas in the architecture of the hotels ranging from Spanish Hacienda, through Mayan Pyramid to Greek Temple but it all blended together perfectly well strung out along Boulevard Kukulcan (the Mayan name for the old feathered serpent god Quetzalcoatl). I stayed in the NH Krystal Hotel in Punta Cancun at the apex of the boomerang, the centre of the action, and couldn't have asked more of a beachfront tourist hotel. The town was orientated towards the youth market, in particular North American youth, with a Planet Hollywood, Hard Rock Café, Hooters bar, with well-endowed waitresses whizzing round on roller skates, Buba Gump's which specialized in prawns, the massive all-night club Coco Bongo, Vegas Showtime, the Rainforest Cafe and Margarita y Marijuana in the main square. For once, I wished I was young again. In a small dock towards the landward end of the north arm of the boomerang, two Spanish galleon style "Pirates of the Caribbean" ships were moored, waiting to press-gang landlubbers for cruises. There was enough kitsch to last a lifetime. But I just had a couple of days and I wanted to see Chichen Itza.

I booked a guided bus tour to see the ancient Mayan city of Chichen Itza which was a two and a half hour drive inland through low, dry, sparsely populated forest. It was one of the largest Mayan cities and the best preserved and restored but it was not entirely typical due to a strong influence on its culture and architecture from the Toltec civilization to the north. It was also developed later and lasted longer than the cities further south in the original Mayan heartland in the tropical rainforests of the Peten Basin in Guatemala. (I was later to visit Copan in northern Honduras which was more typical of the classical Mayan cities in its development and history.) Chichen Itza had originally developed as a substantial city around 600 AD when it appeared to have been a fairly typical Mayan city. In the 9th century AD it had suffered a sudden decline, in common with the cities further south, from which they never recovered. When it underwent a renaissance in the 10th century, it was strongly influenced in its choice of gods, forms of worship and architectural styles, by the Toltec civilization with its headquarters in the city of Tula north of Mexico City. Academics once believed that the Toltecs may have invaded and conquered the area or at least migrated there in substantial numbers but it was now believed that their influence may just have been the result of cultural diffusion – the spread of ideas. In this new incarnation, Chichen Itza became the regional capital of northern and central Yucatan with a port on the north coast at Isla Cerritos, trading for obsidian from central Mexico and gold from southern Central America among other widespread trading links. At its apogee it was estimated to have had a population of over 35,000. And then sometime in the 12th century or possibly even earlier it declined again and by the time the Spaniards arrived, while there were still Mayan people living in the area, they were just farmers and all "elite" activities associated with the temples and palaces had long been abandoned. While there was some archaeological evidence that the city had been sacked and looted at some time, the causes for the sudden collapse of the elaborate culture associated with it were a matter for speculation.

We parked at the Hotel Mayaland near the eastern entrance to the site. Just inside was the Cenote (sinkhole) Xtoloc which had been the source of drinking water for the city. The Yucatan Peninsula was a limestone plateau with virtually no surface water other than where these sinkholes reached the water table. The name of the city meant "at the mouths of the wells of the Itza (the tribe living in the area)". Immediately ahead of us was the most iconic building on the site, the great stepped pyramid El Castillo or as it was sometimes known, the Temple of Kukulcan, the Mayan name for Quezalcoatl. It stood in the centre of a wide plaza which was surrounded by other buildings and at 30 metres (98 feet) high it dominated the square. The temple on top was 6 metres (20 feet) high with Toltec style warriors flanking its entrance and steep staircases ran up each of the four sides: the one on the north side had large stone serpents' heads at the foot of the balustrades, representing Kukulcan. The guide told us that in the early morning and late afternoon at the spring and autumn equinoxes, the pattern of light and shade created by the shape and orientation of the pyramid made it look as if the serpent was wriggling along the balustrade. He also demonstrated an odd acoustic effect created by the pyramid: when he clapped his hands, the sound that echoed back was like a quetzal bird chirping. According to the guide, there was another, older pyramid inside the present one, which at one time visitors had been able to reach through a tunnel which was now closed: the stairs were off-limits too as an American woman had fallen down and killed herself in 2006. The temple on top of the inner pyramid contained a throne, painted red and shaped like a jaguar, jade used to represent its spots. Beside it was a statue of Chac Mool, a purely Toltec character. The pyramid was no doubt used for blood sacrifices, particularly to the sun god. The Maya, like the Toltecs and the later Aztecs, believed that the sun god needed the blood of human sacrifices to persuade him to rise again in the morning. Murals found at another Mayan site, Bonampak, showed the priest-king pricking his tongue and penis with a sharp instrument to add his own blood to that of the prisoners being sacrificed.

But essentially El Castillo was a huge calendar. The Maya appear to have been obsessed with time, perhaps not surprisingly in an area where rainfall was seasonal and unreliable – it was important to be able to predict the right time to plant and harvest crops. They had several different ways of keeping track of time based on the movements of the sun, moon and the planet Venus but there were two main calendars: the Tzolkin, based on a 260 day count which was the sacred calendar, used to determine the time of religious and ceremonial events; and the Haab, the secular calendar, based on a 365 day solar year and used for everyday purposes. The Tzolkin operated as a 13 day cycle in which each day had a number and a 20 day cycle where each day had a name: each day would therefore have a number and a name combination and it took 260 days (the Tzolkin year) for every possible combination of day number and name to occur once. Various theories had been put forward in an attempt to explain the significance of a 260 day "year" including that it was the length of a pregnancy, the time between planting and harvesting maize, and the time between the zeniths of the sun at the latitude where the Olmec people lived, Central America's oldest civilization, who were credited with originally developing the Mayan calendar system. The Haab calendar consisted of 18 months of 20 days each plus a 5 day period of "nameless days" at the end of each year known as "Uayeb". The 18 months each had its own name and the days were numbered starting from zero. (The Mayans were great mathematicians and developed the concept of zero independent of the Old World where it originated in India and didn't reach Western Europe until the Renaissance – the ancient Greeks and the Romans were ignorant of it.) The Haab calendar made no allowance for the extra quarter of a day in the solar cycle (they had no leap years) so it would gradually have got out of kilter with the seasons. The Tzolkin and Haab calendars were coordinated in the Calendar Round which labelled individual days in both systems: the possible combinations ran out after 52 Haab years which equated to 73 Tzolkin years and the cycle began over again. To provide a longer term framework (which incidentally eliminated the leap year problem) they also operated a Long Count calendar based on units of 20 days which were grouped in multiples of 20 to form time periods each with their own name. An individual date could be given by the number of each of these units which had passed since the mythical Mayan creation date, 11th August 3114 BC, when the gods had successfully created man out of maize. They believed that this was the fourth Long Count time cycle following earlier ones when the gods had experimented unsuccessfully with men made out of among other things mud and wood. The largest time unit was the baktun. Previous Long Count cycles were believed to have ended after 13 baktuns.

The current one would therefore end on 21 December, 2012, a date that has been given much significance by New Age doom mongers who have interpreted it as meaning the end of the world, Armageddon. There is nothing in Mayan texts on their stellae (stone pillars inscribed with hieroglyphics), their four surviving codexes (book style written documents) or the Popol Vuh (the so-called Mayan "bible" written after the Spanish conquest and setting out Mayan spiritual beliefs) to suggest that this was anything other than the end of another time cycle like the 52 year cycle of the Calendar Round. There was nothing to suggest that the gods would scrap us and try again with some of the materials now available through new technology, like for example coltan, which would be much more durable than maize and we wouldn't need mobile phones any more because we would actually be mobile phones. However, just up the road, straddling the north Yucatan coastline around Chicxulub, was a reminder that the world can come to an end anytime. The outline of a crater rim 180 kilometres (112 miles) in diameter surrounded by a circular fault zone 240 kilometres (150 miles) in diameter (marked by a line of cenotes [sinkholes]), marks where a massive asteroid or comet, measuring 10 to 15 kilometres (6 to 9 miles) across, smashed into the earth, releasing explosive energy equivalent to 100 trillion tonnes of TNT, over a billion times more explosive than the atomic bombs dropped on Hiroshima and Nagasaki in World War II. This happened 65 million years ago and the blast, followed by the nuclear winter which it created, wiped out the dinosaurs and more than half of all the species on the planet. This was a while ago now, but that didn't mean it couldn't happen again on 21st December, 2012, just as the Mayans didn't predict.

Each staircase on El Castillo had 91 steps which, with the platform on top, made the number of days in a Haab year; the pyramid had nine stepped levels, the staircases dividing those into 18 separate terraces on each façade, representing the months in the Haab year; and 52 flat panels on the vertical faces of the terraces on each side represented the number of Haab years in a Calendar Round cycle. The four sides of the pyramid were exactly aligned with the cardinal points of the compass. Records showed that it had originally been covered in stucco plaster and painted a vivid red.

On the east side of the plaza, the Temple of the Warriors was a substantial, Toltec-style, squat building, the temple standing on a platform atop a truncated stepped pyramid, with a forest of stone pillars in front of and flanking it carved to represent warriors. A statue of the ubiquitous Chac Mool reclined at the entrance to the temple flanked by two columns sculpted as serpents. Around to the north of El Castillo were a number of low platforms: the Platform of the Eagles and Jaguars had panels along its sides showing eagles and jaguars devouring human hearts; the Skull Platform was decorated with grinning human skulls and carvings of eagles tearing open men's chests to eat their hearts – this platform had been used to display the heads of sacrificial victims; and the Platform of Venus may have had an astronomical purpose. The north-western side of the plaza was taken up with the Ball Court. These were to be found in nearly all Mayan cities but the Chichen Itza one was the biggest measuring 166 by 68 metres (545 by 223 feet) flanked by 12 metres (39 feet) high walls. High up on each of the long walls, were stone rings carved with intertwining serpents. Sculpted panels showed teams of ball players: in one of them a player had been decapitated, gouts of blood erupting from his neck. The losing team (or according to one theory, the winners) were sometimes sacrificed to the gods – what Sir Alex Ferguson would give to have that sort of incentive available at Manchester United. Throwing tea cups and boots would be a thing of the past. The game had been played using a solid rubber ball about the size of a man's head, the object being to get the ball through the stone rings using just knees, shoulders and hips: it couldn't have been easy as the holes in the rings weren't much larger than a man's head and they were higher on the wall than a basketball hoop. However, there may have been some other scoring system and possibly other games as some murals elsewhere showed players carrying sticks of some sort. It was obviously a body contact sport as the panels showed the teams padded up like ice hockey players. Built into the east wall were the Upper and Lower Temples of the Jaguar, the lower one with a jaguar throne like the one in the inner pyramid of El Castillo but very much the worse for wear; the upper one, with a faded mural showing a battle scene.

We walked north about 300 metres along a sacbe (Mayan causeway) to the Cenote Sacredo (Sacred Well), another sinkhole in the limestone, which had been sacred to the Rain God, Chaac (no relation to the wanker, Chac Mool) and where sacrifices had been made to him, including human ones. Dredging had brought up a wealth of treasures including gold and jade jewellery from as far away as Columbia and an awful lot of human bones. It was a rather forbidding place, the sinkhole about 60 metres (200 feet) in diameter with sheer sides dropping around 27 metres (89 feet) to the murky, greenish water. We walked back south past the ruined pyramid called El Osario (the Bonehouse) inside which tombs containing bones had been found and the Casa Colorada (Red House), one of the best preserved buildings, where there were extensive carved hieroglyphs referring to rulers of Chichen Itza and a Mayan calendar date corresponding to 869 AD. We arrived at El Caracol, the Observatory, a round building set on a large, square platform. Slits in the walls framed the position of certain celestial bodies, particularly Venus, on key dates in the Mayan calendar. The Mayans were masters of astronomy. They could predict the phases of the moon, equinoxes and solstices, and solar and lunar eclipses all without the aid of telescopes, sextants or clocks. They calculated the Venus "year" to 584 days, as against the actual figure of 583.92. Right at the south end of the site were the misleadingly named Nunnery and Church, the former being a palace, the latter probably a temple to the rain god, Chaac. These buildings were older than the complex around El Castillo, the facades beautifully decorated with stone fretwork and carvings including masks of Chaak on the Church. There were also carved hieroglyphic texts mentioning a ruler called Kakupakal. Mayan writing was the most advanced ever developed in pre-Columbian America and was a mixture of glyphs standing for words and others which combined symbols to form words phonetically. About 800 different glyphs have been identified. Most of it could now be deciphered. Numbers were written with a dot for one, a bar for five and an ellipse enclosing four vertical lines for zero. They used 20 as their base for counting rather than 10 as we do. Further south in "Old Chichen", even older structures were being excavated but that area was cordoned off to the public.

I flew down to San Jose, the capital of Costa Rica, and checked into the Gran Hotel right in the centre of the city. I was in good company:

John F. Kennedy, John Wayne, Jimmy Carter and Pele had all stayed there. It was an elegant, cream coloured, five storey building, built in 1930 with government assistance to provide a major first class hotel for the country. It was still a first rate establishment and amazingly good value for money. In the little, landscaped square outside, was a statue of Costa Rica's first president and on the east side, the attractive neo-classical National Theatre with three statues of the muses on the roof above the entrance. The rather austere Metropolitan Cathedral was just across the road, brightened up by its blue domes. I walked through the Plaza de Cultura, part of which formed the concrete roof of the underground Museum of Pre-Columbian Gold. The plaza was lively with street musicians and vendors and teenagers sitting around posing. I saw a number of almost life-size, black and white plastic cows – I never discovered what they were for. A couple of blocks north, Parque Morazan was shaded by trumpet trees and a statue of the South American independence hero Simon Bolivar stood under a purple jacaranda tree. A concrete bandstand in the centre, where concerts were held, was rather grandiosely called the Templo de Musica. Just across the road a flame tree, palm trees and bamboos in the Parque Espagna, framed by blue sky and fluffy white clouds, were reflected in the blue glass façade of the multi storey National Insurance building which also housed the Museum of Jade. There were a number of statues scattered among the trees and flower beds in the park, including one of Christopher Columbus. A beautiful little whitewashed pavilion with a red tiled roof had its lower walls inlaid with ceramic murals. On the west side of the park, the neo-classical style two storey Edificio Metalico had been pre-fabricated in Belgium and erected here in 1892. It was made entirely of reddish coloured metal panels and housed a school. On the north side of the park, dwarfed by the National Insurance skyscraper beside it, a single storey, yellow painted, colonial style building with an ornate, elaborately carved entrance and portico and red tiled roof housed the Foreign Ministry. A redflowered ceibo tree, planted by US President John F. Kennedy in 1963, just before he was assassinated, towered over it. Just beyond, a former distillery had been converted to accommodate the Ministry of Culture, venues for the National Dance and Theatre groups and the Museum of Contemporary Art and Design. It was a strange, eclectic grouping of building styles but somehow, aided by the park-side setting, it worked. Just to the south, government buildings clustered round the Parque National, planted with trees, with the impressive granite and bronze National Monument in its centre and a fish pond stocked with koi carp. On the north side of the park, the National Library was housed in a modern building completed in 1971: on the south side, the National Assembly occupied three historic buildings, all in different styles, taking up an entire block. Immediately to the south, across the Avenida Central, the National Museum was in a restored 19th century fortress.

In the evening, I had dinner in the Gourme Restaurant in the hotel. Their food was much better than their spelling: I had ceviche, followed by an Argentinean style churrasco steak and several caiparinhas. Afterwards, I walked up to the Nashville South Bar which I had seen earlier, near Parque Morazon. It was a pleasant little spot at first floor level looking out towards the park. I moved on to Key Largo, a lively bar with music on the corner of Avenida 1 and Calle 11, just a block south of the Plaza Espagna. This was a notorious pick-up joint frequented by elderly Gringos and young local girls. Just across the road, the shocking pink (perhaps it was blushing), top-end, Hotel del Rey served much the same function. If you felt like a change of sin, there was an opulent casino on the opposite corner. When I checked into the hotel, I had been given a note saying:

> "Dear Guest. If you decide to walk through San Jose, we advise you to visit areas to the north and east of the hotel because these are the best locations and are safer."

I had taken their advice, although they probably meant in daylight – few Latin American cities are safe at night. However, I didn't feel threatened in San Jose. Although Greater San Jose held about a million and a half people, it somehow didn't feel like a big city. Costa Rica had the highest standard of living in Central America and the best social services. After a Civil War in 1848, the government had decided to abolish the armed forces. In recent years it had had stable, democratically elected administrations. There had been a government policy to deliberately entice retirees from North America and Europe to settle there and some 35,000 had done so as well as a lot of younger English speaking immigrants. A local English language newspaper, the "Tico Times" was aimed at them as well as business visitors and tourists. ("Tico" was the nickname Costa Rican's gave themselves.) Situated in a wide valley in the Central Highlands at 1150 metres (3,800 feet), San Jose had a European spring-like climate all year round. Everything considered, I could see why people would be attracted to settle there.

I had booked a tour into Nicaragua which involved spending 3 nights in the old colonial city of Granada on the shores of Lake Nicaragua. I was to be driven to the border and picked up there by Careli Tours, the Nicaraguan operators. My driver arrived very early – it was a long drive and I had a border to cross. He introduced himself as Chepe (a common local nickname for people called Jose). His English was fairly limited and once again I appreciated the hours I had spent teaching myself Spanish. He was an ex professional footballer and had played in the top National League so we got talking about football. I joked with him about the salaries earned by top footballers now and how I couldn't see David Beckham driving me to Nicaragua. He said that there had been very little money in it locally when he had finished playing ten years ago but he knew some ex team mates and opponents who had gone to Europe and done well for themselves. We followed National Highway 1, part of the Pan-American Highway which ran all the way through South and Central America to the USA. We passed the airport and drove on through coffee plantations and fertile farmland with patches of forest. It was the start of the rainy season and low cloud obscured the volcanoes which peppered the highlands. We stopped for breakfast at a roadside restaurant and had what Chepe said was the traditional Tico breakfast, gallo pinto, which meant "painted rooster", rice and black beans seasoned with onions, garlic, coriander and chopped red peppers, with scrambled eggs and a slice of the delicious local Monteverde cheese, washed down with the local coffee for which Costa Rica was famous.

Back on the road and on the subject of football again, Chepe said that the Chinese had just agreed to gift Costa Rica a new 35,000 seater

National Stadium for football to be built by a Chinese firm using a mainly Chinese workforce. While it would be nice to have the stadium, he said, it was worrying the way the Chinese were moving in on the country, almost as if they were being colonised again. I had read an article in the Tico Times about this just the day before. Under the headline "Doting China Still Costa Rica's Sugar Daddy" it said that:

"The honeymoon is over but China is still showering Costa Rica with gifts. Since cutting ties with Taiwan last June 6, the Costa Rican government has been reaping the benefits that accompany friendship with the growing economic and political giant."

It went on to describe the very high level diplomatic exchanges that had taken place, how China had donated cash as foreign aid, gifted 200 police cars, awarded scholarships and opened up a credit line for small businesses. Discussions were underway about a free trade agreement; about China directing public works projects for water supply, waste water treatment and flood prevention; about the Chinese National Petroleum Organization tripling Costa Rica's oil refining capacity to process crude oil from Venezuela and Ecuador for export to China and carrying out offshore oil exploration; about involvement in the food and agriculture business sectors; and about the possibility of Chinese firms setting up shop in Costa Rica to manufacture textiles and other products for export to the USA, taking advantage of the Central American Free Trade Agreement. As we approached the city of Liberia, I remarked that the lower, dry, ranching country with scattered thorn bushes and acacia trees which we were passing through, resembled parts of Mexico. Chepe replied that Costa Rica was beginning to resemble Mexico in another, more worrying way - Mexican drug cartels were setting up branches to secure the supply route for Columbian cocaine to the USA.

The border formalities at Penas Blancas went surprisingly smoothly and my tour guides from Careli Tours, Luis and Oscar, were waiting for me with a mini-van. We drove north along the shore of Lake Nicaragua, the twin volcanic peaks dominating Ometepe Island soon becoming visible through the haze, far offshore, the highest and still active

Concepcion rising to 1,610 metres (5,232 feet). The lake contained the world's only fresh water sharks, which had almost been commercially fished to extinction but were now recovering, perhaps a mixed blessing as they were fond of humans – in the "with chips" sense. Just outside the town of Rivas, we came on a picket line: bus, truck and taxi drivers nationwide were striking against rising fuel prices. Oscar and Luis joked that they were "scabs" but we drove through unmolested. I checked into the Hotel Dario in the Calle de la Calzada, which ran for a kilometre from the town centre at the Parque Central down to the edge of Lake Nicaragua. It was a beautifully restored old colonial building, with green painted trim around the windows, doors and ornately carved wooden balconies outside the upstairs French windows. My balcony looked out towards the nearby Mombacho volcano, 1,345 metres (4,371 feet) high and still active. The narrow street was lined with mainly single storey, restored colonial buildings, painted in pastel shades of pink, blue and ochre. A figure on stilts in fancy dress was tottering around across the street, surrounded by a bemused looking audience. Granada was the oldest city in mainland America, having been founded in 1524. The San Juan River flowing out of the lake was navigable for small craft all the way to the Caribbean Sea and a relatively narrow isthmus separated the town from the Pacific Ocean, giving Granada a key location for trade and making it very wealthy. This attracted pirates and the infamous Captain Henry Morgan had led an expedition up the San Juan and sacked the city in 1665, burning much of it to the ground. Other pirate raids were carried out periodically over the years when pirates were active in the area. It was almost destroyed again in 1854 by an army led by the Yankee mercenary William Walker, ostensibly fighting for the city of Leon during a civil war but latterly trying to take over the country for himself. After each disaster, buildings had been reinstated or rebuilt: the latest restoration efforts had been aimed at the tourist trade and the end result was a well preserved colonial era gem with a population of around 100,000.

In the evening, I had dinner in the hotel's excellent El Tranvia Restaurant followed by a drink in their Café Bar Chocolate. I was reading the "Nica Times", a clone of Costa Rica's "Tico Times". In 2007, the veteran left wing leader of the Sandanista Party, Daniel Ortega, had been elected President after long years out of power. An article in the newspaper reported him accusing the USA of plotting against him in a re-run of the "Contra War" of the 1980s during the Cold War when the CIA had actively supported the rebel right wing Contra group against the ruling Sandanista government. I remembered the scandal involving Oliver North, who, with the CIA, had operated a clandestine scheme in which arms were secretly sold to Iran and the funds channelled to the Contras. The resulting bloody civil war was another example of the double standards Uncle Sam applied in his crusade to spread democracy around the world. How much the "Teflon" President, Ronald Reagan, knew about the scheme was never established.

In the morning, I set out to explore the town. The centre-piece was the magnificent Cathedral with its golden yellow baroque façade and twin bell towers with red-tiled domes. It had originally been completed in 1539, destroyed by pirates, rebuilt in the current baroque style in 1783, badly damaged by William Walker and restored again in 1862 – almost a historical record of the city itself. The Parque Central was surrounded by attractively restored buildings. I had a coffee in the café-bar of the opulent Hotel Gran Francia. There was a row of horse drawn carriages outside the Hotel Alhambra which had an ornate pink-painted portico with a blue and white Nicaraguan flag flying from the roof, matching the sky. I wandered inside for a look. It was laid out in typical Moorish, Andalucian, style with an inner patio open to the air filled with pots holding flowers, shrubs and bamboo plants, a riot of colour. From the roof terrace there was a panoramic view across the city. I walked round to the Church of San Francisco with its striking blue façade. It had been completed in 1585 and suffered a similar history of destruction and resurrection as the cathedral. Next door in an old Convent there was a fascinating museum with primitive artworks, a scale model of the city, a tableau of papier-mache figures of local Indians cooking and lounging around in hammocks and a collection of black basalt statues from the island of Zapatera in the lake. Down by the lake, the Centro Turistico was a beach front park with paths shaded by trees, sandy beaches, fish restaurants, bars, boats for hire for trips on the lake and children's playgrounds. A little river flowing into the lake looked none too clean so I didn't chance a swim – besides there were the man-eating sharks

The following morning, Oscar and Luis turned up to take me for a cruise on the lake and a visit to the active Masaya volcano. We cruised through the archipelago of tiny islands, imaginatively called Las Isletas, lying off the town. They were clothed in tropical rainforest with masses of flowers, colourful birds and on one some very inquisitive monkeys. Some had mansions on them, mostly holiday homes for the rich and famous. They had been formed around 10,000 years ago from debris thrown out by a massive explosion of the Mombacho volcano, which loomed above the shoreline. We drove the 16 kilometers (10 miles) to the scruffy little town of Masaya nestled at the foot of the volcano of the same name. It stood on the edge of a lake with a crumbling malecon (waterfront promenade) running along it. The town's main claim to fame was a large artisan's market housed in a substantial black basalt building resembling a fort, with turrets and towers. The adjacent municipal open air market had displays of fruit, vegetables, butcher meat, fish, footwear, handicrafts and souvenirs. But the quality handicrafts were in the Artisans' building – leatherwork; woodcarvings, including balsa wood work; hammocks; shiny black ceramics; woven fabrics from a variety of fibres including palm leaves and reeds – made into mats, hats, toys and baskets; and soapstone sculptures. Masaya was reputedly the best place in the country for handicrafts. We drove up to the edge of the crater, 934 metres (3,035 feet) above sea level. This would have driven health and safety officials mad in most parts of the world. Lava permanently bubbled away at the bottom of the crater, hidden by a plume of sulphurous gasses. A notice did offer a warning that if poisonous gasses appeared you were to get the hell out of it but it occurred to me that by the time you realized they were poisonous it would probably be too late. The early Spanish settlers had called it the gate to hell and erected a cross to ward off the evil – that was probably as useful as the notice. A species of parakeet nested in the crater walls – it's amazing where nature finds niches to survive in.

The crater was just the latest active vent in a huge crater extending for miles around it. The capital city, Managua, not far to the north, had been almost destroyed in a massive earthquake in 1972. This wasn't the safest place in the world.

I returned to San Jose by the same route and flew on to Guatemala City. I had read about the City's fearful reputation for violence – murders, armed robbery, mugging and kidnapping - and decided to spend as little time as possible there, just using it as an overnight base for excursions into the Guatemalan Highlands and to the ancient Mayan city of Copan, just across the border in Honduras. Nothing that I saw in Guatemala City indicated that I had got it wrong. The streets were full of heavily armed, navy-blue clad security men. Just near the Marriott Hotel where I was staying, I saw a gun shop with a tasty array of automatic weapons which presumably anyone could walk in and buy. The multi-storey Marriott stood like a fortress in a wasteland of sterile, empty streets – like an outpost of civilization surviving after some apocalypse. There were always plenty of taxis outside and you would have been mad not to use them. I was picked up early by the guide from Clark Tours, Hector, to drive to Chichicastenango (fortunately normally shortened to Chichi), 145 kilometres (90 miles) to the north through the Guatemalan Highlands. There were just another half dozen tour group members in the mini bus – a Spanish American couple from Miami, a Japanese couple and a Swedish mother and daughter. At the start of the rainy season there was a lot of low cloud but the mountain scenery was varied and interesting with pine forested summits, river valleys, fields cultivated for maize and vegetables and emerald green pastures with cattle. We turned off the Pan American Highway at Los Encuentros for the remaining 17 kilometres to Chichi. We were staying at the Mayan Inn, which comprised several beautifully restored double-storeyed colonial houses, each with an interior patio filled with colourful exotic tropical plants, cages of parakeets hanging among them, and Mayan style sculptures. The Mayan Indian who showed me to my room solemnly presented me with a card which said: "Manuel Cutillo. He is your waiter and room attendant." My very own batman: and sure enough, when I appeared for dinner he was there to serve me and again at breakfast next morning. There were no keys to the rooms – Manuel was obviously permanently on guard. The rooms were furnished with antique furniture and there was a magnificent carved fireplace. It was one of the most hospitable places I have ever stayed in, a complete contrast to the menace of Guatemala City.

We had arrived in time for Chichi's famous Thursday market. The central plaza between the picturesque whitewashed churches of Santo Tomas and the Capilla del Calvario was filled with stalls covered with white canvas awnings and laden with flowers, fruit and vegetables – potatoes, carrots, tomatoes – gaudy textiles, gruesome wooden masks, used by the Indians in rituals, pottery and all the everyday needs of the community – food, clothing, shoes, soap, coffee as well as a lot of souvenirs and handicrafts obviously aimed at the tourist trade. The women wore traditional costumes of brightly coloured long skirts and embroidered "huipiles" (tunics), many with hats: apart from the stall-holders, many of them were walking around with traditional textiles for sale draped over their arms, shoulders and heads. The market extended right to the steps of Santo Thomas Church where people, mainly men, were sitting smoking - one was playing a marimba (xylophone). Something that smelled like incense was smouldering in a tin can ventilated with what looked like bullet holes. Inside the church, which dated from 1540, among the candles there were offerings of maize, flowers and bottles of alcohol wrapped in maize husks – I don't think the Church of Scotland would have approved. Along one side of the plaza, the wall of the Municipal Offices was decorated with a mural showing scenes from the civil war which had lasted from 1960 to 1996. Successive right wing dictatorships supported by the CIA had conducted a vicious campaign against left wing guerrillas, aided by Russia and Cuba, many of whom came from the local Indian population. Thousands had died and the government had attempted to herd the Indians into villages which they could police – virtual concentration camps. It had ended after the Cold War ended and the Russians and Americans who had supported the opposing sides lost interest, a semblance of democracy appearing. The mural used symbols from the Popol Vuh, the Mayan bible, which had been written in this area, to tell the story. The final pages of that document have been interpreted as showing a great flood ending the world but it made no mention of the dreaded December 21st 2012 date.

The following morning, we set off towards Lake Atitlan. We stopped in the town of Solola where another bustling market was underway in the plaza outside the Cathedral. An Indian wedding was taking place in the Cathedral, nothing traditional here, the bride wore the full white wedding dress with veil and tiara and the groom was in a smart black suit. The Cathedral was packed with the crowd spilling out onto the steps. The winding, 8 kilometres (5 miles) down to the lake offered spectacular views across the shimmering blue water to the three volcanic peaks on the far side. We were staying in the Porta del Lago Hotel right down by the lake shore in Panajachel, the main town on the lake. The lake had been formed in a massive volcanic explosion about 85,000 years ago, debris from which had been found as far north as Florida. It measured 18 kilometres by 8 (10 miles by 5) and was about 300 metres (nearly 1,000 feet) deep. The hotel looked out at the three more recent volcanoes clustering around the little town of Santiago Atitlan on the far shore, the highest of which, Atitlan, rose to 3,537 metres (11,495 feet). There was a row of thatched roofed, timber restaurants on stilts above the beach beside the pier where boats left to cross the lake. In the evening, I had ceviche and a fillet of tilapia from the lake in one of them– tilapia had been my favourite fish when I had lived on the shores of Lake Victoria in Africa and this brought back memories.

In the morning, we caught one of the open passenger launches shaded with a canvas awning across the lake to Santiago Atitlan, about 18 kilometers (10 miles) away. Near the dock where we disembarked, a row of dug-out canoes were drawn up on the beach – we had passed some fishermen on the way across. A path led up through rows of thatched souvenir, craft and food and drink stalls to the bottom of the main street, Calle Principal. I was accosted by a little Indian girl of seven or eight selling key rings with little figures of birds and animals attached to them by strings of tiny coloured beads, quite a lot of them, draped over her arm. They were well made but whether in Santiago or Shanghai was debatable. I asked her in Spanish how much they were and she replied in English: "Ten quetzales each, Sir." I had discovered that a lot of the Indians didn't speak Spanish, just using the local Mayan language. I suspected that the little girl could speak Spanish perfectly well but used English as the language of commerce. I said that was pretty dear, how about five quetzales? (There were 12 quetzales to the British pound sterling.) She obviously had her business plan well prepared. "I'll tell you what." she said, "How about two for fifteen quetzales?" We eventually settled on eight quetzales for a ring with a quetzal bird attached, with a long green tail, green body, red belly and yellow feet: it was the national bird as well as the name of the currency. She seemed well pleased with the deal and thanked me politely, walking off to accost the next tourist walking up from the boat. The main street climbed uphill between shops, cafes, bars and restaurants, mainly aimed at the tourist trade. After about 500 metres we reached the central plaza where the church built by the Franciscans had been completed in 1582. Inside, there was a plaque commemorating an American missionary priest who had been murdered by a right wing death squad in 1981 during the civil war. On the pulpit, there were effigies of men made of maize, an echo of old Mayan beliefs. In a house in a narrow lane, further along the hillside, we visited Maximon, a strange, hybrid deity worshipped throughout the Guatemalan Highlands. The Spanish had called him San Simon, the Indians Rilaj Maam but the mixed-race compromise Maximon was more common. He was an amalgam of Mayan gods, Judas Iscariot and Pedro de Alvarado (the bloodthirsty Conquistador who had been Cortez's second in command in Mexico and went on to conquer Guatemala), a rather unsavoury crew but in spite of his ancestry he was a very amiable character, fond of a drink and a smoke. In Santiago he took the form of a carved wooden figure wearing silk scarves and with a large cigar in his mouth. The house where we found him was fairly basic – apparently he moved around a lot among a society of caretakers. There was an open fire burning in the courtyard outside and inside, Maximon sat surrounded by packets of cigarettes, cigars and bottles of hard liquor which had been gifted to him. He looked the epitome of a sixty a day and a bottle a day man. If it hadn't been a catholic country, there would probably have been a pile of French letters beside him as well. That was the sort of religion I could subscribe to – I wished him luck.

We caught another launch back to Panajachel and then drove south to Antigua. This was another old colonial gem like Granada in Nicaragua, listed by UNESCO as a World Heritage Site. It was dominated by three towering volcanoes, the highest, Acatenango rising to 3,976 metres (12,922 feet), Agua and Fuego, a couple of hundred metres lower. These provided a spectacular setting (a plume of smoke curled out of Fuego during the day and it emitted a red glow at night) but also a dangerous one. Antigua had been the capital of Guatemala in early colonial days (after an earlier one had been buried in a mudslide from Agua) and had become the most important centre in Central America in the 17th and 18th centuries with 38 churches and a wealth of architectural masterpieces including schools, hospitals and a university. Then in 1773 it was virtually destroyed in a massive earthquake and partially abandoned, the capital moving to Guatemala City where the earth was a bit more stable. In the early 19th century, people started moving back into the city on the back of the coffee boom, restoring some of the fine old houses. In the 20th century the government declared it a national monument which gave impetus to the restoration work. Another earthquake in 1976 provided another setback but the UNESCO designation in 1979 gave the final push. It was now an intriguing mixture of derelict, damaged and magnificently restored 17th and 18th century architectural masterpieces with a population approaching 60,000, a lively tourist magnet specialising in Spanish language schools.

The city centre in the Plaza Mayor was a popular meeting place for locals and tourists alike with a mermaid fountain, shady and colourful planting and benches. The group of buildings surrounding it had been magnificent and even partially restored were still impressive. The cathedral, begun in 1542, had been destroyed in the 1773 earthquake. Its whitewashed façade had been restored with replicas of saints standing in niches. Only the front of the original church, the entrance hall, had been restored: the ruins of the main body stood behind. On the north side of the Plaza, the Ayuntamiento (Town

Hall) was in better condition, stately columns providing a street level arcade, with an arched terrace at first floor level. The imposing Palace of the Captains General occupied the south side of the plaza. Built in 1558, the whole of Central America had been governed from here while Antigua was capital of Guatemala. Fifth Avenue North extended north from the plaza, a pedestrianised street of mainly single storey buildings – shops, restaurants, offices – whitewashed or painted in pastel colours, with red terracotta tile roofs. Ceramic pots with bright flowers and shrubs lined the street and a wooden cart was parked packed with flowers. A creamy yellow arch with a clock tower in the middle straddled the street, the Arco de Santa Catalina. It had been part of a former 17th century convent: the nuns had used it to cross the street in privacy. The yellow painted La Merced Church with its bell tower was straight in front. A large cross stood in a little square in front of it. North-east of the plaza, Las Capuchinas nunnery had been partially restored with cloisters and gardens and an unusual group of nuns' cells built like a tower around a central patio. Outside the walls, an Indian market stretched in a long strip along the pavement, Indian women squatting beside their spread out wares – textiles of all sorts, rolls of cloth, rugs, embroidery, clothes, bags, dolls, jewellery. Further east, in the grounds of the luxury, five star, Casa Santo Domingo Hotel, the gothic style Santo Domingo church was being excavated and restored. The complex of archaeological site, partially restored church and cloisters and some small museums was fascinating, accessed through the hotel's lush tropical garden with parakeets and a large swimming pool. Five blocks south, the Church of San Francisco was another interesting complex. Apart from the fine old restored church and the ruins of a monastery, there was a shrine and museum dedicated to Hermano (Brother) Pedro who had founded a hospital for the poor in the 17th century and been canonised by the Pope in 2002, the only Guatemalan saint. The grounds were full of people so he was obviously still revered.

We returned to Guatemala City and the following morning I set off on the last leg of my trip, a tour of the ancient Mayan sites of Copan, just across the border in Honduras and Quirigua back in

Guatemala. This time there were only three other group members, a lone Japanese man (an endangered species, they usually hunted in large packs) and a mother and daughter who lived in the USA but were originally from Guatemala City. It was a long drive, initially through the highlands and then dropping down to the valley of the Motagua River and following it east along the Carretera al Atlantico which led to the Caribbean Sea. We branched off at Rio Hondo and headed for El Florido on the Honduran border. Copan was just 12 kilometres (8 miles) from the border. Confusingly the little town where we were to spend the night in the Marina Copan Hotel was called Copan Ruinas: in spite of this, it was a pleasant, sleepy town of cobbled streets and colonial style whitewashed single and double storey adobe houses with red terracotta tiled roofs and a good supply of cafes, bars and restaurants catering for tourists visiting the adjacent archaeological site. A lovely old colonial church stood beside the Parque Central in the town centre. In the evening, I had a meal and a drink in the lively Carnitas Nia Lola bar-restaurant, overlooking a ravine at the southern edge of the town.

The remains of the Mayan city were not as impressive or well restored as Chichen Itza but it was a more typical example of the Mayan heartland where Mayan culture reached its highest development during what was known as the Classical Period from about 250 AD to around 900 AD. The city had developed in the valley of the Copan River. Pottery dating to 1200 BC had been found and evidence of an agricultural community there at that time. It wasn't known when substantial buildings and an embryo city first appeared: the first hieroglyphic date found was 426 AD when a ruling dynasty was formed by a man called Great Sun Lord Quetzal Macaw. Inscriptions on stellae suggested he had come from the city of Tical to the north in the Peten Basin and possibly originally from Teotihuacan in Mexico. This dynasty had ruled for the entire period of Copan greatness, the last incumbent (number 17) being recorded as starting his rule 1n 822 AD. Sometime not long after that, the civilization collapsed. At its peak in the 7th century it was estimated to have had a population of around 27,000 and dominated the surrounding region, controlling the valuable trade in obsidian, jade, cacao and quetzal feathers passing through the Motagua river valley.

Before we entered the site, we visited the Sculpture Museum which housed the originals of some of the sculptures from the site and a life-size replica of the Rosalila Temple which had been discovered beneath a newer structure in the Acropolis area of the site. The replica was painted in the original pink colour, parts of the elaborate stucco decorations on the façade picked out in blue. There were sculpted figures at the upper corners of the main building and beside the roof comb on top of it. A sculpted mask of the sun god lowered above the entrance. We approached the site down an avenue of trees with a couple of macaws sitting on branches. The site entrance led into the Great Plaza, a level expanse of grass, peppered with stellae (stone columns) sculptured with the likenesses of the various rulers with hieroglyphics on the sides identifying them and telling about their exploits. Their names were intriguing: King 18 Rabbit featured a lot; Smoke Monkey; Moon Jaguar; Waterlily Jaguar – they sounded like members of the Bob Geldhof family, none of the boring Georges, Hooray Henrys and Williams of the British royal family. The stellae were carved from a soft, greenish, andesite rock which enabled extremely intricate and delicate sculpture to be executed. Apart from the rulers, there were carvings of serpents' heads and gods, such as the rain god, Chaac. South of the Plaza, past a ball court, was the Hieroglyphic Staircase, a flight of 62 steps, 10 metres (33 feet) wide, completely covered in hieroglyphics telling the story of the ruling dynasty. Six richly decorated figures were spaced out up the middle of the stairs, probably representing outstanding rulers and a figure on a stele at the foot of the steps in a feathered cloak was probably King Smoke Shell who had built this version of the staircase. An altar in front of him showed a human head emerging from the jaws of a serpent. South of the staircase platform, up a flight of steps, the main group of temples around two plazas or patios was known as the Acropolis. This had been the religious and political centre of the city, where ceremonies had been held and the kings buried: the tomb of the first ruler had been found under one of the buildings. The Temple of Inscriptions stood at the top of the steps, covered in hieroglyphics. Standing above the East Plaza, the Temple of Meditation had been well restored. After the city had been abandoned, the Copan River had gradually changed course and eroded the east side of the Acropolis. It had since been diverted away but the damage had been done. A giant pine tree grew out of the building on the south-east side of the plaza. The large building on the south side was where the Rosalila Temple had been found, accessed by a tunnel from the plaza. Successive temples had been built here, one on top of the other, by successive rulers, the height gradually increasing over the centuries. In the West Plaza, an altar had sculptures of the first sixteen rulers carved around it. There were marvellous sculptures all over the complex – monkey gods, half man, half bat figures, serpents, jaguars. It had been a magnificent city.

Jared Diamond's book, "Collapse", had a chapter on the decline of the Mayan civilization, including specific reference to Copan. He claimed that four reasons were behind their demise: environmental damage through deforestation and soil erosion; climate change, specifically prolonged periods of drought; warfare with other cities and possibly civil war involving rebellions against the ruling class; and cultural factors, including the rulers' obsession with monument building which would have used scarce resources, diverted manpower from the maintenance of agricultural and irrigation systems and diverted attention from wider environmental threats. He described how agriculture had developed, initially growing maize, beans and squash (and cotton for clothing) on the fertile alluvial soil of the flat land along the river, and then, to feed the ever-growing population, spreading up the surrounding hillsides using the traditional slash and burn technique, moving on to a new area when the nutrients of one area had been exhausted. This led to soil erosion, acidic upland soils being washed down onto the alluvial soils below, reducing their fertility and clogging up irrigation systems. In addition, destruction of the forests reduced rainfall through less evapo-transpiration. Agricultural production declined and examination of skeletons from the 650 to 850 AD period showed signs of malnutrition and disease. By this time they were having to import food from outside their area. Research using sediment cores had enabled a picture of rainfall patterns to be established. Mayan cities had declined at different times, Mirador up on the Mexican border around 150 AD; Tikal in central Peten around 600 AD; and Copan and the rest of the central lowland rainforest cities from 800 to 900 AD. These dates all coincided with prolonged periods of drought. Around 760 AD the worst period of droughts in 7,000 years began, with peaks lasting several years – one particularly dry period starting in 910 and lasting six years may have given the coup de grace to Copan. Warfare had always been endemic between the cities, often motivated by the need for prisoners for blood sacrifices. Murals of later rulers showed them dressed and armed for war. There was archaeological evidence that the Copan royal palace had been burned down around 850 AD, although this could have been the result of civil war. If the priest-kings couldn't deliver good harvests through their elaborate ceremonies and sacrifices, the people would eventually turn on them. They had also contributed to deforestation through their extensive use of stucco on temples and palaces. Stucco was made from burned limestone, requiring enormous amounts of timber to achieve the high temperatures needed. When the Spaniards arrived, there were only a few Mayan families around Copan, living by subsistence agriculture. At the height of the Mayan civilization, it was estimated that there had been at least 3 million people, perhaps as many as 14 million, in the wider Mayan area, centred on the Peten lowlands: by the time of the Conquistadors this had fallen to around 60,000.

The following morning, we crossed back into Guatemala to visit Quirigua, 67 kilometres (41 miles) east along the Carretera al Atlantico from the Rio Hondo junction, before returning to Guatemala City for the last night of my Central American trip. There wasn't much left to see of Quirigua except the magnificently carved and preserved sandstone stellae for which it was famous. These stood in shelters comprising four posts supporting a thatched roof, spread out around a grassy field, the tallest of them reaching 8 metres (25 feet). The stellae dated from after 737 AD, the city's period of greatness. Until then, they had been under Copan's control: but that year King Cauac Sky captured King 18 Rabbit of Copan and beheaded him, enabling Quirigua to become top dog in the area for a while. The stellae were mainly erected to the glory of King Cauac, with figures of the great man himself, wearing elaborate headdresses and sometimes a beard, hieroglyphs telling of his exploits. Others contained zoomorphs, carvings of mythical beasts and jaguars, tortoises, serpents and frogs. The remains of the Acropolis were not nearly as impressive or extensive as at Copan. It was a fitting place to end my Mayan pilgrimage, a case study of how civilizations can suddenly end.

The Maya failed to predict or prevent their own demise and the end of the Mayan Long Count Calendar cycle on 21st December 2012 at the end of its 13th Baktun arrived and life went on. The Doomsday Preppers were disappointed but they argued that the Mayans didn't mean the world would literally end on that day, just that it was the beginning of the end. Anyone convinced that the end of the world is nigh doesn't have far to look for potential culprits. On my trip I had seen what environmental degradation, climate change, warfare and political incompetence could do to a great civilization; I had seen great cities destroyed by volcanic eruptions and earthquakes; and I had seen where the dinosaurs and over half the species on earth had been wiped out by one little asteroid. Shit happens. And in any case, the Mayans were dead right in terms of their own cultural beliefs. A new age has already begun with men made from new materials. Coltan man is already with us. Robots make cars and are being developed to carry out surgical procedures. It's just a matter of time until they're able to replicate themselves. Happy New Baktun.

About the Author

Born in the Shetland Islands, Scotland, James A. Anderson earned an MA in geography, graduating with honors from Aberdeen University in 1967. He went on to gain a diploma in education from Makerere University, Kampala, Uganda, and served as an education officer with the Kenyan government for two years. Next, he became a town planner in New Zealand and, later, in England. He finally moved again to New Zealand in 1997, where he worked as a district planner and a planning consultant until retiring in 2008.

Perhaps it was his Viking blood that drove him to travel extensively whenever he could. And now, after completing a New Zealand Institute of Business Studies course on freelance travel writing and photography, Anderson shares his travel tales in his book *To the New 7 Wonders of the World*, which details the journeys that took him to each of the intriguing destinations on the list.

30610840R00138

Made in the USA
Charleston, SC
21 June 2014